Citizenship, identity and immigration in the European Union

MANCHESTER
UNIVERSITY PRESS

Citizenship, identity and immigration in the European Union

Between past and future

Theodora Kostakopoulou

Manchester University Press
Manchester and New York

distributed exclusively in the USA by Palgrave

Copyright © Theodora Kostakopoulou 2001
The right of Theodora Kostakopoulou to be identified as the author of this work has been asserted by her in accordance with the Copyright, Designs and Patents Act 1988.

Published by Manchester University Press
Oxford Road, Manchester M13 9NR, UK
and Room 400, 175 Fifth Avenue, New York, NY 10010, USA
http://www.manchesteruniversitypress.co.uk

Distributed exclusively in the USA by
Palgrave, 175 Fifth Avenue, New York,
NY 10010, USA

Distributed exclusively in Canada by
UBC Press, University of British Columbia, 2029 West Mall,
Vancouver, BC, Canada V6T 1Z2

British Library Cataloguing-in-Publication Data
A catalogue record for this book is available from the British Library

Library of Congress Cataloging-in-Publication Data applied for

ISBN 0 7190 5998 4 *hardback*

First published 2001

08 07 06 05 04 03 02 01   10 9 8 7 6 5 4 3 2 1

Typeset in Sabon
by Northern Phototypesetting Co. Ltd, Bolton
Printed in Great Britain
by Bookcraft (Bath) Ltd, Midsomer Norton

(14912)

Contents

Acknowledgements

This book has had a long period of gestation owing to circumstances which often were beyond my control. The book has certainly benefited from it, though I have occasionally suffered. Its genesis is to be found in a PhD Dissertation submitted to the Department of Government, Essex University, in 1995. At Essex University, I enjoyed intellectual stimulus and learned from conversations with fellow graduate colleagues, members of staff and my students in Law and Government. Ernesto Laclau, Sheldon Leader and the other members of the Centre for Theoretical Studies provided an intellectually stimulating environment within which many of my ideas were shaped. Their discussions and comments on earlier ideas are greatly appreciated. Albert Weale and Richard Bellamy have also provided helpful comments and suggestions. Their thorough observations led me to clarify my own position and their advice has proved invaluable over the years. I have also learned a great deal from 'virtual' conversations with Robert E. Goodin. His correspondence was a source of inspiration and his overall support and friendship have been a gift for which there could truly be no adequate thanks.

I am very grateful for comments and criticisms on earlier drafts or parts of this manuscript, by Iris Marion Young, Simon Bulmer, Mick Moran, Adrian Favell, Benjamin Arditi, Tariq Modood, Max Silverman, Bob Brecher, Avner de-Shalit, Wendy Donner, Jo Shaw, Floya Anthias, Gabriella Lazaridis, Gino Naldi, Martin Laughlin and John Peterson, among others. None of these named should be held in any way accountable for the arguments, analyses, opinions and deficiencies of this study. I also thank my students at Essex and East Anglia Universities, and at Manchester University for their encouragement and cheerfulness.

Parts of this book have appeared in papers I have written over the last few years, although all have been substantially rewritten. Chapter 3 is adapted from the essays 'Nested "Old" and "New" Citizenships in the EU: bringing Forth the Complexity', *Columbia Journal of European Law*, 5, 2000, 389–413, and 'European Citizenship and Immigration after Amsterdam: Openings, Silences, Paradoxes', *Journal of Ethnic and Migration Studies*, 24:

4, 1998, 639–56. An earlier version of Chapter 5 originally appeared as 'Towards a Theory of Constructive Citizenship in Europe', *Journal of Political Philosophy*, 4: 4, 1996, 337–58. Chapter 6 is based on my paper 'Is There an Alternative to "Schengenland"?', *Political Studies*, 46: 5, 1998, 886–902. I thank the editors and the anonymous reviewers of these journals for their comments. I also wish to thank the editorial team at Manchester University Press for their interest in my work.

Finally, I owe special thanks to my parents and my partner. The book is dedicated to Alexander, Erini-Beatrice and Euclid with the hope that, as adults, they will be treated with the dignity and respect that every human being deserves.

Introduction

This book aspires to contribute to the literature on the theory and practice of European political integration by providing a systematic theorisation of Union citizenship and European migration policy, and a set of proposals for institutional reform. The subject matter of this study is a thorough examination of the process of community-building in the European Union, that is, the politics of 'belonging' and 'exclusion', as they find their juridico-political expression in citizenship laws and immigration policies, from the standpoint of normative political theory. This entails an inquiry into: (a) the question of socio-political membership in the emerging European polity and the issue of European identity, (b) the theory and politics of EU citizenship and (c) the issue of immigration, since there is a close connection between the ways a polity responds to the challenge of migration and its values, collective understandings and institutions.

Two distinctive features of the contemporary situation make it particularly appropriate – and, indeed, urgent – to engage in normative theorising on the emergent institutional designs of European citizenship and immigration. One is the fact that the scale, complexity and novelty of Europe cannot be adequately understood with the aid of traditional theoretical tools. European developments have challenged some standard positions in political science, legal theory and international relations. Certainly, in the fields of citizenship and immigration, the European Union is not a suitable plane for the application of existing theoretical paradigms on citizenship, immigration and community, for these have been firmly rooted within the spatial framework of the state. In addition, perspectives which tend to locate community and citizenship in the cultural community are running up against the fact that the European Community is a deeply diverse community 'beyond tradition'. In such a community 'feelings of togetherness' will most probably be the outcome, rather than the cause, of practices of closer co-operation. The process of creating a European civic space, a dynamic system of governance beyond the nation-state, facilitates the reflective awareness of the limitations of existing perspectives and highlights the need for new intellectual frameworks to capture the novelty and complexity of the EC/EU. This explains why scholars have recently embarked upon a search for a political and constitutional theory 'beyond the sovereign nation-state'.[1]

While academics search for viable models which can reflect the complexity of rapidly changing environments, political actors at the national level have embarked upon a process of 'soul-searching'. The problems concerning the ratification of the Maastricht Treaty and the subsequent period of national retrenchment, the Nordic accession debates and the many deficits of the European Union have sparked a debate concerning the social legitimacy of the European edifice. But whereas some partners are undergoing a process of reconceptualisation of what is involved in being a 'state' and what membership in the Union entails others, quite surprisingly, appear to be rediscovering themselves as nation-states in externally interdependent, internally heterogeneous environments. Scholars and commentators have picked up these signs and called for critical reflection on European integration in an interdisciplinary way (Weiler, 1995, 1996, 1997; Shaw and More, 1995; Shaw, 1996; Stone Sweet and Sandholtz, 1997; Armstrong and Bulmer, 1998).

Situated in such an era, this study seeks to respond to these challenging calls. The lens of normative political theory will enable the critical examination of constitutive categories and conceptual frameworks by highlighting the historicity of their construction and possibilities for their reconceptualisation. It will also facilitate the analysis and critical evaluation of European institutions and discussion as to how these may be reformed. After all, awareness of the limitations of European institutions does not contradict the process of reform; it is a condition of the possibility for it. At the same time, a critique of existing institutions is more powerful and meaningful if it is accompanied by alternative ideas and designs.

My concern with conceiving alternative realities and institutional designs stems from my belief that every reality is an observed, constructed and dynamic reality and therefore reformable. Existing institutional arrangements do not exhaust the range of possibilities and, depending on one's perspective, can be viewed either as a status to be maintained or a setting that calls for change. It is in this specific context that my approach can be called 'constructivist'. The concern with relating knowledge to socio-political change is important for two reasons. First, 'Europe' seems to cry for a shift of attention 'from values to mechanisms for implementing them' urged by Goodin (1993: 176). Second, for too long debates on European integration have neglected the ethical dimensions of the European project by emphasising either functional imperatives or state interests and intergovernmental bargaining. The lens of normative political theory will redress this deficit by addressing the ethics of the structuration of the European polity and the possibilities for its democratic transformation.

The study also wishes to partake in the newly emergent but fast-growing search for a new explanatory framework in the Union. Intergovernmentalism and neofunctionalism – the two paradigms which have dominated integration theory literature since the mid-1960s – have yielded important insights about the process of European integration, but have been unable to capture the complexity of the political evolution of European governance. By viewing the EC/EU as an international relations phenomenon, they have underscored its polity-like dimensions and confined their research agenda to identifying the rationale for interstate co-operation. But European integration is a contested, uneven and complex process which cannot be reduced to functional exigencies or governmental interests. Moravcsik's liberal intergovernmentalism (1993, 1998) and Keohane's liberal institutionalism (1989) are sophisticated refinements of intergovernmentalism in so far as they pay attention to the process of domestic interest formation and to institutions and their impact on state behaviour, respectively, but they are still nation-state-centred. Federalism exhibits a similar bias towards the state by envisaging a European supranational state or a state-like European polity. Indeed, a distinctive feature of both intergovernmentalist and federalist approaches is that they have been primarily preoccupied with the fate of the nation-state – that is, with the preservation of nation-states (intergovernmentalism) or their withering away and the creation of a putative supranational state (federalism).

It is doubtful whether European governance can be explained on the basis of concepts taken from national statehood. Nor should its study be reduced to the departure from the nation-state/return to the nation-state dualism. Acknowledging the limits of the old debates, approaches derived from the literature on public policy analysis and comparative political science have broadened the research agenda by examining European policy-making, the day-to-day politics of the Union and questions concerning the authoritative allocation and distribution of resources (Hix, 1994, 1998; Marks, Hooghe and Blank, 1996; Richardson, 1996; Risse-Kappen, 1996). From this perspective what is at stake is not just questions of integration as such, but the multifaceted dynamics of the policy process, the role of European institutions and their impact on specific institutional outcomes and issues concerning the formation of a European polity.

The importance of institutions as shapers of outcomes has been highlighted by the 'new institutionalist turn' in EU studies which dates back to Scharpf's (1988) 'joint-decision trap' thesis.[2] Albeit diverse in their methodological and epistemological assumptions, the rational choice and historical institutionalisms comprising the institutionalist literature[3] have provided important insights into different aspects of EU governance, such as the power relations among the European political actors and legislative procedures, the European Parliament's alleged conditional agenda-setting power, the activism of the European Court of Justice (ECJ), the single market, social policy, structural funds and so on. Sociological institutionalism, on the other hand, has only recently began to inform EU research design. By putting emphasis on collective systems of meanings, norms, practices, symbols, culturally specific understandings and their effect on actors' interests, identities and behaviour, sociological institutionalism can help us unravel the assumptions underpinning European governance, examine the impact of Europeanisation on national cultures and traditions and address the thorny issues of democracy, legitimacy and identity in the Union. This research agenda coincides with the social constructivist research programme articulated by more recent reflections in international relations theory (Jorgensen 1997; Christiansen et al., 1999)

Whereas some believe that a more synthetic approach based on some sort of methodological convergence among the three institutionalisms is needed (Aspinwall and Schneider, 1998) – or, more generally speaking, a multidimensional approach which can capture the multifaceted phenomenon of European integration – others view 'Europe' as 'the first truly postmodern' political form (Ruggie, 1993: 140; Ward, 1996, 173–94; Caporaso, 1996). And although the decisive breakthrough in the debate is yet to be achieved, there is hardly any doubt that the complexity, sophistication and uniqueness of the new juridico-political order merit a new conceptual framework.

Unlike traditional international organisations, the European Community represents a unique legal order which has become an integral part of the legal systems of the Member States and which their courts are bound to apply (Case 6/64 *Costa v ENEL* [1964] ECR 585). In an attempt to tame the tired doctrines of nationalism, sovereignty and economic autarky associated with the old statecentric order (Urwin, 1995: 1), the High Contracting Parties established in 1957 a supranational body which is empowered to make decisions that are binding on Member States against their will and to create rights which individuals and undertakings can enforce before national courts (Case 26/92 *Van Gend en Loos* [1963] ECR 1; Case 106/77 *Simmenthal v Amministrazione delle Finanze Dello Stato* [1978] ECR 1453). Proceedings may be brought against defaulting Member States before the Court of Justice without the states' prior consent and sanctions may be imposed in cases of non-compliance with the Court's judgement. Moreover, the preliminary reference procedure under Article 234 EC has established a unique marriage between national and European legal orders in so far as national courts view Community law as part of their national laws and their actual practice.

Finally, in contrast to the reversibility or easy reversibility of traditional international law agreements, the High Contracting Parties have created a Community of unlimited duration.[4] True, the Community is ridden with conflicts as perspectives, agendas and interests fail to coincide. But what is important is that these tensions and disagreements are married into visions of a polity whose members are obligated to ensure fulfilment of their obligations and to abstain from any action that jeopardises the objectives of the Treaty. The safety of the European adventure and the exclusivity of the club are closely guarded by conditioning admission of new members on acceptance of the *acquis communautaire*.

Given the Community's unique legal and institutional structure, the question that arises is how it is possible to develop a research agenda suited to the construction of a novel political order which resists reversion to the old sovereign state and its organising principles and affirms the openness of the future. How could we go about formulating a way of thinking which is critical and yet visionary? In the subsequent section, I discuss some concepts and themes which underpin the discussion in this book and which could be taken as (by no means exhaustive) points of departure for the articulation of a political theory of European integration.

Eight themes for a political theory of European integration and outline of the book

1 The dominant paradigm of sovereign statehood is not an appropriate lens through which to view the new European order in the making. Projections of the old paradigm to the Union lead to the erroneous conception of the European Union as an aspiring superstate competing with the Member States. If, on the other hand, political imagination is freed of the conceptual constraints of the statist paradigm, a search could then commence for those tools required in order to capture European developments. This is not just an intellectual exercise, for the postcolonial misery owes much to a similar inability on the part of political actors to imagine new forms of political community beyond the inherited statist paradigm.

   Eschewing determinist assumptions, there is no reason why the process of integration should lead to a more centralised form of government. European integration is not quest for ultimate statehood (but see Mancini, 1998). Rather, 'Europe' constitutes a unique design which could politically develop along the patterns of co-operative federalism without a state. In such a non-statal form of governance, a gain in functions at one level does not necessarily imply a loss at another. But it does necessitate the reassessment of central organising principles, such as the principle of sovereignty.

2 The EU legal order has contributed to the questioning of the monistic, absolute and indivisible conception of sovereignty upon which traditional legal theory is founded. Suggested alternatives include MacCormick's (1993, 1996) conception of interactive normative orders, Bankowski's adaptation of systems theory (1994: 164) and Sorensen's notion of different types of sovereignty games in the international system (1999: 590–604). Medieval categories have also exerted a certain attraction, with their 'patchwork of overlapping and incomplete rights of government' and 'parcelized sovereignty'.[5] While one can find similarities between the feudal and European political orders, such as the experience of fragmentation, overlapping jurisdictions and plural allegiances, transplantation of neo-medieval metaphors into the European field would obscure what is really at stake in the Union; namely, the institution of co-ordinate and

strategically interacting levels of government. In the Middle Ages, feudal institutions spread and jurisdictions overlapped in a disorganised manner, boundaries were disputed and obligations were ignored. In marked contrast, the Union is characterised by the emergence of a polycentric conception of sovereignty which accommodates multilayered governance, allows for many centres of collective decision-making and the exercise of joint responsibility for certain functions. This may be captured by the idea of nested sovereignties – an idea that underpins much of my discussion on constructive citizenship (Chapters 1, 3 and 5) and a non-restrictive European immigration policy (Chapter 6).

3 The survival and success of sovereignty as an organising principle of national states have much to do with presumptions of their organic unity: states have been portrayed as unitary, undifferentiated and integrated bodies lending an overarching identity to their citizens and compelling their unqualified allegiance. Although most theorists on nationalism underline the modern character of nations, associated either with the emergence of standardised culture (Gellner, 1983), or the process of state formation more generally (Tilly, 1975), or European belief systems and movements (Kedurie, 1993), or invention of traditions (Hobsbawm, 1990) or the emergence of print capitalism (Anderson, 1983), the idea that ethno-history determines the quality, scope and intensity of national identity still exerts considerable influence. According to Smith (1986, 1991), 'ethnic mythomoteurs' – that is, myths, symbols, memories and traditions – may be revived, reinterpreted and recombined, but can neither be fabricated nor invented. However, the tendency to explain the distinctiveness and intensity of nations on the basis of some shared essential attributes and timeless qualities leads to essentialism and the misreading of the political nature and the dynamics of national identity formation. Moreover, if such an approach is transplanted to the European Union, the prospects of the formation of a European identity appear bleak. What are the chances for the development of a European imagined community? What does being a member of the emerging Euro-polity mean after all?

Tempting as it may be to search for answers to those questions within the framework of civic nationalism which views the nation as a community of equal citizens united in a patriotic attachment to a shared set of political values, this model is also inappropriate for two reasons. First, civic national *demoi* have been hegemonised by majority cultures. The dictum that to belong is to conform, to 'take on the essential elements of national character' holds true even in civic territorial states.[6] Second, movements of 'new' citizenship in Europe have demonstrated the failure of state-induced homogenisation by means of a national culture. The pluralism of modern life and the deep diversity of the European Union necessitate a serious rethinking of the connections between citizenship, nationality and culture.[7] Embracing the diversification of attachments and the dynamics of multiple identifications leads to a conception of a European identity which is symbiotic with other existing forms of identification.

The literature on European identity has paid insufficient attention to the dynamic character of European identity formation. 'European identity' is viewed as either something that exists, but needs promotion, or as something that the European Union lacks. Very rarely it is seen as something which is in a process of formation. As a result, analyses tend to exhibit a nostalgia for a 'politics of place' in which community and identity are fused and, quite often, make the people's subjective orientations a standard of evaluation without questioning the quality, depth and consistency of such attitudes. Instead of building my argument on essentialist assumptions about a given European identity or examining the implications of its 'alleged lack' for EU governance, I make central to my argument an inquiry into the institutional reforms and politics which can enhance identification with Europe and sustain the affective allegiance of its citizens (Chapter 1).

The European Union's own official discourse and policy on the question of European identity is quite ambiguous. Despite the official rhetoric on citizenship and aspirations to move towards a civic inclusive mode of identity, the EC/EU adheres to a civic but exclusionary mode of identity (Chapter 2). Positive steps in the areas of citizenship, abolition of discrimination, sex equality, social rights and reduction of regional economic disparities have been overshadowed by an agenda shaped by the logic of exclusion. Third-country nationals residing legally and permanently in the Union are excluded from the free-movement provisions and the other benefits of Union citizenship. The logic of exclusion is further attested by the incremental development of a restrictive European immigration regime, which until quite recently has lacked democratic legitimacy, accountability and judicial supervision, and the substantive nature of the policies agreed (Chapters 2 and 3). But if the political future of Europe lies in establishing a politically constituted, democratic public space, which is respectful of the Other (Derrida, 1992) and is committed to the 'creation of a joint citizenship' (Tassin, 1992: 188–9), then both the theorisation (Chapters 4 and 5) and empirical implementation of such citizenship (Chapter 5) are crucial.

4 Despite differences of opinion concerning the theorisation of Union citizenship and its implications for national citizenship, most scholars believe in the resourcefulness of this institution. Meehan's (1993) pioneering work on European citizenship has highlighted the complexity brought forth by the intersection of subnational dynamics, national and supranational dynamics of European citizenship. However, the challenge of multiple citizenship (Heater, 1990, 1998) is not simply to allow for multiple standards of citizenship and institutional pluralism, but to transform the scope and nature of these citizenships. European citizenship is not simply a neo-national model of citizenship with a European dimension added in

(Leca, 1990). Despite its present limitations, European citizenship has a radical potential which may well lie in the transcendence of the nationality model of citizenship.

'Citizenship' as used in this book refers to the 'bundle' of rights and responsibilities, practices and expectations, benefits and resources, virtues and identities stemming from juridical or associative (i.e. *de facto* citizenship) membership of an individual or a group in multiple, overlapping and strategically interacting political communities formed at various levels. Although citizenship has had an individualistic dimension in so far as it has been used to describe the relationship between the individual and the polity, the European citizenship design needs to accommodate group membership and group-differentiated citizenship (Young, 1989, 1990). Civic identity and civic virtues are also crucial not only as devices for containing nationalism and the antagonisms generated by competing ethnic, cultural, religious and regional identities, but also as the building blocks of a stable democratic polity. These ideas are developed within the framework of constructive citizenship (Chapter 5).

5 Since citizenship is the juridico-political expression of membership in a community, its inclusive or exclusionary character is intimately connected with conceptions about the source and justification of political membership. In the literature, three candidates have been proposed for understanding membership and community: ascription, consent and the fuzzier notion of discourse. Ascription prioritises 'thick' communal attachments (i.e. ties of blood and history, culture, common language, ethnic origin, territory or of common allegiance to a royal sovereign). As such, it is bound to lead to domination and exclusion. The Lockean-inspired principle of consent seems to avoid this problem by making membership a matter of free and mutual choice. But because contractual communities are modelled on 'natural' (in the sense of national) communities which may not accept an individual's membership, consent does not preclude exclusion.

Habermas (1992) aspires to disentangle membership in a political community from ascriptive identities. This disentanglement is pertinent to the politics of EU citizenship and several scholars have sought to apply Habermas's idea of communicative rationality to the Union (Lehning, 1997; Closa, 1998). Given that Habermas's argument is premised on the existence of a single political culture and not a heterogeneous political community, however, I argue below that the formation of a heterogeneous and democratic European public necessitates an alternative conception of what 'belonging' and 'community' means and a rethinking of what binds the people together in a political community (Chapters 4 and 5).

6 The debate on European democratisation has been broadened so as to include issues concerning the social legitimacy of the Union (Weiler, Haltern and Mayer, 1995; Weiler, 1996, de Burca 1996), alongside more traditional questions concerning the EU's democratic deficit. It is often

said that a democratic Europe is impossible, because there is not a European people which is prior and independent of the process of its political constitution.[8] Others point out that 'Europe' lacks the structural preconditions for democratic will formation, such as a European political discourse, a nation-transcending political public sphere and so on (Grimm, 1995: 297). Against this backdrop, scholars swiftly conclude that the achievement of the democratic constitutional state can for the time being be adequately realised only in the national framework.

Such line of reasoning assumes that the national framework is the only and/or the best institutional framework for democracy to work. National democracies can rest their legitimacy on a 'unified will of the people', whereas 'Europe' lacks a similar homogenising identity. What is being overlooked, however, is that democracy may have been contingently wedded to the territorial state, and that the constitution of a European *demos* is both a project and a process (Habermas, 1995). As such, all it requires is the citizens' concern and their participation in the process of a collective design of institutions which reflect their aspirations, accommodate their differences and meet their similar or distinct needs. After all, the Union may be a polity with the potential to do what national democracy cannot: that is, to 'cultivate respect for a politics of democratic governance by pluralizing democratic energies, alliances and spaces of action that exceed the closures of territorial democracy' (Connolly, 1993: 66). Any assessment of the chances for a democratically constituted European polity must therefore take into account the various transformations in democratic practices that have occurred in the European arena – and, in particular, the opening up of the public sphere.

The 'opening up of the public sphere' refers to the multiplication of 'access points' for subnational, national and transnational groups to enter the policy-making process (Mazey and Richardson, 1993: 18). Being both complex and open, the unique institutional structure of the Union invites the formation of 'overlapping policy networks', as multiple interests groups, be they functional or territorial, try to gain access to the Commission and the European Parliament. The Commission's increasing reliance on the scientific knowledge and expertise of interest groups, even on information provided by them about possible breaches of Community law in certain policy sectors, has attracted much attention. Certainly, this does not mean that the situation is one of equal pluralism. Nor are all policy areas equally exposed to the input of organised interests. What the group mobilisation indicates is the opening up of possibilities for more participatory politics (Hirst, 1990: 7) and opportunities for empowerment of those actors who have been disadvantaged at the national level by exercising their influence on a zone of law-making that is 'relatively autonomous' from national political agendas and goals. The emergence of transnational co-operation among political groupings creates a sense of a public forum and has been a valuable experience of 'European' political socialisation, in so far as EU lobbyists realise that the key to success is to think transnational or multinational. These developments in turn facilitate 'partnership-based forms of action' which promote co-operative dialogue, consultation and co-ordination (Mazey and Richardson, 1993: 48). The Union has also prompted a redefinition of policy-making and influenced its content at the national level. 'Europe' does not only shape the intellectual and normative framework of public policy (Mény, Muller and Quermonne, 1996: 11), but domestic policy becomes increasingly the hybrid result of processes of interaction and negotiation among the various levels of governments. So instead of having any preconceptions as to where the proper locus of democracy should be and assuming that an integrated polity by nature is less democratic than its constituent units, it might be more fruitful to examine the various possibilities the Union offers for decentralised decision making, active participation and the airing and institutionalisation of differing views.

True, democracy requires also the *demos'* involvement in the making of political decisions. But the latter process can qualify as fully democratic only if the *demos* includes all adult members of the association – except transients and the mentally defective (Dahl, 1989). According to Dahl, inclusiveness of the *demos* is an essential criterion of the democratic process. In this respect, the civic inclusiveness deficit of the Union – that is, the exclusion of third-country nationals who have been residing on a lawful and permanent basis in the territories of the Union from the benefits of Union citizenship – strikes at the heart of any discussion on European democracy and citizenship, and underpins the discussion in this book.

7 Long-term resident third-country nationals have not been viewed as equal participants in European societies and the emergent European polity by national executives (Chapter 2). Instead, they have been part of the 'problem of immigration' which national executives have sought to tackle through ad hoc and informal intergovernmental co-operation in the beginning (1986–91), then intergovernmental co-operation in the context of the Union (1992–98) and, finally, in post-Amsterdam Europe by relinquishing competence on issues of circulation and residence to the Community. Irrespective of the rationale for the incremental Europeanisation of migration policy (i.e. state inability to control migration flows, the circumvention of national constraints on migration control (Guiraudon, 2000), or state demands for compensatory powers of control at the external frontiers in exchange for the removal of controls at the internal frontiers), the crux of the matter is that it has traditionally been assumed that polities can introduce restrictive and discriminatory immigration policies without causing any damage to democratic principles. In Chapters 6 and 7, I argue that democratic theory and practice can no longer avoid confronting questions of membership and identity of the political community,

and the 'burden' of fashioning a democratic identity. This necessitates a rethinking of the issue of immigration in the Union and the questioning of official discourses which portray immigration as a security issue to be tackled through stringent policing of the Union's external frontiers and internal policies of control and surveillance.

A number of studies have contributed towards a greater understanding of the politics of immigration in the Union either by combining theoretical and empirical perspectives on migration flows, or by providing an overview of legal–institutional developments, or by placing European migration in the context of international migration. Yet the discussion rarely moves beyond the level of 'diagnosis' towards alternative institutional designs. Comparative research – be it on the varying conceptions of national identity in Western European countries; on citizenship, nationality and immigrations; on official immigration discourses; on naturalisation policies in Europe; on racism and the rise of anti-immigrant parties – confirms that the future is not bright for migrants in Europe. Suggested alternatives consist of recommendations on how to promote more democratic control of (albeit limited) migration. But rarely do they entail 'a politics of vision' founded on the hypothesis that immigration may be a blessing, and not a curse. By engaging with both vision and reality, theory and critique, I develop a theoretical paradigm for migration policy in the Union (i.e. economic migration, family reunification, asylum). My institutional recommendations on this matter delineate the broad themes of a principled, enlightened, justiciable and non-restrictive European migration policy (Chapter 7).

8 Coherent and principled institutional designs in the fields of European immigration and citizenship can succeed only if they are able to shape people's preferences, inform identities and encourage motivations. Since the identities of citizens are bound up with the institutions in which they are involved, a consideration of subjectivity and its mode of being in the context of the Union is essential (Chapter 7). After all, nationalism, in its various varieties, xenophobia and the rise in new racism can hardly be understood without attention to processes of collective identity formation.

Post-structuralist, anti-essentialist studies of identity formation have shown that identities are the outcome of complex and contingent practices of articulation. They are not objectively given – that is, the reflection of necessary essences – but the product of complex systems of identification mediated through difference. This means that there can be no identity unless difference (or, to be more precise, differences) have played their defining role. On this reading, subjectivity is a *process*: identity is formed and transformed through communication with others. Acknowledging the relational character of our identities, the difference within ourselves and around ourselves and letting go of aspirations to have a fully objective identity is the key to uncovering new ways of being together. For Connolly, such an acknowledgement is essential for the cultivation of an 'ethic of agonistic respect' which like a bridge connects but does not unite (Connolly, 1991a). And as Abu-Lughod (cit. in Moghadam, 1989: 96) has noted, 'to recognise that the self may not be so unitary and that the other might actually consist of many others who may not be so Other after all is to raise the theoretically interesting problem of how to build ways of accepting or describing differences without denying similarities or turning these various differences into a single, frozen difference'.

Single frozen differences and rituals of enmity and exclusion have been the effect of modern territorial states. Political subjectivities have been constructed through systems of signification and boundary-producing practices which emphasise the states' exclusive ownership of the territory instead of dwelling; control, exclusion and the securitisation of migration instead of connection; cultural conformity for migrants and their families instead of their equal participation in the fullness of public life; the territorial state's monopoly of control over signification instead of the deterritorialisation and pluralisation of identities (Chapter 7).

But to define the self in the context of the Union as essential and unitary is to underestimate the importance of shared experiences and the commonness of the European project. To neglect the importance of cultivating an interest in the future of the polity and fostering an ethic of the Other is to dispute the possibility of a European civil society and a European identity, or at least of such conceptions of European civil society and identity as those furnished in this book.

Notes

1   Compare Curtin (1993); Harden (1995); Seurin (1995); Petersmann (1995); Weale (1995); MacCormick (1993); Walker (1996); Shaw (1999).
2   Scharpf (1988: 271) describes the joint decision trap as
      an institutional arrangement whose policy outcomes have an inherent (non-accidental) tendency to be sub-optimal – certainly when compared to the policy potential of unitary governments of similar size and resources. Nevertheless the arrangement represents a 'local optimum' in the cost-benefit calculations of all participants that might have the power to change it. If that is so, there is no 'gradualist' way in which joint-decision systems might transform themselves into an institutional arrangement of greater policy potential.
3   The discussion here espouses Hall and Taylor's (1996) distinction among sociological, historical and rational-choice institutionalisms.
4   The most interesting metaphor is that provided by Weiler (1993).
5   Strayer and Munro (1959); Somers (1994). For a critique of uses of neo-medieval metaphors in the European Union, see Wæver (1995).
6   For the opposite view, see Miller (1993, 1994).
7   On this, see Connolly (1996); Goodin (1996).
8   This is the 'no-*demos*' thesis adopted by the German Constitutional Court in

Cases 2 BvR 2134/92 and 2159/92, *Brunner v European Union Treaty* [1994] 1 CMLR 57: namely, that there can be no democracy without the existence of a European *demos*. For a critique, see Weiler (1995). Preuss (1995:108, 1998) has also remarked that a European *demos* will be the product, and not the precondition, of European democracy.

1

European identity

The European Union is not sure who it is. It has found an identity, but it is not certain whether this is its 'true' identity. Its main business is to find an identity which is capable of inducing feelings of belonging and the involvement of European peoples. This is not an easy task. If the EC/EU were simply a political form of interstate co-operation, be it in the form of a Grotian 'society of nations' or de Gaulle's idea of a 'security community', then the question of a European identity would not arise or would, at best, be secondary. It is because the EC/EU is more than a forum of transnational decision-making, a policy-generating mechanism and a 'security community' that the issue of European identity features prominently on the European policy agenda.

As an emerging polity, the EC/EU has to foster a sense of solidarity among European peoples who would not hesitate to participate in the project of European unification and support it in times of crises. After all, in order to make 'Europe' work, you need 'Europeans' (Shaw, 1997) – or, at least, people who are not so unwilling to accept European integration so as to posit insurmountable obstacles to it. In addition, the position of the European Union as an international actor would be strengthened by the creation of a collective identity *vis-à-vis* other parts of the world. This outward dimension of a European identity has been explored by the literature on European external relations and security (Wæver, 1995, 1996; Laffan, 1996; Buzan et al., 1998).

But what kind of identity does the EC/EU need to foster? The answer to this question is not straightforward, for it is generally acknowledged that we lack the necessary conceptual and theoretical tools in order to theorise European identity. This might explain why most academics tend to view European identity as the 'mirror image' of national identity and apply concepts, models and practices associated with the nation-state and/or federal systems to the EC/EU. By so doing, they tend to endow the EC/EU with state-like and nation-like qualities. Whereas hardly anybody would disagree with the dictum that 'one does not fall in love with the common market', it is unclear why the European peoples should identify with a European flag and anthem, myths and symbolisms relating to 'Europe's unique cultural past' or 'Europe's destiny'. Such accounts criticise 'Europe' for failing to become the object of unqualified allegiance and overlook the problems that might arise if it became the overarching locus of identification. There is such an inbuilt bias towards national statism in the literature that it becomes difficult to imagine a process of formation of European identity which does not resemble the nineteenth-century process of national identity or community-building (Smith, 1992; Wilterdink, 1993) or, indeed, to conceptualise European identity itself in novel terms.[1]

Against such a background, it is not surprising that the feasibility of European identity is put into question. It is said that the formation of a European identity is an impossible task because Europe is too diverse and 'lacks emotional resistance and historical depth' (Smith, 1992: 70–4, 1995). The absence of the known homogenising elements, such as a *lingua franca*, a uniform system of education, mass media, a European public opinion and so on, are seen to create insurmountable obstacles to European identity-building. In the search of the appropriate building blocks for the creation of 'a living cultural awareness of truly pan-European dimensions' (Garcia, 1993), the model of national integration by contract, nevertheless, remains an attractive candidate (Howe, 1995: 34–42; Laffan, 1996: 102–3; Weiler, 1997).

In this chapter I take issue with these assumptions and examine the impact of the politics of European identity upon the nature of the emerging Euro-polity and the project of European integration. The purpose of this chapter is thus twofold. First, to examine the conditions of possibility for a European identity and, secondly, to provide a systematic theorisation of European identity. In this respect, I draw a typology of European identity options based on differing assumptions on what 'Europe' stands for and what 'political community' means. As the discussion proceeds, it will be made clear that it is imperative to make a judgement about which of these approaches is preferable and on what grounds.

Conditions of possibility for a European identity

The European Union as an evolving form of governance beyond the nation-state

The relationship between a European identity and other existing forms of identification has been the subject of much controversy. This is because positions in the debate over European identity are defined by the answers they give to some other questions, such as: (i) What is the nature of a European identity?; (ii) What is its function? (iii) What is the role of the nation-state and national identity in the process of European unification? (iv) How can we conceive of the latter process and what is its *telos*? And as to be expected, opinions diverge considerably over these issues. Let us briefly examine these

views before proceeding to address the relationship between European identity and other existing identifications.

For many, the creation of 'an ever closer Union' signals the creation of a
modern Leviathan which will annihilate national sovereignty, generate
bureaucratic apparatuses, minimise accountability, undermine democracy
and erode the current sense of nationhood of the Member States. These fears
were manifested in varying degrees in the post-Maastricht ratification crises,[2]
the 'Maastricht ruling' of the Bundesverfassungsgericht (12 October 1993, 2
BvR 2134/92, 2 BvR 2159/92 (*Brunner v European Union Treaty*), and the
British Conservative opposition to the 'deepening' of European integration.
In part, this resistance is due to a dogmatic adherence to the principle of
national sovereignty as a basic political value (Pinder, 1995 [1991]: 6). Certainly, one cannot discount the role that ideology has played in this process.
In the UK, English nationalism underpins the Conservative opposition to
'Europe': 'the Conservative Party's discourse is instinctively that of national
identity' (Wallace, 1995: 50). This explains why Conservative Euro-sceptics
in the early 1990s saw it as a categorical imperative to defend British national
sovereignty against the federal scenario which, in their opinion, has been
based upon the false appreciation that the nation-state in Europe is dead.
Similar worries exist in France about the prospect of a European federation
in which the nation will lose its identity as a sovereign political unit, or about
the prospect of 'a Baroque or Gaudiesque construction, multilevel and mul-
tispeed, manipulated above all by Germany' (Hoffmann, 1993).

Interestingly, such worries flourish despite the general acknowledgement
that the traditional, monistic conception of sovereignty needs rethinking in
light of contemporary developments, such as the internationalisation of capital, the growth of virtually stateless, multinational firms, the emergence of
social and regional movements, international mobility and the absence of
empirical evidence suggesting that states are 'withering away'. True, states'
functions have been redefined and decision-making is constrained by virtue
of their participation in an interlocking network of bargained situations
(Mann, 1993; Muller and Wright, 1994: 1–11). But states retain a nodal
decision-making position. As Wallace (1999: 505) has observed 'government
remains national, though significant aspects of governance now operate
above (and below) the nation-state level'.

State involvement in the European integrative project confirms this. The
Member States remain the 'masters of the Treaty' – that is, are authorised to
shape the crucial 'moments of European constitutional choice', be they primary law (i.e. the Treaties), amendments of the Treaties or decisions concerning the accession of new members to the Community, and Community
law is 'normatively and politically dependent on law and practice in member
states' (MacCormick, 1995: 101). The EC/EU's legislative input crucially
depends on the Member States who are also responsible for the administration and implementation of its rules. Additionally, national interests are well

represented in the European Council and the Council of the European Union (i.e. the Council of Ministers), whose meetings are characterised by an 'ethos of consensus': efforts are made to reach agreement and accommodate the dissenting viewpoints even when decisions are to be taken by qualified or simple majority voting.

Community membership may not undermine statehood – 'the Treaties contain a variety of formal indications for this' (Dashwood, 1998: 202), but neither has it left it unchanged. Domestic legal systems and administrative practices have become 'Europeanised' and national laws have ceased to be purely domestic. Rather, they are hybrid, that is, the result of the implementation of Community legislation. Several issue areas falling within the exclusive domain of national policy have been incorporated within the authoritative purview of the EC/EU (Schmitter, 1996: 124–5). Additionally, the European Court of Justice (ECJ) has circumscribed the Member States' capacity to 'exit selectively', that is to say, to avoid their obligations under the Treaty (Weiler, 1991). The EC/EU and the Member States are therefore entangled in a dynamic process of reciprocal interaction and continuing evolution in relation to one another simultaneously with their respective motion and change in relation to other possible environments. Needless to say, both partners are not unified and homogeneous systems: they are sites of contestation and conflict. But this does not deny their involvement in a process of reciprocal influence, the 'osmotic' relationship between the Member States and the Community (Schuppert, 1995: 349–50). As Schuppert (1995: 350) has put it,

> if reciprocal influence is the key to understanding the process of European development, it cannot be a case of either waiting for the EC to take the step of becoming a federal state or, alternatively, of anxiously observing the process of the erosion of the nation-state in order not to miss the moment which finally marks the loss of sovereignty.

This is essentially a call to rethink our inherited terminology and to devise concepts that can reflect both the distinctiveness of the new evolving form of governance beyond the nation-state and the transformation of the state without overlooking the creative tensions, dialectical struggles and conflicts entailed by such processes. It also presupposes a shift of focus from the *telos* of European integration (i.e. the end product to be predicted on the basis of deterministic laws) to its process-like nature. But will the development of a way of thinking which prioritises 'system interaction' and 'system change' rather than the familiar models of the state, political community or supranationality lead to the reformulation of the doctrine of state sovereignty? And, further, how will this affect the relationship between European identity and national identities?

'Statecentrists' – that is, those who believe that the European project is (and should be) all about interstate co-operation and diplomacy – will not be convinced about the need for a rearticulation of the principle of state sovereignty. Alan Milward's (1992) sophisticated study of the origins of European integration has shown, for example, that the choice of the paradigm of integration over that of interdependence can be explained on the basis of sovereign states pursuing their national interests. By embarking upon a series of historical case studies – ranging from the Belgian coal industry to the change in the British policy towards Europe as a result of the rise of the German industry and the car production levels, Milward et al. (1993) have demonstrated that the 'evolution of the Community has been an integral part of the reassertion of the nation-state as an organizational concept'. Stanley Hoffmann has also defended the enduring existence of the nation-state as a community of belonging and identity – provided, of course, that integration is confined to a low-level interstate co-operation in certain limited fields. Hoffmann's 'co-existence thesis' tends to underplay the increasing interdependence of international politics and the penetration of the Community legal order into domestic orders.

The ambivalent evolution of the European Community in the 1990s, whereby states neither remained resistant to the Community's intrusive pressures nor became absorbed by a European federation, has led Taylor (1991, 1996) to revise the intergovernmentalist paradigm by developing the model of consociational confederalism. Consociational confederalism acknowledges the need for common solutions to persistent problems and mutual co-operation without succumbing to the supranationalist solutions proposed by the neofunctionalist or federalist perspectives. Along not so dissimilar lines, Moravcsik's liberal intergovernmentalism purports to explain the interaction between states and international organisations, such as the EC/EU, by exploring the relationship between national interest formation and interstate bargaining. Accordingly, European integration is accounted for on the basis of the lowest common denominator intergovernmental bargains, in which the pursuit of national interests reflecting domestic policy preferences leads to institutional outcomes which serve the long-term interest of the Member States (1991, 1993: 514, 1998).[3] On this reading, the EC/EU increases 'the efficiency of bargaining by providing a set of passive, transaction-cost reducing rules' (Moravcsik, 1993: 517).

Despite the (often striking) differences among the various intergovernmentalist perspectives, all of them, nonetheless, share: (i) a belief in the resilience of the nation-state; (ii) the tendency to view European integration through the lens of the state which is assumed to be a rational actor having objective interests (neo-realism) or reflecting aggregated domestic preferences which are defined exogeneously (liberal intergovernmentalism); (iii) the tendency to focus on selective data so as to validate the theory. Convinced that there can be no viable and effective political framework beyond the nation-state and that states are the exclusive nexus between domestic politics and international relations (Chryssochoou et al., 1999), state-centric theorists tend to 'mobilize notions of the past in order to explain developments in the future' (Koopmans, 1992: 1049). By so doing, they overlook the artificiality and historicity of nation-state as a mode of political organisation and resist any suggestion to 'look first at the different levels of government activities, without any preconceived idea as to where the sovereign state is, or should be' (Koopmans, 1992: 1049). There are three reasons for this. First, given that sovereignty is seen as constitutive of statehood, its dilution or its possible dislocation from the state cannot but have significant repercussions for the continued existence of modern territorial states. It would take us 'beyond the sovereign state' (MacCormick, 1993, 1995). Secondly, bearing in mind that modern states are seen to embody the democratic will of the people as a nation, that is, as an intergenerational community founded on sacred ties and trust, any limitations imposed on 'national sovereignty' by bodies other than those in which sovereign power is vested might lead to the weakening of the national community of belonging and identity.[4] Finally, since the idea that sovereignty can neither be transferred nor shared is deeply engraved in the Member States' political cultures, it would be unrealistic to expect that national political elites would readily admit that: (i) there may not exist certain core prerogatives whose sum total equals sovereignty; (ii) sovereignty is not a zero-sum game where a gain in capability at one level implies a loss at another. Political expediencies often force governments to maintain the illusion that they can meet the exigencies of the global political economy and of international politics in ways that suit their own national interests and sovereign prerogatives. In other words, it is not so important that governments are in control as that they appear to be in control.

In response to the first point, it can be said that if sovereignty is seen as an essential attribute of statehood, then the transfer of certain competences to the Community does not automatically reduce overall state power; it could even increase it if it brings other gains (Newman, 1996: 13). But if sovereignty is seen as a bundle of competences that can be gradually pooled or transferred to supranational bodies, then the transfer of certain competences reduces state power. As the French senators submitted to the Constitutional Council: 'if sovereignty is no longer anything but an addition of competences, if one can successively remove them as one would the leaves of an artichoke, at what point, or at what degree, do we derive at the heart?'(cit. in Hoffmann, 1993: 72). Is there 'a constitutionally defined tolerance threshold to the transfer of powers to European institutions' (Bonnie, 1998: 524)? Hoffmann's distinction between areas of 'low politics' and 'high politics' – that is, competences which are not integral to state power could be transferred upwards and those which form the 'heart' of the artichoke – could be useful in this connection. In its decisions on the compatibility of the Maastricht and Amsterdam Treaties with French constitutional law, the French Constitutional Council referred to certain 'essential conditions for the exercise of national sovereignty', core sovereign powers, such as immigration policy, foreign policy, defence policy and monetary policy, whose transfer to the Community would require prior constitutional amendment (Decision 92-308 DC 9 April 1992; Decision 97-394 DC 31 December 1997) (see also Mayall, 1999). Such an approach, however, fails to define 'core' and 'peripheral' powers in a reliable way and underscores the possible 'politicisation' of peripheral powers and their reclassification as core powers.

A different approach would have to recognise the peculiar and exceptional nature of the 'artichoke' (provided that we retain the simile): it is capable of mutating, regenerating new leaves and does not have a heart. On this reading, sovereignty is not an inherent quality of statehood, but is a discursive category designed to legitimise state power by inventing timeless foundations and essences (Weber, 1995; Sorensen, 1999). It may be defined as an empty space since it is not actually inhabited. This does not mean that sovereignty does not exist. It exists, but it is located within the radically open domain of discourse.

In the UK, discursive games on parliamentary sovereignty featured prominently in the academic scene in the 1980s and early 1990s and rallied supporters in reaction to 'Europe'. According to Dicey, 'parliamentary sovereignty' or the Parliament's legislative omnipotence means that the Queen in Parliament has the 'right to make or unmake any law whatever' (the positive aspect), and 'no person or body is recognised by the law of England as having a right to override or set aside the legislation of Parliament' (the negative aspect) (Dicey, 1959: 40). Although legal sovereignty is subordinate to the political sovereignty of the nation (i.e. the belief that ultimate power rests with the electorate), and the two notions are often blurred, criticisms of the political notion of sovereignty on the grounds that it conceals executive rule and party domination and/or it is no longer apposite to political realities left legal sovereignty unaffected. More importantly, it was the legal conception of sovereignty – that is, the idea of unlimited legislative authority and a hierarchical legal relationship between the legislature and the courts (i.e. no court within the UK can set aside an act of Parliament) – that hampered the recognition of the primacy of EC law over conflicting national law. True, this issue has finally been resolved (see the *Factortame* saga and *Secretary of State for Employment, ex parte Equal Opportunities Commission* [1994] 2 WLR 409), and the British judiciary has accepted the supremacy of EC law.[5]

Despite this resolution, worries nevertheless remain about the migration of legislative authority into the European level under the control of an 'indeterminate and intangible political sovereign that can be identified only through the diffuse procedures of the European Union' (Bradley, 1994: 91–4). Such concerns echo Dahl's (1994) fundamental democratic dilemma': namely, the compatibility between the ability of a national political unit to exercise democratic control over the decision of the polity on the one hand, and the need for a more effective decision-making in response to an increasingly internationalised world on the other (also points (ii) and (iii) on p. 18). In his reflections on the Maastricht Treaty, Dahl highlighted the trade off between democratic values and system effectiveness, but he also conceded that in the European Union a sort of transnational polyarchy might gradually come into existence (Dahl, 1994: 32).

Dahl's argument concerning the inverse relationship between 'system effectiveness' and 'citizen effectiveness' (i.e. democratic control) relies on the cumulative verification of the following two hypotheses. First, citizens do actively participate in national deliberative processes and can effectively influence the conduct of their government. In other words, the quality of democratic governance at the national level is quite high. Secondly, the Community is not distinguished by a comparable level of democratic control because: (i) decisions are taken by faceless, distant and intangible political bodies whose accountability to either European or national Parliaments is weak, (ii) there exists no transnational participatory political culture, (iii) intergovernmental bargains and deals struck by big states are likely to disregard the interests of small states; (iv) when the Council decides by qualified majority voting, possible outvoting of a state deprives the citizens of that country from exercising control over both the content and financing of policies within the EC's competence.

As regards (i), reservations can be raised about the tendency to exaggerate the democratic qualities of national democracies. Citizens do have the power to choose who will govern them at the ballot box but, arguably, there is more to democracy than voting on election day. True, electoral participation has stagnated, party identification has declined and participation in direct and uninstitutionalised forms of political action, such as petitions, demonstrations and political boycotts on the other hand, does not have a crucial impact upon governmental decisions or the exercise of political power. In other words, the state of democracy at the national level is far from perfect. European polities must take democracy seriously and remedy imbalances in participation and representation, accountability and openness, equality and citizenship. European integration can perhaps aid this process of democratisation by consolidating the democratic culture of the public domain at the supranational level and by empowering individuals and collective actors. This leads me to hypothesis (ii) about the democratic credentials of the European Union.

Although it is fashionable to talk about the 'democratic deficit' of the EC/EU, be this an accountability deficit, transparency deficit, information deficit or social legitimacy deficit, we tend to forget that national governments bear a great deal of responsibility for it. A historical look at the process of European integration unravels both the origins of horizontal distributions of power among the European institutions and the determination of national governments to preserve their pre-eminence and to control the trend towards supranationalism. More importantly, Member States' representatives, acting as the legislature of the Community, have chosen to act 'not in a

manner of the presumed openness characteristic of liberal democratic parliamentary regimes, but of a closed, secretive, unaccountable system' (Lodge,
1994: 346). The Amsterdam Treaty has made some advances in this respect
but, as we shall see below, the process of the democratisation of the Union is
far from complete. Despite these problems, European integration, nevertheless, offers possibilities for the creation of a network of subnational bodies
and for citizen empowerment. One notices, for example, the extent to which
subnational actors have embraced the European project in an attempt to shift
the domestic balance of power. For them, 'Europe' is a unique opportunity
to make their voices heard and a tool for inducing changes in domestic law
and policy (see the introduction and p. 36 below). In this respect, it might be
more fruitful to examine the interactions between the Member States and the
Community without assuming that national communities offer the best
framework for democracy.

It may be objected here that 'the fact that even a huge majority of the electors in polity A can be outvoted by the electors of polities B and C shows that
integrated polity is less democratic – although not necessarily undemocratic'
(Weiler, 1991: 2470). Weiler's argument depends on the presupposition that
there exists a single and unified national voice in polity A, which is represented by the national government with respect to taxation, education, foreign policy and so on, and that governmental interests reflect electoral
preferences. But doubts can be raised about both the unity and the repre-
sentativeness of the national voice. Even in the exceptional case of a victori-
ous party at a general election enjoying the support of a majority of electors,
it would be incorrect to argue that there is a huge majority on specific policy
issues. It is also problematic to extrapolate opinions for specific policies
from voting behaviour since the latter may be determined by factors other
than personal opinions about rival election manifestos. In addition, citizens
do not normally endorse the whole manifesto of the party they support at
the polls. Moreover, governments often masquerade a narrower private
interest as general interest. And even within the governing elite it is not
uncommon to find that conflicting views and preferences exist as to which
particular policy option should be the 'national' one. Weiler does not only
exaggerate the democratic pedigree of national governments, but he also
underscores the fact that the boundaries between the domestic and international or supranational domains have become very malleable and porous.
National decisions and policies produce inputs into other states' political
systems and states frequently design their policies having the policies of their
neighbours and competitors in mind. Finally, Weiler tends to assume that
national publics are homogeneous while, in reality, all national *demoi* are
fragmented. Citizens in polity A, who may or may have not voted for the vic-
torious party, could thus find that their interests and preferences in certain
policy areas, such as consumer protection, environment or social policy, are
best reflected by the governments of polity B or C, or other international

agencies, policy networks and so on. But if electors in polity A are beginning to see that they have more in common with electors/groups in polity B than with their own government and lend support to or derive benefits from decisions taken by other governments in the Council, from Community initiatives or initiatives taken by other groups or policy networks elsewhere in the Union (in the special case that a minority in polity A is aligned with electoral minorities in polities B and C), then the argument about the alleged loss of democracy must be rethought. Notwithstanding its present democratic imperfections, the EC/EU could be seen as enhancing democratic principles by enabling the creation of a complex web of relationships beyond borders and, hence, the formation of a heterogeneous *demos* beyond the nation-state.

European identity and national identities: a tale of symbiosis

But if this is the case, are not statecentrists and Euro-sceptics alike justified in fearing that European integration will compromise the identity of the Member States and weaken nationhood? The neo-functionalist predictions about the gradual transfer of peoples' loyalties from the national to the supranational level were predicated on the assumption that the new supranational institutions would possess and demand jurisdiction over the pre-existing national states (Haas, 1958) and the underestimation of the pervasiveness and deep-rootedness of national identities. Intergovernmentalists are quick to point out that the formation of a European identity or, at least, of a deep European identity unavoidably competes with pre-existing and deeply rooted myths and memories. But in this competition 'Europe' lags behind since it lacks myths and symbolisms, that is, the essential material out of which collective identities are made.

On that view, the nation-state remains the ultimate locus of political authority and the overarching locus of identification. National identities are strong because they satisfy deep human psychological needs, such as the need to 'belong' somewhere and to overcome the futility and transience of human existence through the dream of collective immortality. This line of reasoning, however, often portrays the nation as a unitary, seamless transhistorical cultural community which is imbued with timeless qualities. In the same vein, national identities are seen as the product of either timeless essences (the primordialist approach) or the combination of modern socio-political conditions and the premodern, ethnic elements within nations (the ethnonational approach). Both approaches are essentialist in so far as they assume some underlying and enduring basic structure or substance which transcends historical variations and change. Even depictions of national identity as a civic identity and therefore of the nation as a democratic community of citizens have not managed to escape the trappings of a naturalistic conception of ethnicity and homogeneity.

What is overlooked by these perspectives is that the nation is only one of the communities, imagined or not, to which individuals happen to belong.

There are several forms of identification beyond and below the nation-state, which are capable of generating a sense of belonging to a community. As the literature on postmodern subjectivities and identity politics has shown, individuals inhabit multiple worlds simultaneously, interact in various contexts and grow as personalities by developing various identifications in relation to all these contexts. Multiple identity is normal: 'individuals have a more or less extensive repertoire of identity options which they call upon or engage within different contexts and for different purposes' (Wallmans, 1983: 70). Despite the monocultural ideology of the nation-state, Black British, Muslim British, Scottish and Welsh people have all experienced the process of shifting in and out of various subject positions, the moving in and out of multiple 'homes'. Similarly, participants at supranational or international levels, and members of transnational pressure groups (e.g. Amnesty International, Greenpeace, Save the Children, Oxfam) do not unquestionably give moral primacy to the nation over all other human associations. This does not mean that all identifications are equally intense and durable. Some identifications will be more durable than others, but none is fixed: all are subject to negotiation and re-articulation through various narratives and specific forms of collective action. One may be a member of a neighbourhood watch scheme, the Anglican church, a trade union, identify oneself with Scotland, seek the protection of the British embassy when travelling abroad and be European-minded when environmental interests or social rights are heard and acted on in Brussels. Different contexts yield different 'sorts' of experiences which in turn induce different identifications. More importantly, it is our living within these multiple worlds that makes us distinctively us.

Critics may object here that what really matters is not so much whether individuals have multiple personal identifications as the recognition of the pervasive character of collective identities. Since 1992, *Eurobarometer* has been tracking the development of a shared European identity among the citizens of the Union by asking them regularly whether they see themselves as nationals only or nationals and Europeans. Interestingly, the figure of the respondents who identify themselves as both nationals and Europeans has not fallen below 40 per cent since 1992 (this figure is 41 per cent according to *Eurobarometer*, 49, Spring 1998), but it has not become more widespread over the years either. Indeed, in Portugal (62 per cent), the UK (60 per cent) and Sweden (59 per cent), people are still most likely to see themselves as their own nationality only. In contrast, in Austria, Spain, Portugal, Greece and Ireland, identification with Europe has increased. This data lends support to the argument that Europe cannot compete in popular consciousness with deeply rooted national identities. As Smith has argued, 'at the collective level it is not the options and feelings of individuals that matter, but the nature of the collective bond' (Smith, 1995: 123–4). This bond is seen to have an enduring quality and exert a powerful presence over the lives of individuals: 'for the moment, the ethnic and national levels of identification will take priority' (Smith, 1993: 134).

In response, it can be argued that it is not the objective nature of the bond itself but the articulation of discourses about it which gives national identity its force and leads to the production of subjectivities. And although one cannot deny that collective identities, be they national, ethnic or cultural, do matter, my argument has sought to question how they should matter. By recognising the artificiality of identities, their contradictory and multiple nature, one can expose the domination and overarching power underlying the social construction of national identities. Since people can cultivate political loyalties and have identifications which extend beyond and across state borders, subnational, national, transnational and supranational identities can interact in ways that create political options.

The dispersal of political allegiance over various political units does not only highlight the plural and flexible character of one's commitments, but it also undermines the nation-state's monopoly in lending an ultimate political identity to its citizens and demanding unqualified allegiance. This should not necessarily lead to the weakening of a strong sense of commitment and loyalty – unless, of course, what is implied by the latter is a strong sentiment of national patriotism that subjugates the civic ethic of responsibility and critical reflection to unqualified allegiance. Notably, this sentiment, in its historical peculiarity, is evoked in citizens in order to ensure spontaneous acceptance of governmental enactments and policy options mostly on the grounds of necessity (national expediencies) and trust (those who know best care about the interests of the country), and not on the basis of conscious insight and merit. But in this case, patriotic allegiance amounts to nothing else than uncritical surrender of every right to authority. If, on the other hand, political allegiance is conceived as concern, active engagement and commitment to common projects, then the possibility of being loyal to a combination of political units cannot be ruled out. Of course, conflicts may arise. But in such a case, the pre-eminence given to any of them cannot be determined *a priori*, as intergovernmentalists seem to believe. It depends, instead, on the reflexive assessment of the quality of the claims involved (Laski, 1917: 19).

To sum up, the claim that European and national identities are uneasy bedfellows tends to reinforce the misconception that identities are unitary, fixed and inflexible. Such an essentialist conception of identity is coupled with a nationalistic populist appeal which praises the unity and homogeneity of the nation. By treating ethnic/cultural heterogeneity as a problem and multiple identity as an unhealthy choice, national identification is seen as the dominant identification which should override other allegiances in scope and power. But if a European identity is neither structurally nor theoretically incompatible with national identities, what kind of impact might the changing content and the shifting boundaries of the Union have upon the formation of a European identity?

One 'Europe' or several 'Europes'? Does the indeterminacy of
Europe hinder the formation of a European identity?
Throughout history 'Europe' has been characterised by the mutability of its
content and its shifting boundaries. In other words, there have been several
'Europes' within Europe: the Europe of Greek mythology and Hellenistic
ideas; the medieval Europe; the Christian Europe; the Europe of the
Enlightenment; the colonial Europe; the racial definition of Europe as an
Aryan continent; the Atlantic Europe; the capitalist Europe and so on. This
historical indeterminacy of Europe is coupled with political indeterminacy.
The discussion above has mapped some of the conflicting views as to what
the European Union is and what it should be. In addition, there exist various and differing interpretations of 'Europeanness' at national and subnational levels, since political actors interpret European developments in
distinctive ways in accordance with the requirements of domestic political
scenes and their unfulfilled expectations.

Such processes of articulation and re-articulation of Europeannness are
prominent in Eastern Europe and will become even more so with the accession of Central and Eastern European (CEE) countries to the Union. In the
search for a new political identity after the collapse of communism, these
countries are keen to present themselves as the 'kidnapped, displaced and
brainwashed West', to use Kundera's term (1984), thereby seeking to redeem
their culturally and historically legitimate Western identity which was
allegedly lost under communism.

Political forces within Western Europe have also tried to identify the speci-
ficity of Europe in narratives on Europe's unique cultural heritage, on myth-
ical essences and fictitious commonalities that various national or ethnic
collectivities might possess. Others tend to put emphasis on the spirit of the
Enlightenment – that is, the values of modernity (autonomy, tolerance,
liberty). But such appeals to a 'European heritage' are selective: they overlook the crucial experiences of colonialism, European totalitarianism, the
Holocaust and decolonisation, as well as Europe's multicultural realities
(Pieterse, 1991; Delanty, 1995, 1996).

Arguably, 'Europe' does not need to be filled with Euro-centric myths in
order to act as an integrating device.[6] Nor does the idea of European unity
need to appeal to ideas such as the protection of the European cultural heritage – 'the unique amalgam of Greek humanist, Roman–legal and Christian
spiritual values', in order to develop as a political doctrine. For such significa-
tions can only ignite European racism and xenophobia by culture-baiting
ethnic minorities as 'aliens' and essentialising differences between European
and non-European worlds. Right-wing political discourses by calling for a
'Europe for the Europeans' have portrayed Europe's ethnic residents and citizens as radically 'Other', and thus as a threat to the 'relative ethno-cultural
homogeneity' of Europe. This new face of racism in Europe, named 'cultural
differentialist' or 'mixophobic' (Balibar and Wallerstein 1991; Taguieff, 1994:

124), draws upon the theme of the 'European civilisation' and Europe's original ethno-cultural identity in order to depict Europe's immigrant population
as culturally different. On this basis, GRECE (Groupement de recherche et
d'Etudes pour la Civilisation Européenne), the cultural wing of the French
'New Right', advocates a return to an original European identity which is
purified from the 'Judeo-Christian elements of egalitarianism'; and the
'emptiness' of humanism and universalism (de Benoist, 1985, 1994). One
cannot, thus, overlook the danger of exclusion and discrimination entailed by
such essentialist representations of Europe and of European identity.

The existence of many representations of 'Europe' and interpretations
of 'Europeanness' should not be taken to suggest that the formation of a
European identity is an impossible task. It simply shows that 'Europe' neither
obeys a single unifying logic, nor can it be reduced to an essence. Ideas about
Europe and European identity can be found, produced and reproduced in a
wide array of discourses marked by political power. This highlights the
urgency and importance of the formation of a civic and inclusive European
identity which is embedded in political institutions, rules, procedures, practices and understandings.

A typology of European identity options

The discussion thus far has focused on the possible conditions for the formation of a European identity. This section will conceptualise European
identity by drawing a typology of European identity options based on differing perspectives about the meaning of European identity and community-
building in the European Unity. The juxtaposition of various modes of
European identity will yield interesting insights for the politics of European
identity formation and will elucidate the salience of this issue for the political development of the Community. I begin with the Euro-nationalist mode
of European identity.

The Euro-nationalist mode of identity
The Euro-nationalist approach is distinguished by the application of the
nationalist framework of analysis to the question of European identity. The
EC/EU is modelled on the patterns set by the formation of national communities in the ninetennth century and European identity mirrors the pattern of
national identity-building. Although the creation of a organic and involuntary community of 'Europeans' is seen as the end product of European integration, opinions diverge over the desirability of such a goal and the
prospects of its success. Two candidates appear to provide the overall framework of analysis for European identity: ethno-nationalism and civic nationalism. By putting emphasis on the past and the existence of naturalistic bonds
among people, the former approach is rather pessimistic about the chances
of the formation of a European identity and community. A civic national

approach, on the other hand, is forward-looking and optimistic. It views the emergent European community as a community with a shared destiny which is built upon the combination of political structures and abstract principles which do not reflect the particularity of its constituent units. However, both approaches are premised on the enfeebled sense that European identity must resemble national identity.

A prime exponent of the former approach is Anthony Smith. Smith acknowledges the pervasiveness of national identities and remarks that 'Europe' is deficient compared to deeply rooted ethno-national myths, symbols, values and memories of the nations and ethnies that make up the area of Europe (1991, 1992: 55–76, 1995). According to Smith, 'the only way in which a truly united Europe could emerge is through a slow formation of common European memories, traditions, values, myths and symbols in the image of the ethnie and the nation' (1995: 142). A European identity could thus be the product of a unifying ideology within the Community furnished by a 'Pan-Europeanist' movement aiming at unifying in a single cultural and political community several member states on the basis of European patterns of culture (families of culture) (1992: 171, 1993: 129–35, 1995). The term 'families of culture' refers to the partially shared and overlapping political and cultural traditions, such as Roman law, parliamentarism, democracy, Renaissance, humanism, empiricism and rationalism, romanticism and classicism, that have over the centuries cross-fertilised many areas and peoples in Europe (1995: 130). Drawing on this common European heritage, a pan-European nationalist movement could thus forge common myths, symbols, values and memories, thereby establishing the foundations for a new type of collective identity which overarches but does not abolish individual nations (1992: 175). Smith concedes, however, that 'since neither of these conditions seem likely to obtain in the foreseeable future and that in the meantime the national state remains resilient and there is no sign of any diminution in ethnic awareness and self-determination, there would appear to be little cultural and emotional space for a new Pan-European level popular supernational identification to develop' (1995: 143).

Smith's ethno-national approach to European identity formation may be criticised on several grounds. First, Smith views the European project through the lens of traditional nation states and existing national identities, despite the absence of empirical evidence lending support to a statal or national vision for Europe. The European community is a community of diversity and its institutions have been built and evolve in the absence of strong legitimating narratives. Interestingly, it has managed to lay down norms guiding behaviour and state action in the absence of both coercive apparatuses and quasi-religious justifications.

Secondly, Smith tends to subscribe to a monolithic and rather essentialist conception of national identity; one which is constructed around a hard premodern ethnic core. This 'rootedness' of national identities explains both the permanence and intensity of national identities. But by modelling European identity upon national identity and by conceiving European identity as a cultural identity, Smith ends up projecting the deficiencies that have accompanied the construction of national identities (i.e. the built in we–they syndrome, practices of exclusion and defamation of foreigners, ill-treatment of minorities and so on) onto the European identity. This is likely to yield undesirable political implications not only for Europe's ethnic population, but also for the nature of the emerging polity in Europe.

Although Smith criticises the political conception of European identity for its 'artificial' and 'memoryless' character, he provides no convincing justification as to why: (i) 'Europe' needs a 'secure ethnic base with a clear cut set of common historical memories, myths, symbols, values and the like' (1993: 134); (ii) European identity should be conceived as a collective cultural identity for which Europeans should make sacrifices, rather than a political identity. Needless to say that a European 'family of cultures' is crossed by the most diverse currents; it is prey to contradictory standards and values.

Critics may object here that a political European identity would be too thin or weak to induce the transfer of individual loyalties and attachments from the national to the European level. In other words, politics and culture cannot be kept separate, for the secret of collective identities is memory. Political engineering may 'invent traditions' and create myths, but if these myths are to be sustained they must be able to appeal to and mobilise the citizens of Europe by conjuring memories and experiences. In response, it may be argued that the themes of shared traditions and partially shared heritages are not the only repositories of the myths and symbols required for European identity-building. There exist also subversive memories of suffering, of slavery and colonialism, the Holocaust, wars, conflict and exclusion as well as symbols of freedom and resistance which could enhance identification with the European project and generate a determination to improve existing arrangements. Indeed, I would submit that the value and significance of the European project does not lie in Europe's past; it lies, instead, in the possibilities for new beginnings which transcend past failures. Subversive memories and narratives based on a critical reading of the past are thus more appropriate building blocks for a European identity than retrospective narratives of a shared past which tend to promote nativist senses of belonging.

Smith is aware of the danger of exclusion. In addressing the possibility of a European identity being forged through opposition 'to a disaggregated Third World', he remarks that 'the forging of a deep continental cultural identity to support political unification may well require an ideology of European cultural exclusiveness' (1992: 76). Smith is led to this conclusion because: (i) he views national identities as the expression of necessary relations and essences which predetermine the outcome of their articulation; (ii) he treats the process of community and identity-building in the European Union as the 'mirror' image of national community and identity respectively.

It must be noted here that Smith is not alone in believing that collective identities are defined with reference to whom or what they exclude. If exclusion is structurally necessary for the production of identity, then the EC/EU would have to identify itself in juxtaposition to others. Although this argument recognises that identities are constituted through the encounter with others, it rests on the incorrect assumption that identity is only possible by abjecting the other. As such, it conflates difference and opposition. In reality, what is required for the production of identity is encounter, communication and recognition with reciprocating others. Through encounters we recognise that we are different from others, learn things about ourselves, try to come to grips with unanticipated events and gain new perspectives, thereby becoming 'other' to ourselves. Exclusion of the Other is thus a contingent consequence of political discourses. These normally thrive in the absence of effective political opposition. In this respect, 'Europe' does not need to barricade itself and demarcate itself against the Other (i.e. non-Europeans) in order to gain or maintain a sense of identity. Rather, it can create a sense of identity by becoming other than itself, that is, by coming to terms with the 'weight of its past', learning from it, and re-writing it in the process of constructing a decent democratic future.

Unlike Smith, Paul Howe conceives of the emerging community in the Union as a modern liberal community based on the abstract belief that others are of the same community (Howe, 1995). Inspired by the North-American nation-building, Howe adopts a 'future-oriented' approach which founds the emerging community in Europe on some common political values and shared final ends. As he put it, 'the people of Europe may not be willing themselves to be part of a new nation, but they are acquiescing, and will probably continue to do so, as political structures that typically precede such a development are put into place' (Howe, 1995: 34, 37).

Howe may reject Smith's ethno-national approach in favour of a civic form of nationalism, but it is, nevertheless, still the framework of the nation-state that informs his account of community and identity-building in the Union. By conceiving of the 'community of Europeans' as a community destined to become a fully fledged European nation, he underscores the extent to which the civic nationalist paradigm has been susceptible to ethno-cultural interpretations and exclusionary practices. Political values are often entangled with their particularistic cultural anchoring, and discrimination or exclusion of the Other usually finds expression in a discourse stressing a conflict of values. Modern liberal national communities are simultaneously civic and ethnic. It is this covert particularity of the civic nation which makes the application of the civic nationalist paradigm to the Union particularly unattractive. Howe concedes the problems entailed by the insider/outsider distinction, but he hopes that the development of a 'powerful European political consciousness' which values multiculturalism might in the long run 'soften attitudes towards immigrants, refugees and others visibly different from the European majority' (Howe, 1997: 311–12). Notwithstanding this acknowledgement, however, Howe (1997: 314) is not prepared to abandon the model of the nation-state as a lens for viewing European integration.

In light of this discussion, it may be concluded that the main weakness of the Euro-nationalist mode of European identity is that certain conceptual categories and ideological assumptions associated with the national-statist paradigm are simply replicated at the European level, without being rethought and adjusted to the institutional peculiarities of the Union.

Constitutional patriotism

Constitutional patriotism may be a more attractive candidate since Habermas seeks to separate political membership in a community (*demos*) from ascriptive identities (*ethnos*). According to Habermas, a common European political culture based on the rule of law, separation of powers, democracy, respect for human rights and so on, would guarantee the flourishing of equally legitimate cultural forms of life (1992, 1996a, 1996b). This mode champions active dialogic participation and the flourishing of a European public sphere. By separating *demos* from *ethnos*, Habermas envisages the formation of a European political identity shared by all citizens, regardless of their own national identities and subcultures, and makes democratic citizenship the main integrative device in the Union. More importantly, this idea is compatible with a European community organised either in statal terms (Mancini, 1998), or along the lines of a balanced and flexible system of co-operative federalism without a state.

On closer inspection, however, constitutional patriotism may not succeed in severing the ties between *demos* and *ethnos*. The reason is that project of decoupling of citizenship from ascriptive identities still relies on the subtle, continued relationship between the two. Constitutional principles are not ethically neutral; they have a particularistic anchoring in so far they are rooted in interpretations from the perspective of the nation's historical experience and the point of view of the majority culture. Habermas admits this: 'every legal system is also the expression of a particular lifeform, not merely a reflection of the universalist features of basic rights' (1993: 138). Although this does not preclude critique and the overall adjustment of the political culture, it does confine critical exchanges within the 'architectonics of the constitutional state'. The latter are not exposed to critical questioning by other interpretative communities or become the subject matter of debate by old and new citizens alike. Immigrants are thus expected to be 'politically acculturate' and 'engage in the political culture of their new home' (1992: 17). But they must not question in public the specific interpretations of substantive principles or culturally and historically specific understandings they embody. Indeed, Habermas insists that the 'democratic right of self-determination includes the right to preserve one's own political culture', and political integration does exclude fundamentalist cultures of immigrants (1993: 147).

These conditions are set because Habermas believes that individuals, be they citizens, residents or newly arrived migrants, are cocooned by single and unified worlds which make them what they are. Having preconstituted identities, individuals then enter the public sphere in order to agree on a framework which regulates their actions and relations. Agreement on the rules must be possible under conditions of undistorted communication. Bearing in mind, however, that the worlds that people inhabit are multiple, fragmented and contradictory, and the prospects for unimpeded communication are pretty slim in the real world (Squires, 1993) – even more so in the Union where deliberation and communication is often seen by participants as an opportunity to hold on to their entrenched positions in order to meet domestic political expediencies and not to succumb to the force of the better argument, this mode of European identity has weaknesses.[7]

Critics may also object that constitutional patriotism is not able to sustain a European political community since it is rather weak in the affective dimension. Being rational and reflexive, it may fail to elicit subjective identification with the Union and create strong bonds of attachment.

A corrective European identity

It is for this reason that Weiler and others have opted for a 'mixed' approach of accepting the normative ideas of constitutional patriotism and at the same time affirming the particularistic ethno-cultural traditions of the Member States. National identities are valued as symbols for collective action, resources for identity-building and markers of communal intergenerational projects promising authenticity and collective immortality.

Weiler (1994, 1995, 1996, 1998) argues that a European civic public can co-exist with national publics without threatening to displace them. Whereas national citizenship would be the realm of affinity and a symbol of nationhood, European citizenship would be the realm of law and Enlightenment ideals (the 'variable geometry' approach). Double membership in a national ethno–cultural community, on the one hand, and a supranational, civic and value-driven *demos*, on the other, would tame the appeal nationalism continues to offer but which can so easily degenerate into intolerance and xenophobia (Weiler, 1994: 23–4; 1997: 508–9). On this reading, the formation of a supranational political community based on shared values and citizenship will neutralise the vices inherent in national-statist communities: 'it will serve as a civilising force which keeps the eros of nationalism at bay' (Weiler, 1996: 527).

This position is shared by Bellamy and Castiglione (1998) who add that the construction of the EU is a two-way process: a process of preserving national identities in Europe but also of making the nations of Europe more European. In such a European 'mixed commonwealth', communitarian commitments and distinctive identities can co-exist with a cosmopolitian regard for universal principles of rights and fairness (cosmopolitan communitarianism). One wonders here whether the tension generated by these opposing elements can so easily be overcome. At present, communitarian (i.e. national) definitions of membership have compromised the civic and universalist ethos of the European public (Article 17(1) EC). To put it differently, the affirmation of ethno-cultural narratives concerning national identities could lead to the 'nationalisation' of the European supranational community – and not to the 'Europeanisation' of the nation-state. The exclusion of third-country nationals from the benefits of Union citizenship and the present restrictive immigration regime are good cases in point.

In any case, the differentiation between national organic cultural and European *demoi* may appease anxieties about possible absorption of national citizenship by European citizenship, but it is based on the distinction between civic and ethnic nationalism. Because this distinction has emerged within the context of the nation-state, reservations could be raised about its transfer to the European context. After all, several states would not portray themselves as organic cultural communities, notwithstanding their adherence to *ius sanguini* principles. This perspective overlooks civic constructions of the nation which define 'belonging' in political terms and freeze the mutability of the nation-state in an era of globalisation and international migration. As I have argued above, these developments have put into question traditional assumptions about the unity and supposed homogeneity of civic publics and have forced states to consider seriously demands for respect for 'unassimilated otherness' (the challenge of diversity) and for political inclusion (the challenge of membership).

A functional European identity
The neofunctionalist perspective envisaged that the expansion of elite co-operation and the development of habits of co-operation in solving common problems would eventually transform social expectations and values. In the European 'would-be polity', individual attachments would shift away from traditional attachments to nation state to a supranational system which is responsive to individual and societal needs (Haas, 1958). The crucial test of the whole enterprise is efficient performance, for structures exist to satisfy the functional needs of individuals and societies. On that reading, Europe remains a 'nominal community of deeds' (Schmitter, 1996: 150) in which individuals will switch their 'non-rational political loyalties' for informed calculations of their objective interests.

Accordingly, emphasis is put on economic rationality and technocratic governance: the European unification process is legitimised by good performance and efficient problem-solving. Majone (1996, 1997, 1998), the prime theorist of the regulatory model at the European level, views the supranational institutions as a 'fourth branch of government' – that is, as independent regulative agencies with far-reaching delegated powers. On this reading, standards and criteria of legitimacy derived from the theory and practice of parliamentary democracies will not be suitable candidates for assessing the legitimacy of the Community, since the latter is based on efficiency-oriented institutions which are not really equipped to deal with redistributive issues. The basic criterion for their legitimacy is thus a functional one: efficient performance and the ability to perform better than the Member States in a complex and changing world.

The problem with this approach is not so much its overreliance on practical results and efficiency as its exclusive reliance on these indicators. Community membership is based on calculated self-interest, and the EC/EU is reduced to a policy-generating mechanism. This results in the underscoring of the polity-like features of the Community and it is likely to yield minimalist agendas. It is certainly the case that certain policy areas, such as European Monetary Union (EMU) and the autonomy granted to the European Central Bank (ECB), rest on a vision which is informed by the regulatory approach, and short-term successes and popular initiatives in the fields of sex equality, social policy, environment and consumer protection and so on promote identification with Europe. But this process is also prone to reversal in the face of crises, enduring problems and long-term failures. Arguably, a functional European identity cannot sustain a political community and create such bonds of fellowship among Europeans so as to justify sacrifices on the part of some for the interest of the whole. What is needed is a sense of community which is unaffected by cycles of enthusiasm and disenchantment and transcends cost-benefit calculations and narrow self-interest.

The contractualist mode of European identity

Defenders of the Gaullist vision of 'a Europe of fatherlands' tend to view European integration as a high and self-sustaining level of diplomatic and socio-economic exchanges – not as a union of citizens or a polity in its own right. In their view, European citizens are rooted in national cultures. In this respect, a genuine European identity is to be resisted – or, at best, can be accommodated as a 'thin' identity overlaying deeply rooted national identities

According to the contractualist, the Member States are the driving forces of integration in the European Union and therefore the scope and terms of European citizenship must be determined by them in accordance with their nationality laws. In this sense, one can talk about a 'hegemony' of the particularistic framework of nationality over the supranational institution of Union citizenship. People of immigrant origin would continue to be excluded from the normal channels of policy-making and from the benefits of Union citizenship, despite the fact that this creates a two-tier Europe; namely, a Citizens' Europe juxtaposed to that of Metics (that is, of long-term resident third-country nationals, recently admitted economic migrants, guestworkers and refugees). As objects of national administrative polices (with the exception of Denmark, Ireland, the Netherlands, Sweden and Finland where non-citizens can participate in local government elections), migrants would have to meet the requirements of increasingly restrictive naturalisation policies if they want to become citizens of the Union. But even when they are proved to be 'worthy of admission', they are required to embrace the culture of the host community and/or its 'way of life'.

Integration into the fabric of the host society is achieved through either assimilation (this strategy characterises the French individualist paradigm) or integration (it characterises British, Scandinavian and Dutch multiculturalist paradigms). Assimilation to the culture of the host state requires a deep transformation of their identities, in that they have to abandon who they are and conform to the attitudes and culture of the majority community. As the 'melting pot' metaphor indicates, obliteration of differences is often seen as a requirement of full membership. Membership is defined on an individual basis, and there is no institutional recognition of minority groups. The integrative response to difference on the other hand, accepts and tolerates difference so far as it is confined to the private realm. As far as the public realm is concerned, it is a matter of indifference whether communities affirm their right to be different in private. In public, migrant and ethnic communities are expected to embrace the nation's ideals, to be loyal to the state of which they are nationals and identify with the common culture of citizenship – even though its terms have been defined exclusively by the dominant national collectivity. In this respect, demands for the public recognition of difference (i.e. bilingual education) are seen as promoting cultural separatism, and not as a quest for public acceptance of their identities and culture.[8] In addition, 'institutionalised racism' in police, education and the health care system, which remains unaffected by national legislation, confirms their unequal membership.

Restrictive immigration rules are instrumental in perpetuating the second-class status of people of immigrant origin, despite official pronouncements, such as 'fewer immigrants, better race relations'. The reason being, is that by 'accepting public concern about immigration as a legitimate grievance and seeking to remedy that grievance by restricting the entry of black and Asian people, governments have reinforced the view that such people are undesirable' (Spencer, 1994: 309). In the Union, the abolition of internal controls has led to the establishment of compensatory controls at the external frontiers aiming at keeping migrants and asylum seekers out. In the subsequent chapters, I examine the origins and development of the intergovernmental restrictive migration regime. What is important to mention here is that, according to the contractualist approach, individuals can develop an identification with 'Europe', but this would most certainly be a weak one, since the Union is basically a 'states' Europe' rather than a 'people's Europe'.

The constructivist mode of European identity
The constructivist approach conceives of the emerging community in the Union as a political design and of European identity as a task. This means that European identity is not a thing-like entity which might or might not exist, but emerges out of a complex web of institutionalised practices of

co-operation and participation. European identity is thus a process and a project to be achieved as the 'grand conversation' concerning the political restructuring of Europe goes on. Because it is neither established once and for all, nor always firmly in place, but always continually happening (i.e. constructed and reconstructed in accordance with the evolution of the EC/EU), it must be nourished by institutions, practices, rules and ideas embodying a commitment to social transformation and democratic reform.

A constructive European identity is not merely a constructed identity. It is also underpinned by ways of thinking about community and identity-building in the Union which transcend the various patterns of nation-state building. From this it follows that a constructive European identity is neither opposed to national identities, nor does it become identical to them. European and national identities differ in both intensity and nature and can be reciprocally complementary by virtue of their differences. Whereas national identities tend to be affective, a European identity could be more evaluational and reflective. Through interaction, communication and the exchange of information, a European identification would induce individuals to learn, make political judgements, readjust their cognitive structures and behave in ways that are congruent more with their value systems than with their feelings or psychological needs. European identity is thus associated with a critical reflective attitude rather than with a satisfying, self-defining experience. As integration deepens, a sense of pride in the Union's achievements may develop, but what is important is that European identity does not originate from this feeling.

Critics may object that such a rational and reflexive conception of European identity might not be strong enough to sustain a sense of community in Europe precisely because it is not accompanied by a 'quasi'-religious mythology. Although I respond to this criticism below, I must mention here that nothing I have said so far denies that the European Union needs to foster narratives, operative myths and symbolisms. Given that all collective identities are entangled in stories, the success of a European identity will depend on the development of symbolisms and stories. But these are more likely to be critical narratives about Europe's past and the past of Others and subversive stories.

Since the formation of a European identity is a political process, the delimitation of the boundaries of the European political community carries within it an ethical responsibility; the responsibility to respect the Other (i.e. ethnic residents, third-country nationals and refugees), to welcome her/him as Other and to seek community with them. The above-mentioned modes of European identity premise community on some sort of commonality or similarity, rather than difference. Even when they are committed to diversity they merely carve out a precarious area of diversity on the margins of a predominantly assimilationist culture (Parekh, 1998). There is a generalised apprehension about giving public and institutional status to difference, for this is seen as a recipe for the disintegration or fragmentation of community.

In contrast, the constructivist approach regards the European political community as a community of difference, for it is within diversity and through diversity that we seek community (see Chapters 4, 5 and 6). As such, it does not seek to create a 'European man'. Nor does it have as its goal the creation of *e pluribus unum* (i.e. a European people). Instead, it seeks to convert subjects and citizens whose lives have been monopolised by national collectivism into critical citizens of the Union, and believes that both majority and minority communities in Europe should be the rightful shapers and makers of the public culture and Europe's possible futures.

Clearly, membership of such a political community cannot be conditioned upon possession of state nationality. We cannot go forward by going backwards. By calling for the disentaglement of the supranational institution of European citizenship from its present quasi-nationalist trappings, the constructivist mode of European identity seeks to face up to the challenge of how to construct a community in a genuinely mutlinational, polyethnic, multireligious, polycultural and polyglossic environment. The significance of this moment for democratic politics in general lies not so much in the separation of the political act of the institution of a European *demos* from the particularistic identities of its constituent units (i.e. states, regions, communities, groups, etc.). Rather, it lies in the construction of a genuinely pluralistic 'European Home' which is neither a monopoly of 'mono-nationality', nor 'ethnocidal'. By transcending the limitations of the narrow nationality model of citizenship, the constructivist option promises to foster the creation of a community of expectations and civic engagement in the Union – that is, of a democratic polity that takes 'difference' (i.e. ethnic, religious, cultural) seriously, yet critically, and is inclusive.

The crucial questions then are: what norms and institutions will be appropriate for achieving just and heterogeneous and inclusive European public? What will 'citizenship' mean in such a context, and what kind of civic culture should impart the formation of a heterogeneous European public?[9] What sort of reforms does the democratic restructuring of the EU entail? How can one articulate a principled and fully justiciable common immigration policy which looks fundamentally to the future because it is based on an enlightened understanding of global migration flows and the causes of the international refugee crisis? And, finally, to what extent is this alternative future possible? Answering these questions is the main task to which the rest of this book is devoted. After all, whether a constructive European identity can foster and sustain a sense of community in the Union depends as much on the kind of institutions and practices of membership that are in the making as on the design of credible models of citizenship and immigration.

Notes

1 See Schlensinger (1992); Smith (1992); Wilterdink (1993); Laffan (1996).

2 The Danish rejected the Treaty on European Union which was signed in February 1992 in a national referendum. A second referendum yielded a narrow majority in favour of ratification. In Germany, the constitutionality of ratification was considered by the Federal Supreme Court; see Cases 2 BvR 2134/92 and 2159/92 *Brunner v European Union Treaty* [1994] 1 CMLR 57. In France, the Constitutional Council declared the Treaty incompatible with the Constitution. Ratification was achieved after constitutional amendment; Maastricht I, Decision 92-308 DC, 9 April 1992; Maastricht II, Decision 92-312 DC, 3 September 1992; Maastricht III, Decision 92-313 DC, 23 September 1992.

3 Moravcsik's theory has been criticised for underestimating the role of supranational institutions, and in particular of the ECJ; for overlooking the day-to-day supranational innovations in the field of policy-making by focusing on the historical moments of constitutional choice; for overrationalising a much more haphazard process; for failing to provide a theory of the origins of state preferences: see Wincott (1995: 601); Armstrong and Bulmer (1998: 30–1).

4 Contemporary Euro-sceptic discourses tend to blend elements of popular nationalism with appeals to parliamentary democracy as being antithetical to heteronomous governance. As such, they have created a chain of equivalence among state, national and popular sovereignty, whereby limitations on state sovereignty at the European level come close to limiting the sovereignty of the people at the national level, thus threatening the very idea of democracy: (Seurin, 1994: 627).

5 According to McEldowney (1994: 30–3) '*Factortame* is the clearest indication that EC membership is no longer compatible with Dicey's classical doctrine of Parliamentary sovereignty'. And yet, politicians and judges have sought to justify this on the basis that the Parliament itself has voluntarily agreed to limitations of its sovereignty by the European Communities Act 1972: *Factortame Ltd v Secretary of State for Transport* (No. 2) [1991] 1 AC 603. So in so far as Parliament has made the choice to be bound by the Community method and has the right by subsequent legislation to abrogate that duty and withdraw from the Community, its ultimate sovereignty has not been affected; on this, see Craig (1991).

6 For a review of Euro-centric narratives on Europe and cultural essentialist ideas of identity, see Pieterse (1991); Delanty (1995).

7 As Calhoun (1995: 75) has observed: 'Habermas's scheme can recognise conflicts between principles – between equality and freedom, say, or justice and non-violence – though it presumes these principles to be ultimately commensurable. It cannot recognise conflicts over what counts as a moral decision. Habermas assumes that ethico-political principles are similar to discourses about truth claims and that it must be possible for all to result in rational consensus.'

8 In France, fear of separatism on the part of ethnic minorities or 'ghettoisation' is played out any time the Jacobin conception of French national identity is questioned. See Safran (1991). Maxim Silverman (1992: 32–3) notes, in this connection, that assimilation is always ambivalent; it presupposes that 'there is both an initial difference which must be obliterated (i.e. you must be like us) and an initial difference which can never be obliterated (i.e. you can never be like us)'.

9 The term is borrowed from Young (1990).

2

The institutional construction of European identity

In Chapter 1 we saw that the character, scope and orientation of European identity depends on the nature of the emergent European polity and on 'what kind of community' one has in mind. The typology of European identity highlighted the problems in conceptualising European identity as: (i) a badge which will supplement deeply rooted national identities; (ii) the cement for the formation of '*e pluribus unum*'; (iii) a boundary which sets European and non-European citizens and worlds apart. I suggested that European identity should be conceived of as a task directed towards the formation of a political community which is open and inclusive towards ethnic migrants and other minority communities and more participatory. This discussion also raised several questions about the institutional implementation of European identity and its future development which will be confronted here as well as in the following chapters.

In this chapter I trace the development of EU law and policy on identity and citizenship and assess the European Union's response to this challenge in light of the six modes of identity outlined in Chapter 1. My aim is not to establish an external, universal standard against which the inadequacies of the European Union's identity and citizenship agenda can be measured. Such an exercise would inevitably sidestep the institutional peculiarities of the EC/EU and underscore its incremental evolution. Instead of relying on a moral architecture which separates 'good' from 'bad' policies, I will attempt a normative critique that 'works within'; that is, I will evaluate the steps that EU institutions have taken towards the institutionalisation of European identity by adopting a historically and institutionally grounded perspective. Such an approach is likely to be sensitive to the dynamics of the Union's institutional structure and development and will highlight both the limitations and unrecognised possibilities of the European policy on identity.

The emergence of European identity on the European political agenda

The European Community emerged in the context of postwar economic reconstruction and against a background of popular movements championing federalist ideas. In its early days, it represented the organisation of industrial-sector communities setting up integration in limited, but vital, economic fields (i.e. coal and steel). The avowed objectives of the founders of the European Coal and Steel Community (ECSC [18 April 1951] 25 July 1952) included the prospect of a 'European federation'. The political dimensions of the integrationist framework featured in the Schuman Plan (1950), which was anchored in the belief that closer co-operation between France and Germany would furnish a 'broader and deeper community among peoples long divided by bloody conflicts' (preamble to the Treaty of Paris, 18 April 1951).

The Treaties of Rome (1957) which established the European Economic Community (EEC) and the European Atomic Energy Community (EAEC or Euratom) signalled the transcendence of the sectoral approach to integration and affirmed the political character of European integration. The EEC's aim was to establish a common market based on the four freedoms of movement (i.e. capital, goods, services and persons) and on the gradual convergence of economic policies. The Treaty was not merely an economic text; it was a stage in the process towards political union. As Hallstein had noted, 'we are not integrating economies, we are integrating politics. We are not just sharing our furniture, we are jointly building a new and bigger house' (cit. in Urwin, 1995 [1991]). Undistorted competition within a larger market was seen as a catalyst for monetary stability, economic expansion, social protection, the raising of the standard of living and quality of life, economic and social cohesion, and solidarity among the Member States (Spaak Report, May 1956).

The co-existence of economic and socio–political aims has, undoubtedly, created genuine dilemmas and has thwarted the development of Community policies, such as social policy, consumer protection and so on by making them adjuncts to economic policy/market integration (Weatherill, 1996). However, the co-existence of economic and socio-political aims also helps eschew overly deterministic accounts of the EEC. By this, I mean accounts which depict the internal market as an end – not as a means to a broader socio-political end – and portray the beneficiaries of the free-movement provisions as 'market citizens' (Everson, 1995: 84–5).

Since its early days, the Community has recognised that freedom of movement is not merely a functional prerequisite of the common market. The fifth preamble of Council Regulation 1612/68 characterised the right to move as a 'fundamental right' of workers to improve their standard of living which must be exercised in 'freedom and dignity'. Workers are not seen as mere factors of economic production, but as human beings.[1] It is for this reason that the principle of non-discrimination, which lies at the heart of the free-movement provisions, extends beyond the workplace to the broader social environment of the host Member State, and has been advanced at the expense of national sovereignty, since all those who previously nccdcd state permission in order to enter, reside and engage in economic activities on the national territory were granted the right to do so. Bearing in mind that European citizenship implies the existence of a direct legal bond between the Community and a class of persons to which certain rights and special obligations may be attached, it may be argued that the Treaty establishing the EEC certainly established an 'incipient form of European citizenship' for certain classes of persons (i.e. workers, professionals, service-providers and their families) (Plender, 1976).

Generally speaking, the development of EC policy on identity and citizenship can be divided into the following distinct phases:

- 1957–72: the common market and the removal of obstacles to freedom of movement for people;
- 1972–84: the conceptual paradigm shift – political union and European identity;
- 1984–91: a 'people's Europe' and the 'states' Europe';
- 1992–96: citizenship of the Union and 'Otherness';
- 1997– : strengthening the 'citizen dimension of the Union' and security identities.

The discussion which follows will address the first four phases, whilst the last phase will be considered in Chapter 3 which discusses the Amsterdam reforms.

1957–72: an incipient form of European citizenship

The Paris summit in 1972 is taken to be the starting point for the analysis of European identity and citizenship since it marks a paradigm shift from economic to political union and the emergence of European identity on the Community's policy agenda (Van den Berghe, 1982; Wiener 1998). True as this might be, I believe that the 1957–72 period is still worthy of consideration, for two main reasons. First, in this period the 'incipient form of European citizenship' was given substance through the introduction of secondary legislation. Secondly, through this legislation national executives grafted their conception of who the Europeans are on to the emerging European institutions. This conception became ossified and has biased subsequent developments in the fields of identity and citizenship. But let us examine these issues in more detail.

The 1958–72 period is characterised by attempts to realise the ambitions of 1958 as far as possible by removing customs duties between the Member States and establishing a common external tariff (CET) (the customs union was achieved on 1 July 1968); eliminating quantitative restrictions and measures having an equivalent effect; and enabling employed persons to go freely to another Member State to take a job under the same conditions as nationals of that country. Secondary legislation was introduced to implement the free-movement provisions: Regulations 15/61 and 38/64, Regulation 1612/68 of 15 October 1968 (amended by Regulations 312/76 and 2434/92), and Directive 68/360 of the same date. In order to encourage the mobility of Community workers the rights of entry and residence for family members were secured (Regulation 1612/68 Article 10), and Regulation 1251/70 of 29 June 1970 granted workers (and their families) the right to remain in the territory of a Member State after having been employed in that State. Since the aim of the Treaty was to remove all obstacles to the free movement of persons, the Council introduced two regulations on the social security of migrant workers in 1958. These have been superseded by Regulation 1408/71, as supplemented by Regulation 574/72. In addition, by adopting a 'rights-based' approach to freedom of movement the European Court of Justice (ECJ) embarked upon a process of creating an extensive case law which gave rise to directly effective rights for individuals. As an active integrationist, the ECJ contributed decisively to the transformation of the Community into an area of freedom and mobility for Community workers and their families, professionals and providers of services.

Whereas this 'foundational period' (from 1958 to the mid-1970s) is characterised by an inexorable dynamism toward enhanced supranationalism, from a pure political-decisional point of view, it also signals a shift towards intergovernmentalism (Weiler, 1991). The 'Luxembourg Compromise' of 29 January 1966, which asserted the importance of unanimity when 'vital national interests' are at stake and resolved the so-called Empty-Chair crisis, demonstrated the Member States' eagerness to resist the integrationist agenda by resuming control of the process of norm-creating at the European level (Weiler, 1991). One such example of hegemonic control over the process of norm-creation has been the confinement of the personal scope of freedom of movement of workers to workers who are nationals of the Member States.

The Treaty refers simply to workers as the main beneficiaries of the free-movement provisions (Articles 48-51 EEC (39-42 EC on renumbering)). No distinction is made as to whether these should be residents in the territory of the Member States, nationals of the Member States irrespective of the place of their residence, both nationals and residents, or workers who are either nationals or residents (Hartley, 1976: 24–5). By enacting secondary legislation to give effect to the right to free movement, however, the Council confined the right to free movement to workers who are nationals of the Member States (i.e. Regulations 15/61 and 38/64, Regulation 1612/68 and Directive 360/70). This discursive articulation 'fixed' the scope of economic rights in a way that might had not been intended by the Treaty. This decision can hardly be explained on the basis of rational motives (this does not mean that it was unreasonable), for one would expect that decision-makers would have considered seriously the effects of the exclusion of an active part of Europe's labour force from free movement. After all, the maintenance of visa requirements for non-national residents would impede the abolition of passport controls and thus the realisation of the single market.

But such considerations were overshadowed by shared understandings and assumptions about immigration which had shaped the thinking and behaviour of national executives. In domestic political scenes, concerns about the 'problem' of immigration and the 'social repercussions of coloured migration' had already began to replace earlier discourses extolling the economic benefits of immigration and its contribution to postwar economic recovery and the expansion of European economies (Cohen, 1987; Collinson, 1993a). In Britain, for example, the redefinition of immigration appeared quite early. The 1962 Commonwealth Immigrants Act established a voucher system linking entry to prior employment offer, and the 1968 Commonwealth Immigrants Act deprived East African Asians, who could not claim a close connection with the UK, of their right as British passport holders to enter the UK freely. The 1968 Act also introduced for the first time the concept of 'patriality': entry was confined to those with an ancestral connection with the UK. According to Gilroy (1987: 45), this 'codified the cultural biology of race into statute law as part of a strategy for the exclusion of Black settlers'. Since migrant workers were not regarded as equal participants in European societies they could not be rightful beneficiaries of freedom of movement.

The Member States' decision to exclude such workers was clearly political. It repressed other possible solutions and established an 'objectivity' which, as we will see below, proved very difficult to undo – namely, that free movement applies only to workers who are nationals of the Member States. As the moment of the original contingency began to fade, the system of possible alternatives, including the conditioning of free movement on residence, became concealed. The states' favoured interpretation became sedimented – that is, became routinised in ideas, practices and law, thereby rendering alternative options inconceivable. The sedimentation was so complete that the original dimension of power through which that instituting act took place was far from visible. However, sedimentation and concealment of the alternative juridical and political options does not mean that they are cancelled out of existence. As we shall see below, under the right conditions, the contingent nature of the original decision could be recovered and the alternative juridical options reactivated.

In the period under examination, national governments did not only manage to institutionalise exclusion at the heart of the European project, but were also free to determine unilaterally the precise scope of freedom of movement of workers via their definition of nationality. Several categories of persons were excluded from the benefits of the Treaty on the basis of unilateral definitions of nationality, and the Community institutions accepted the

Member States' exclusive competence in the sphere of determination of nationality, despite the fact that the scope and application of Community rules depends on that determination (O'Leary, 1992: 35). The Declarations submitted by the UK on the definition of the term 'nationals' for Community law purposes are good cases in point. In the first Declaration, which was made at the time of the signature of the Treaty of Accession of 22 January 1972, the UK excluded from its definition of nationality for Community purposes UK citizens who were inhabitants of overseas dependencies or former dependencies (i.e. non-patrial Commonwealth and Colonial citizens). This Declaration has been criticised on ethical and legal grounds. On ethical grounds, because non-patrial citizens of the UK from Gibraltar (predominantly white) were considered to be UK nationals for Community purposes whilst other non-patrial citizens of the UK and Colonies were excluded (Bohning, 1972: 154). As regards the legality of the Declaration, Bohning has contended that it 'was incompatible with the Treaty of Rome and its derivative legislation to have one nationality definition for domestic purposes but to exclude from it certain sections of the population for EEC purposes' (1973: 83–4). Along similar lines, the second Declaration submitted by the UK in 1982, following the enactment of the 1981 British Nationality Act, excluded certain categories of persons who enjoyed the right to abode under domestic law from the benefits of the Treaty, while at the same time enabled Gibraltarians who did not possess the right of abode under UK law to benefit from the Community provisions on freedom of movement. By exercising hegemonic control over the scope and terms of membership in the emerging European community, the Member States thus succeeded in grafting notions of 'who the Europeans are' onto the emerging institutions.

1972–84: European identity

In this period co-ordinated efforts were made towards political integration. Already in 1969, when the international monetary system was threatening to collapse, the Heads of State and Government meeting in the Hague decided that the Community should progressively transform itself into an economic and monetary union. The demise of the Bretton Woods system in 1971, the floating of the European currencies coupled with the increase of oil prices in 1973, caused serious social and economic difficulties. The Werner Report on European Monetary Union, drawn up in 1970 by the then Prime Minister of Luxembourg, and the launch of European Political Cooperation (EPC) in the same year, were instrumental in invigorating a political vision for 'Europe'.

The Paris Summit (October 1972) introduced an ambitious programme for the establishment of a political Union. But a European political community needed first and foremost Europeans. EC officials realised that popular identification would be achieved only if the European enterprise became less elitist and more 'citizen-friendly'. The 'Europe of goods' had to be transformed into 'a people's Europe'. At the Copenhagen Summit in 1973, the nine

Member States adopted a 'Declaration on European Identity'. This document set out, for the first time, principles for the internal development of the Community thereby furnishing a framework for the formation of a political conception of European identity.

'European identity' was defined on the basis of the principles of the rule of law, social justice, respect for human rights and democracy, and in relation to: (i) the status and the responsibilities of the nine member states *vis-à-vis* the rest of the world; (ii) the dynamic nature of the process of European unification (Annex 2 to Chapter II, 7th Gen. Rep. EC, 1973). The document was analytically shallow and the political definition of European identity was intertwined with Euro-centric statements invoking a common European civilisation whose survival had to be ensured (Annex 2 to Chapter II, 7th Gen. Rep. EC, 1973). Notwithstanding such references, the Declaration was important in that it set out guidelines and objectives which might be taken as pointers for the grant of special rights to citizens living in a host Member State. It also reflected the Member States' determination to build a Community of law and democracy which 'measures up to the needs of the individual and preserves the rich variety of national cultures' (Annex 2 to chapter II, 7th Gen. Rep. EC, 1973). But a closer inspection reveals that the declaration on European identity comprised an 'inconsistent quintet':

- special rights for Community citizens;
- references to a common European cultural heritage;
- confirmation of the Community as an entity on the international plane;
- a civic European identity in a Community of law, democracy and social justice;
- exclusion of 'non-national residents': the confinement of special rights to nationals of the member states was taken for granted.

Clearly, the Community could never succeed in reconciling all these elements: the formation of a civic European identity was entangled in Euro-nationalist themes, and the exclusion of third-country nationals contradicted the ideal of democracy and social justice. The aspiration to institutionalise a principled European identity was certainly there, but the contractualist mode of European identity exercised a strong hold upon the process of European identity formation. This inconsistency widened the gap between declared principles and goals and the actual practices of Community institutions.

In December 1974, the Paris Summit Conference endorsed the idea of a European identity and gave it more concrete substance by specifying policy objectives, such as elections for the European Parliament on the basis of direct universal suffrage, special rights for citizens of the nine Member States and the creation of passport union. The Paris Summit also instructed the Prime Minister of Belgium, Leo Tindemans, to draft a report on all the necessary measures required for the creation of a Europe of citizens. The Tindemans Report on European Union proposed the protection of the rights of Europeans, and identified three areas for action: (i) protection of fundamental rights in view of the gradual increase in the powers of European institutions; (ii) consumer rights; (iii) and the protection of the environment. The Hague European Summit (1976) examined the report, but with no positive outcome.

Interestingly, it was not so much the report's recommendations as the emergence of the concept of 'passport union'[2] that aroused interest in European citizenship. Passport union entailed the adoption of a uniform passport, harmonisation of the rules affecting aliens and the abolition of controls at internal frontiers. The replacement of national passports by a uniform passport was seen to symbolise a definite connection with the Community and ensure the equality of treatment for all passport holders by non-member countries irrespective of their nationality: it would 'confirm the Community as an entity *vis-à-vis* the rest of the world and revive the feeling of nationals of member states of belonging to that entity' (Bull. EC, Supp. 7/1975: 7). In the same vein, the symbolic appeal of measures, such as a Community flag and a European anthem, was envisaged to increase affective and cognitive support for European integration. Optimism and excitement precluded the realisation that this was basically a pre-political phase as far as European citizenship was concerned since a federal European Community had not been developed and its democratic basis was deficient (Spencer, 1990). Rhetoric was fervent. The introduction of a uniform passport in 1981[3], and the prospect of the abolition of internal controls, coupled with the Council's decision concerning direct elections to the European Parliament (OJ EC, 278, 8/10/77: 1–11), were celebrated as 'first steps towards European citizenship becoming a reality'.

Evidently, the emphasis on the cultivation of symbolic ties of belonging to the Community was inspired by the process of national identity-building. Indeed, EC policy on identity and citizenship in this second period mirrored the patterns set in the nineteenth-century formation of nation-states (Buzan et al., 1990: 215) in three important respects. First, the adoption of a uniform passport was underpinned by the desire to manifest externally the newly emergent legal bond between the Community and individuals so that non-member countries would recognise the Community as an entity and offer identical treatment to all Community passport holders irrespective of nationality (Bull. EC, Supp. 7/1975, 2.2.3: 9). This was essentially an attempt to create in the external domain effects similar to those created by nationality in the nation-state paradigm. Secondly, it was generally believed that state citizenship would not simply co-exist with Community citizenship, but it would eventually become subordinate to it (Bull. EC 12-1972, point 1104; Bull. EC, Supp. 7/1975). Thirdly, drawing on the process of state-building, Community officials sought to construct a European identity though symbolisms and 'consciousness-raising' initiatives and by invoking an essential European identity, built on the basis of 'centuries of shared history and common cultural and fundamental values' (see Commission Communication on a People's Europe, Bull. EC, Supp. 2/88).

Confronted with the need to develop a European identity and citizenship, but lacking a clear political vision of 'Europe', European policy-makers opted for the familiar, existing model of national state-building. They subscribed to the Euro-nationalist mode of identity, thereby lending credence to Majone's (1991: 92) argument that the ability of policy-makers to innovate often depends more on their skill in utilising existing models than on inventing novel solutions. By borrowing the existing tools, they aspired to solve the problems arising from the process of the formation of a European identity of the Union without realising that the favoured solutions essentially negated the existence of these problems on a conceptual level.

The utilisation of theoretical tools and policy ideas from the statist paradigm also had another unforeseen consequence: it amplified the tension between the Commission's and the ECJ's supranationalism and the Council's intergovernmental agenda. More specifically, the prospect of the establishment of a European citizenship which would eventually override state citizenship coupled with the Commission's call for the harmonisation of national visa and immigration policies aroused the Council's antagonistic reaction. It is noteworthy, here, that the Council had already reacted against an earlier Commission initiative on the grant of local electoral rights to Community nationals residing in a Member State other than their own (Bull, EC 10-1972) as national governments objected to the relaxation of the national citizenship requirement for franchise. By deploying delaying tactics and insisting the matter should be tackled by a working group on special rights, it forced the Commission to shift its attention from electoral rights to the establishment of local consultative councils for migrant workers in the member state of their residence.

The European Parliament, which had already criticised the lack of political rights (OJ 1977, C200/25) and had suggested a comprehensive list of citizens' rights (OJ 1977, C299/77), recommended the grant to Community nationals of the right to vote and to stand for election in the member state of residence after five years of residence (OJ 1982, C87/61) in 1982. A year later, it urged the Commission to present a legislative proposal under Article 308 EC (Resolution of June 1983, OJ 1983, C184/28). But the Commission failed to act, arguing that such a proposal would fail to obtain the Council's unanimous approval. As a result, European citizenship remained undeveloped in this period. The endemic conflict between supranational impulses and intergovernmental resistance hampered the search for optimal solutions to problems and true innovations. Change in European integration could take place only in an incremental fashion by resurrecting past initiatives.

1984–91: the duality of 'Europe' – a people's Europe v. a states' Europe

New impetus to the creation of a political union was given by the adoption of a Solemn Declaration on European Union by the European Council in Stuttgart in June 1983. A year later, the Fontainebleau Council set up two

committees with the mandate to examine the practical measures required for
a closer European Union. The first ad hoc Committee, under the presidency
of Mr Dooge, focused on the completion of the Internal Economic Area
(IEA) and on institutional affairs. It submitted an interim report to the European Dublin Conference in 1984 which proposed, among other things, the
use of qualified majority voting and the strengthening of the European Commission and the European Parliament. The second ad hoc Committee for a
People's Europe, chaired by Mr Adonnino, proposed measures designed to
bring the Community closer to the citizens and the young people, and to
foster a European identity. The Adonnino Committee submitted two reports
in March and June 1985, respectively. The first proposed the simplification
of control at land frontiers among the Member States; separate entry channels for Community citizens at seaports and airports; the generalised use of
the uniform European passport; better personal allowances; the mutual
recognition of diplomas and qualifications to ensure the effective exercise of
the right of establishment. The second focused on special rights for citizens,
culture and communication, information, youth and education; the twinning
of towns and cities and the strengthening of the Community's image and
identity. It suggested that citizens' involvement in the Community would
increase as a result of the introduction of a uniform electoral procedure for
European Parliament (EP) elections and voting rights in EP elections for
citizens residing in another Member State, a right to petition the European
Parlliament and the establishment of an Ombudsman.

The Committee also urged the Member States to grant voting rights to
Community nationals at local elections in the country of their residence. The
Committee's proposals aroused interest and public awareness about European citizenship, and formed the blueprint for the creation of Union citizenship in 1992. But assumptions and ideas belonging to the previous
Euro-nationalist phase had, nonetheless, survived: the Committee proposed
the adoption of a flag and an anthem (the 'Ode to Joy' from Beethoven's
Ninth Symphony), and the use of stamps as vehicles for drawing attention to
the Community. Such symbolic measures, however, were accompaniments of
special rights for citizens – and not the basis for a European identity. Could
this be taken to constitute the beginning of a cognitive shift toward the development of a citizenship *'problematique'* which was no longer firmly rooted
within the prevailing assumptions of the statist paradigm?

Support for this hypothesis may be derived from the following two initiatives. In October 1986, the Commission supported the idea of local electoral
rights for Community nationals (Bull. EC, Supp. 7/86), arguing that such
a measure was a logical prerequisite of a 'People's Europe' and, in 1988,
submitted a proposal for a Directive on Voting Rights for Community
nationals in local elections in their Member State of residence (Bull. EC,
Supp. 2/88: 29). Qualifying periods of residence were to be set by the
Member States. Although the MS objected to possible relaxation of the

nationality requirement for local elections, the Commission's proposal introduced a crucial and topical normative dimension to 'the developing practice
of citizenship' (Wiener, 1997, 1998).

The second initiative concerned the status of non-EC migrants (i.e.
third-country nationals). In March 1985 the Commission submitted a background paper and a resolution concerning the socio-political rights of
migrant workers, their educational needs, harmonisation of migration law
and the combating of racism. This initiative challenged the Council's hegemonic determination of the personal scope of the freedom of movement
by stating that non-Community workers should be granted free rights and
enjoy equal treatment given that 'minority communities are today a permanent part of Western European life'. The Commission thus reactivated the
suppressed juridical option of making residence the qualifying criterion for
free movement.

It is also worth noting here that when the Commission used its powers
under Article 118 EC (137 on renumbering) to establish a prior communication and consultation procedure on migration policies in relation to third-
country workers (Decision 85/381, OJ 1985, L217/25), several Member
States filed complaints with the ECJ, arguing that the Commission had
exceeded its competence and impinged on the Member States' sovereign
power in the fields of immigrants and immigration rules. The ECJ ruled that
the Commission had exceeded its procedural powers to the extent that its
consultation procedure aimed at the securing of conformity between draft
national measures on the one hand and Community policies and actions on
the other (Joined Cases 281/85, 284 and 285/85, *Germany and others* v
Commission [1987] ECR 3203). On the issue of whether migration policies
towards non-EC nationals fell within the social issues under former Article
118 EC, the Court decided positively on the reasoning that the employment
situation – and, more generally, the improvement of living and working conditions in the Community – was affected by Member States' policies towards
third-country nationals. But with respect to the other part of the Commission's decision on the cultural integration of non-EC migrants, the Court
ruled that the Commission had exceeded its powers.[4]

The Single European Act (SEA), which entered into force on 1 January
1987, gave new impetus to the idea of Community citizenship and made visible the exclusion of resident third-country nationals. The principal aim of
the SEA was to overcome a double crisis: externally, the loss of global economic competitiveness of the EEC, owing to the rapid growth of the 'Asian
Tigers', a process known as 'Euro-sclerosis'; and internally, the stagnation of
economic and political integration. Compared to the Draft Treaty on European Union, articulated by the European Parliament under Spinelli's guidance in 1984, the SEA was a modest document. Notwithstanding its
weaknesses,[5] the SEA, nevertheless, revived the idea of the Single Market
(Article 8a EEC) and laid down a timetable for its completion by the end of

1992. To facilitate this completion, Article 100a (Article 95EC) was inserted, permitting decision-making by qualified majority. This article formed a new legal basis for harmonisation measures in fields which affected the establishment and functioning of the internal market. The Community's competence expanded to the areas of research and technology, environmental protection, economic and social cohesion, and improvement of living and working conditions. In institutional matters, the Community's supranational profile was enhanced by the reduction of the unanimity requirement in the decision-making process, the increase in the powers of the European Parliament via the introduction of the co-operation procedure and the creation of a Court of First Instance to assist the ECJ. European political co-operation obtained a formal legal basis (outside the Community Treaties), and the European Council was given formal status.

The preamble references of the SEA to human rights, democracy, equality and social justice gave a clear political dimension to the Community and formed the basis for new initiatives and institutional reforms. For instance, in 1988 the Commission proposed a directive on voting rights for Community nationals at local elections on the grounds that 'the integration process was indirectly eroding the democratic rights of some Community nationals' and 'ran counter to the SEA's objective of promoting democracy' (Bull. EC, Supp. 2, 1988: 29). And in 1989, the European Parliament proposed the extension of free movement to all resident workers irrespective of nationality. It also recommended that non-EC migrants should have the same rights of family unification as EC nationals, should enjoy protection from discrimination in employment and social matters and should have the right to vote in local elections (OJ 1989, C 69). As expected, the Council did not welcome the Parliaments's liberal recommendations. National governments were reluctant to relinquish competence over third-country nationals to the Community and, in any case, could not embrace the ideal of a multicultural European polity given the fact that they had institutionalised restrictive immigration policies and exclusion of settled migrants in domestic arenas.[6]

Indeed, driven by the advent of the SEA and the prospect of the establishment of the Single Market, the Member States stepped up the informal and ad hoc intergovernmental co-operation in home affairs which they had initiated in the mid-1970s in response to a range of 'international crime' issues, such as transborder terrorism, public order matters and drug trafficking. The aim of the intergovernmental co-operation in immigration and asylum matters was twofold: (i) to restrict the entry of foreigners and achieve a much more stringent policing of Europe's outer frontiers and (ii) to police migrant communities via various forms of internal control, such as security service co-operation, identity checks, the creation of a police information and intelligence database that would allow exchange of information on illegal aliens, 'subversives' and 'aliens considered likely to compromise public order' (para. 5.1, TREVI, June 1990).

A number of ad hoc and para-Communitarian bodies and agencies, such as the TREVI Group (1976), the Ad Hoc Group on Immigration (1986), the Schengen Group (1985), the Ad Hoc group on Europol (1992) and the Ad Hoc Group on Organized Crime (1992) assumed competence over immigration and asylum. A states' Europe was thus being created parallel to a people's Europe with little democratic debate. The TREVI Group was established in 1976 in order to co-ordinate action against international terrorism. In 1988 its remit was extended to the fields of undocumented immigration, asylum inflows, police and security co-operation. TREVI drew up a list of 50 countries whose nationals required visas to enter the Community. In 1988, the Member States extended the list and agreed on 55 countries whose nationals required visas to enter and on a common list of 'undesirable aliens'. The Ad Hoc Group on Immigration, which was set up in 1986 in order to tackle the 'abuses of the asylum process', recommended the imposition of fines to airlines bringing in undocumented asylum seekers and the co-ordination of the processing of asylum requests. Its input in immigration and asylum policy has been significant: it drafted the *Convention determining the State responsible for examining applications for asylum lodged in one of EC Member States*[7] (Dublin Convention, 30 ILM 425 (1991)), has been involved in the drafting of the External Frontiers Convention[8] (Commission Communication, COM(93) 684 Final, Brussels, 10 December 1993), 'the clearing houses' for asylum and immigration (CIREA and CIREFI) and EURODAC (European Automated Fingerprint Recognitions System).

The adoption of the Schengen Agreement (14 June 1985) by France, Germany, the Netherlands, Belgium and Luxembourg set out a framework for the gradual abolition of checks at their internal borders. Internal liberalisation of the movement of persons (Article 14 EC) was to be accompanied by measures of external and internal control, such as the harmonisation of immigration policies, stringent policing of the external borders, police co-operation, co-ordination of the efforts to combat illegal immigration, the introduction of a visa for the Schengen territory and the creation of a Schengen Information System (SIS) derived from the national police registers. These developments, seen by many as attempts to build a 'Fortress Europe' (Bunyan, 1991; Ford, 1992: xix–xxii) – that is, a European Community with a 'hard outer shell' against Third World immigrants and refugees – gave rise to complaints by human rights groups (e.g. Amnesty International, the Netherlands Institute of Human Rights) and migrant organisations (e.g. the Joint Council for the Welfare of Immigrants).

Following the European Summit at Rhodes (June 1988), the so-called Group of Co-ordinators was set up in order to co-ordinate the ongoing activities of these groups. The Group, consisting of high-ranking officials and a member of the Commission, drew up the Palma Document which recommended, among other things, the harmonisation of external frontier controls; a common list of countries whose citizens would need a visa and a list of 'undesirable' aliens; harmonisation of the provisions for granting visas and adoption of a common European visa; co-operation and exchange of information about undesirable aliens among law-enforcement agencies and customs; harmonisation and simplification of the procedures for the examination of applications for asylum and so on. This Document signalled the beginning of a shift from ad hoc interstate co-operation in migration-related matters to a more formalised and coherent framework.

The Schengen Implementing Convention, signed in June 1990 and coming into force on 26 March 1995, covered the same ground as the Palma Document and fleshed out the vision about 'Europe' that national executives had in mind. Under the Convention, external borders can be crossed legitimately only during fixed hours and at officially recognised border crossing points as defined in Article 1. The Convention also entailed provisions on the abolition of border controls (Article 2), the policing of external borders (Article 6) and the establishment of a common visa policy for long-term visits (Articles 9–17); the adoption of a short-term visa which grants a right to free circulation for a period not exceeding three months (Article 21); internal controls (Article 22); expulsion of aliens (Article 23); carrier sanctions (Article 26); determination of asylum applications (Articles 28–38); police co-operation (i.e. police forces will assist each other in detecting and preventing crime such as narcotic drugs (Articles 70–76), firearms and ammunition (Articles 77–91) and other crimes, and will have the right to pursue criminals and drug traffickers into the territory of a neighbouring Schengen state); and the establishment of a computerised Schengen Information System (SIS) consisting of national information-gathering units and a co-ordinating and supervising joint unit (Articles 92–119). Access to SIS was reserved for police and authorities responsible for border checks and responsibility for the accuracy, up-to-date nature and lawfulness of the data lay with the Contracting Party which inserted the data in the system.

The European-wide consensus on the exclusion of non-European immigrants and refugees was at odds with the citizenship 'problematique' featured on the Community's agenda in this period. Whereas intra-Community migration was regarded as a fundamental freedom and the cornerstone of European citizenship, non-EC immigration was portrayed by official discourse and policy as an 'invasion' to be feared and resisted. This symbolic framing of immigration reflected (and, in turn, helped maintain) the wider political and ideological regime which portrayed non-European migrants as 'unwelcome' intruders and as 'a law and order' issue. Embedded understandings thwarted policy development and innovation in this field: national executives chose to replicate the national path of exclusion and restrictive immigration policies at the European level. The appropriateness of the latter for the Union was never called in question. Nor was the negative impact of these policies upon democratic values and the formation of a civic and inclusive European identity noticed by the Commission. As a consequence, the strategic framing of immigration as a law and order issue could not but feed forward and structure subsequent political processes and identities.

The Maastricht settlement

The co-existence of two different modes of European identity within the same institutional setting – namely, the contractualist and exclusionary mode of identity, promoted by informal intergovernmental co-operation on immigration and asylum, on the one hand and the civic mode of European identity on the other – did not puzzle European policy-makers. In fact, intergovernmental co-operation in immigration matters was seen as a tool for European identity and community-building, not as a challenge to it. Although the Commission would have preferred a Treaty commitment to formal and actual harmonisation on migration issues, it had welcome the Schengen initiative as a laboratory for the Community. This suggests that the two modes of European identity were neither completely separate nor completely subordinate to one single principle.

The absence of an integrated logic on European identity was evident prior and during the negotiations for the Intergovernmental Conference (IGC) on political union which opened on 15 December 1990. Whilst national executives were agreeing on 'soft law' instruments and planning future common action on home affairs and judicial policy, the Parliament adopted the Declaration on Fundamental Rights and Freedoms (12 April 1989). Although the Declaration was not legally binding it, nevertheless, gave impetus to the idea of citizens' rights and of a Community Bill of Rights. The Parliament also called for the extension of free movement and the grant of political rights to all legal residents (OJ C183, 15/7/91) and did not hesitate to highlight the democratic deficit of intergovernmental co-operation in migration-related issues (*Europe*, 1750, 1751, 13 December 1991). The Spanish Prime Minister Gonzales suggested the inclusion of European citizenship in the new Treaty9 and the Commission articulated an ambitious text on Union citizenship (Commission opinion, 21 October 1990).

The final text of the Treaty on European Union (TEU) agreed at Maastricht (signed in February 1992) gave constitutional status to Union citizenship and enhanced the supranational character of the Community. The Community's competence was extended to the areas of education, culture, consumer protection and development policy. The powers of the Parliament increased through the introduction of the co-decision procedure (under which the Parliament can veto legislation on the third reading) and the extension of the scope of application of the co-operation procedure. The Parliament was also given the power to approve the members of the Commission prior to their appointment, and extra powers to scrutinise Community finances. A new impetus towards inter-regional co-operation at the European level was given by the creation of a Committee of the Regions. Although the members of the

Committee were to be appointed by national governments and its powers were only consultative and advisory, its creation marked the involvement of subnational government in the shared adventure of European integration (Everling, 1992). But progress came at a price; owing to the strident opposition of 'minimalist' Member States, such as the UK, common foreign and security policy (CFSP) and co-operation in justice and home affairs remained outside the Community framework. This tripartite structure consisting of a supranational pillar and two intergovernmental pillars gave rise to criticisms about the creation of a 'Europe of bits and pieces' (Curtin, 1993). Others, however, welcome the peculiar combination of supranationalism with intergovernmentalism as a sign of the emergence of a 'mixed commonwealth' (Bellamy and Castiglione, 1997, 1998).

Within the supranational pillar, formal political (albeit not direct) ties between the citizens and the Union were established though the institution of Union citizenship inserted in Part II of the Treaty. Although the significance of Union citizenship as a new form of citizenship beyond the nation-state cannot be underestimated (see Chapters 3 and 5), supranational actors viewed it instrumentally as the means toward the realisation of the two major objectives of the new Treaty: it enshrined the political character of the Community and strengthened its democratic legitimacy. More importantly, since the establishment of genuinely democratic structures within the Community could not be guaranteed owing to the Member States' resistance, the brunt of fulfilling the normative expectations of the citizens of Europe shifted towards measures designed to elicit popular support by making the Community a visible reality in their lives. On that view, Union citizenship does not constitute a fundamental break with the inherited functional and Euro-nationalist approach to European identity and citizenship; rather, it was the continuation of the inherited logic concerning a people's Europe. However, three transmutations had also taken place. First, Community officials had realised that identification with the Community could not to be ordained, but had to be achieved through political and economic reforms and by fostering a new universalist ethos which would help transform the active economic actors' rights into citizens' rights. Secondly, although legally defined and institutionalised, Union citizenship should be an evolving and adaptive institution (Article 8e EC (22 on renumbering)). Thirdly, Union citizenship would supplement and not replace national citizenship, thereby contributing to the creation of a multi-layered form of governance without a state (Schmitter, 1996). As a complex and multilevelled polity, the Union is obligated to 'respect the national identities of its Member States, whose systems of government are founded on the principles of democracy' (F.1 TEU), and must contribute to the flowering of the cultures of Member States, while respecting their national and regional diversity too (Article 128 EC (151 on renumbering)).

The TEU provisions on citizenship and the broader context
Following the precedent set in 1968, the Member States confined the personal scope of free movement to Community nationals. According to 8 EC (Article 17 on renumbering) 'every person holding the nationality of a member state shall be a citizen of the Union'. Nationality is to be defined according to domestic nationality laws, and long-term resident third-country nationals are excluded from membership in the European political community. The only citizenship rights conferred on them are the rights to petition the European Parliament and to refer to an Ombudsman appointed by the Parliament. This shows that preservation of state sovereignty rather than promotion of individual rights or democratic legitimacy underpinned the scope and content of Union citizenship (O'Leary, 1996b: 91). The second paragraph of Article 8 EC entailed an abstract reference to citizens' duties which has yet to materialise.

Free movement and residence   Article 8a EC (18 on renumbering) reaffirmed the Union's commitment to free mobility: citizens have the rights of free movement and residence in the territories of the Union, subject to limitations on grounds of public policy, public security or public health (Articles 39(3), 46(1) and 55 EC and Directive 64/221) (see Chapter 3). Non-active economic actors enjoy the rights of free movement provided they possess adequate resources so as not to become a burden on the social assistance and sickness insurance (see Chapters 3 and 5). The family members of those who have exercised their right of free movement enjoy the right of residence. Entry visas may be required for family members of Union citizens who are nationals of third countries.

Electoral rights   Article 8b EC (19 on renumbering) conferred upon Union citizens the right to vote and to stand as a candidate at EP elections and local elections in the Member State in which they reside under the same conditions as nationals of the host member state.[10] These rights basically extend the principle of non-discrimination on the grounds of nationality to the sphere of political activity by removing the nationality requirement for the exercise of electoral rights. By enabling Community nationals to take part in political life, electoral rights ensure democratic participation and equal treatment and promote a sense of European identity (see the Commission's proposal for *A Council Directive on voting rights under Article 235*, Bull. EC, Supp. 2/88: 28).

Two directives were adopted pursuant to Article 8b(1) EC and (2) of Directive 94/80/EC on rights relating to municipal elections (OJ L368 31/12/94: 38) and Directive 93/109/EC on elections to the Parliament (OJ L329 30/12/93: 34–8). Their aim was not to harmonise national electoral laws, but to facilitate the effective exercise of political rights by Union citizens. Directive 94/80 grants all citizens of the Union local electoral rights in the Member State in which they reside, but permits Member States to reserve access to the public office of major and deputy mayor to their own nationals. Although this derogation has been justified on the grounds that the duties that these offices involve may extend beyond the municipality (e.g. participation in the election of parliamentary assemblies), substantial derogations are, in principle, incompatible with the non-discrimination rule. Exceptionally, a Member State may restrict the exercise of electoral rights to those Community nationals who have been resident for a minimum period not exceeding five years in the case of the right to vote and ten years in the case of standing as a candidate, if the proportion of Community nationals exceeds 20 per cent of the total population (Article 12 of Directive 94/80/EC). Luxembourg has taken advantage of this exception and Belgium has also imposed a minimum period of residence in a limited number of municipalities (Article 12(2) of Directive 94/80/EC).[11]

The implementation of Directive 93/109 on elections to the Parliament ran more smoothly. This directive gave Union citizens the opportunity to choose whether they wished to exercise their electoral rights in their state of residence or their state of origin, but in Member States with a large proportion of Community nationals eligibility for participation may depend on a longer period of residence. The Directive does not affect national provisions concerning the political rights of nationals who reside outside its electoral territory, as a uniform electoral procedure for election to the Parliament did not come into being. Although the development of such a procedure would enhance the political authority of the Parliament and consolidate the democratic legitimacy of the Union, conflicting views among the Member States coupled with the requirements of unanimity on the part of the Council and of an absolute majority in the Parliament for the adoption of such a legal act hindered its development.

Diplomatic protection abroad   Under Article 8c EC (20 on renumbering) Union citizens are entitled to protection by diplomatic and consular authorities of any Member State in third country where the citizen's own Member State is not represented. Unlike the above-mentioned citizenship rights, this provision does not grant an enforceable right of protection: interstate co-operation in crucial for its implementation. Guidelines for the Protection of Unrepresented EC nationals by EC missions in Third Countries were adopted in 1993 (coming into force in July 1993) and, in December 1995, the Representatives of the Governments of the Member States adopted two Decisions regarding protection of Union citizens by diplomatic and consular representations. Since not all the Member States have made the necessary arrangements, their implementation has been delayed. Similarly, the Member States' decision to issue an emergency travel document for EU nationals who lose their travel documents while in a third country has not yet taken effect (25 June 1996)(OJ L168 6/7/96: 4).

Non-judicial means of redress   Article 8(d) EC (21 on renumbering) (in conjunction with Article 138(d) and (e) EC (194 and 195 on renumbering) provided that Union citizens and legal residents of the Union have the right to petition the Parliament and apply to the Ombudsman. The former entitlement already existed in the Parliament's internal rules of procedure, but it was upgraded into a right with a specific legal basis. The importance of both rights lies primarily in the fact that they institutionalise 'political opportunity structures' (Kitschett, 1986: 58) as a means of building a European civil society and enhancing the democratic credentials of the Union. Petitions to the Parliament must relate to an issue falling within the jurisdiction of the Union (this includes second- and third-pillar issues, too) and, with the exception of individual cases, may trigger infringement proceedings by the Commission for violations of Community law or provide a stimulus for political action by the Parliament or the Commission. This presupposes a dialogue between the EP's Committee of Petitions and the Commission.

The task of the Ombudsman is to investigate complaints concerning alleged maladministration in the activities of Community institutions (with the exception of the Court of First Instance and the ECJ acting in their judicial capacity). Detailed rules concerning the Ombudsman's duties were adopted 9 on March 1994 (the Statute of the Ombudsman). The Ombudsman conducts enquiries, either on his or her own initiative or following a complaint. (S)he is completely independent in the performance of duties and acts in the general interest of the Union and its citizens. Complaints must be made within the time limit of two years and must have been preceded by the appropriate administrative steps. Complaints must not concern facts already ruled upon by the Court or matters pending before the Court. The Ombudsman treats the complaint as confidential, conducts enquiries and if a conciliatory solution cannot be found, informs the institution concerned (which must respond within three months) and makes draft recommendations. The institution concerned must then forward its response to the Ombudsman within three months (see the *Interinstitutional Agreement on the Ombudsman's duties*, Bull. EC, 10/1993: 118–19). The Ombudsman will then send his final report to the Parliament and to the institution concerned and include in it any recommendations. (S)he informs the complainant about the outcome and may also send a report to the Parliament. Although the Ombudsman's findings do not carry any formal legal weight, they, nonetheless, have important effects in the field of fundamental rights and have proved valuable to individuals who have suffered from 'maladministration'.

Evidently, the material scope of Union citizenship appears quite limited. With the exception of electoral rights, the Union citizenship provisions enshrine previously existing rights in primary law. Other important rights, such as cultural rights, environmental protection, equal opportunities and social rights which featured in the Commission's draft text on Union citizenship were omitted from the final text owing to governmental resistance. Naturally, this fuelled criticisms that Union citizenship is largely 'a symbolic plaything without substantive content' (see d'Oliveira, 1995), and generated an 'expectations gap' on the part of the citizens of Europe.

The disjunction between normative expectations and outcomes was somewhat mitigated by the increase in the Community's powers in the social and employment spheres and the inclusion of the principle subsidiarity in the Treaty. As regards the former, the Social Fund's remit was widened and a whole new section on education and vocational training was adopted. The Agreement on Social Policy set out in Protocol 14 (from which the UK opted out) laid down the objectives for a Community social policy in accordance with the guidelines contained in the 1989 Social Charter. The Social Agreement contained provisions on: the role of management and labour; the rights of part-time, temporary and full-time permanent workers to improved living and working conditions; health and safety at work; information and consultation; equal pay for equal work; equal labour market opportunities and sex equality at work; and the occupational integration of people excluded from the labour force. However, other important rights, such as the right to join a union, collective bargaining and the right to strike were not mentioned. Whereas the Social Agreement has advanced the idea of a European social citizenship and formed the basis for legislative initiatives, such as Council Directive 94/45/EC *On the introduction of European works councils* and Council Directive 96/34/EC *On parental leave*, the introduction of subsidiarity in the Treaty carried the promise of enhancing citizen participation at local and regional levels.

As a substantive principle, subsidiarity entails a presumption in favour of local decision-making: decisions should be taken as closely as possible to the citizens (Article A TEU). In procedural terms, subsidiarity guides the allocation of competences among the various levels of government. Both definitions of subsidiarity are of crucial importance to the evolution of the Union and to the promotion of democratic citizenship. In particular, if citizenship is conceived of as the legal act of doing, and not simply the legal status of being, decentralised allocations of power, in principle, offer more opportunities for democratic participation. In addition, possible distribution of power in the Union would render state-centric visions of the Union obsolete. Notwithstanding these observations, it is true to say that subsidiarity has been an essentially contested concept: it has featured in many language games and has been marshalled to support several different visions of the Union's future. In the UK subsidiarity has highlighted the 'issue of overloading' of the Commission (Taylor, 1996: 78), whereas in continental Europe subsidiarity is viewed as a tool for Community action, and has triggered an interest in European regionalism and multilayered Union governance.

True, the genuine decentralist meaning of subsidiarity has been compromised owing to the absence of any reference to the allocation of competences between national and subnational levels of government in Article 3b EC (5 on renumbering). Bearing in mind, however, that the rationale behind subsidiarity was to reassure national governments that the conversion of the

Community into a Union would not be followed by an open-ended transfer of powers to the Community (Teasdale, 1993: 188), this is not surprising. 'Minimalist' and 'maximalist' interpretations of subsidiarity were thus combined in an ambiguous way in Article 3b EC (Article 5 EC on renumbering), which states that in areas of concurrent competences action should be taken by the Community only when a given objective can be attained more effectively at the Community level than at the level of the individual Member State. The ambiguity surrounding the definition of subsidiarity in Article 3b was compounded by the problem that the test of comparative efficiency would undoubtedly involve political judgements as to whether a matter was more efficiently dealt by the Community or the Member State. This sparked a debate on the role of the ECJ in this area: would the ECJ have powers of procedural review (this would require the Commission to give reasons as to why a given legislative proposal was in conformity with Article 3b (Emiliou, 1992b: 78)) or, alternatively, would it engage in substantive review, thereby applying and interpreting subsidiarity as a rule of EU constitutional law (Partan, 1995: 63-80)?

Whereas these reforms in the fields of European citizenship and subsidiarity could be seen as points of departure for new developments, national executives saw them more as points of convergence between what existed prior to the TEU and what could be created without damaging their interests in both the domestic and European arenas (the convergence hypothesis). This is attested by the formalisation of intergovernmental co-operation in justice and home affairs issues within the context of the Union, which is discussed below.

Justice and home affairs co-operation
The TEU formalised intergovernmental co-operation in justice and home affairs, but in a more diluted form since links with Community institutions were created (O'Keeffe,1995b: 35). Title VI of the TEU, the so-called 'third pillar', institutionalised interstate co-operation in the fields of asylum policy, external frontier controls, immigration policy and policy regarding nationals of third countries, judicial co-operation in civil and criminal matters, the combating of drug addiction and international fraud, customs and police co-operation. Under Article K6, the Parliament was to be informed and consulted and the Commission shared the right of initiative with the Member States in all areas except judicial co-operation in criminal matters, customs and police co-operation. A system of judicial review was only optionally provided for under Article K3(2)c for third-pillar conventions. The possibility of 'Communitarisation' of asylum policy, external border controls, immigration policy and policy regarding nationals of third countries, the combating of drug addition and fraud and judicial co-operation in civil matters by transferring them into the Community pillar was provided for via the *passerelle* provision of Article K9. However, this provision was subject to a 'double-lock' procedure

requiring unanimous decision by the Council and adoption by the Member States in accordance with their constitutional requirements. Visa policy was the only area transferred to Community competence under Article 100c EC. The various ad hoc groups were subsumed by a Co-ordinating Committee (K4 Committee), which was subdivided into three senior steering groups (i.e. security and law enforcement, police and customs co-operation are the areas of competence of the second steering group) and to several other working groups. The K4 Committee was competent to give opinions to the Council on its own initiative and contributed to the preparation of the Council's decisions. Unanimity was the basic decision-making procedure of the intergovernmental title which lacked any enforcement mechanisms.

This suggests that the Member States were determined to use the repertoire of already established operating procedures instead of taking advantage of the new institutional openings. The process of secretive and non-transparent policy-making continued and flourished in the absence of effective parliamentary and judicial controls. The Commission's input was limited, and the Parliament's right of consultation took the form of reports submitted to it *ex post facto*. Progress in this area was hampered not only by structural weaknesses of the third pillar (i.e. the requirement of unanimity) but also by the unwillingness of national executives to press on with harmonisation by adopting legally binding instruments. They opted, instead, for a form of approximation of national policies via non-binding resolutions and recommendations – instruments which had not been provided for under Title VI of the TEU. More importantly, the substance of the instruments which were agreed, such as the Resolution *On manifestly unfounded applications for asylum; the* Resolution *On a harmonized approach to questions concerning host third countries* which institutionalised the 'host country rule';[12] Resolution *On Minimum guarantees for asylum procedures* (OJ C274, 19/9/96); Council Recommendations on *The status of long-term resident third country nationals* (OJ C80/2 1996) and *On combating the illegal employment of third country nationals* by imposing criminal and/or administrative actions on employers (Bull. EU, 6-1996, 1.10.7), all confirmed fears that the EU was moving towards restrictive asylum and immigration regulations.

The reliance upon past policy responses and operating procedures ensured the continuation of the restrictive character of the asylum and immigration regulations and filtered out any considerations about the latter's impact upon democracy and identity-building in the Union. National executives did not think seriously about the consequences of their decisions at a time when transparency, democracy and legitimacy had become major concerns at the Community level. The Parliament did not hesitate to draw attention to the weaknesses of the third pillar and criticised the lack of effective parliamentary and judicial control in an area in which citizens' rights were directly affected (Resolution A3-01123/92, 7 April 1992, No. C125/81). It also called for the extension of free movement to long-term resident third-country nationals (Resolution A3-0284/92, 21 December 1992, No. C337/211), and its Committee on Civil Liberties and Internal Affairs went on to suggest that immigration and asylum policies should be a matter of joined responsibility of national parliaments and the Parliament – with a formal framework of co-operation between them (Resolution A3-0215/93).

In contrast, the Commission having looked upon the Schengen initiative rather favourably as a laboratory for EU developments (Collinson, 1993a: 152) welcomed the JHA framework as an effective means for sustaining momentum on co-operation in these policy areas. Instead of calling for insti-tutional structures which could help fashion a democratic and inclusive identity,[13] its efforts were concentrated on preparing the ground for a Com-mmunitarised procedural framework which could facilitate policy harmoni-sation in immigration and asylum policy. Not long after the entry into force of the Treaty, it took the initiative of suggesting the transfer of asylum policy to the Community via Article K9. In its report to the Council (*On the possi-bility of applying Article K9 to asylum policy*, SEC(93) 1687 Final, Brussels, 4 November 1993: 5–6), the Commission listed the advantages for applying Article 100c EC – namely, enhancement of transparency and efficiency in decision-making, legal certainty, parliamentary involvement and judicial con-trol. In the 1994 Communication to the Council and to the Parliament on immigration and asylum policy (COM(94) 23 Final, 23/02/94), the Com-mission went a step further to suggest a comprehensive, effective and coher-ent migration strategy based on: (i) measures to counter migratory pressure; (ii) effective control of immigration; (iii) the improvement of the legal status of third-country nationals by creating the right socio-economic conditions for successful integration and combating racial discrimination and xenopho-bia.[14] Despite their weaknesses, the Commission's initiatives indicated that the new Justice and Home Affairs (JHA) framework had not established a complete institutional closure. It had opened opportunities for procedural change. It also had another unintended consequence: it exacerbated the democratic deficit of the Union and gave greater visibility to the uneasy rela-tionship between the discourse and practice of democratic rights on the one hand, and the problem of exclusion entailed by 'Fortress Europe' on the other. By so doing, it called in question the web of official discourses and policies which had sought to construct a European identity at the intersec-tion of ideas borrowed from the process of national identity-building, ideals, efficiency concerns and socio–legal practices which promoted subjecthood instead of democratic citizenship, exclusion instead of inclusion and dis-crimination instead of equality.

Conclusion

By deciding to confine the scope of the free-movement provisions to work-ers who were nationals of the Member States in the late 1960s the Member

States grafted on to European institutions their notions of who the Europeans are. This decision must be understood against the background of shared understandings and nationalist concerns which portrayed ethnic migrants as unwelcome guests and/or a 'problem'. As it became sedimented, it biased the process of the institutional construction of a European identity by filtering out alternative considerations about a civic and inclusive mode of European identity.

Despite aspirations to build a democratic, civic European identity, the policy on European identity is full of ambiguities and incoherence. Uncertain of their convictions EC policy-makers vacillated between the Euro-nationalist (i.e. preserving Europe for the Europeans), functional (i.e. making Europe a tangible reality in the lives of European citizens) and contractualist modes of European identity. Political constraints and intergovernmental resistance is not the sole reason for this. Lack of ideas and the failure to imagine European identity through anything other than the lens of national/statist identity-building also played a crucial role. The intellectual borrowing of ideas and assumptions from the national–statist paradigm and the transfer of practices from the domestic environments to the European level resulted in cognitive limitations and normative closure. The differences among the various modes of European identity were not perceived and their intrinsic limitations were not considered. In addition, Commission officials failed to reflect critically on the meaning of membership in the emerging Euro-polity and the normative implications of what was being institutionalised. However, the closure was far from complete. The European Parliament's critical interventions were a source of normative vision as they criticised existing arrangements in the fields of citizenship and immigration and often advanced discursive alternatives. Although this vision was not acted upon, it was sometimes followed by proposals for legislation or by the Council's agreement on initiatives that had been previously blocked.

The process of the institutional construction of European identity is thus marked by such 'generative gradualisms' as well as by compromises between 'the inadequate' (proposed by the Council) and 'the not clearly thought about' (on the part of the Commission) in migration-related matters. It is also true to say that the TEU's provisions on Union citizenship lack a clear conceptual framework and a cohesive vision. In addition, the enabling capacities of this institution have been overshadowed, and to some extent undercut by the Council's restrictive and law-enforcement approach to immigration, asylum and the position of third-country nationals. The co-existence of the citizenship *'problematique'* with elements belonging to a less advanced phase of European integration (i.e. intergovernmental co-operation in the context of the Union) and to a different mode of European identity (i.e. contractualist identity) meant that the novel properties of the former could be reinterpreted and used to reinforce a weak civic but exclusive mode of European identity. What were European policy-makers missing? And what did they have to do differently given the opportunities for revision of the Treaties at the 1996 IGC? It is to these questions that I will now turn.

Notes

1 See Advocate-General Trabuchi's opinion in *Fracas v Belgium* (Case 7/75) [1975] ECR 679.
2 This was in implementation of point 10 of the final Communiqué issued at the Paris Summit (9-10 December 1974) (Bull. EC, Supp. 7/1975).
3 Resolution of 23 June 1981 (OJ C241 19/09/81: 1), completed by Resolution 482Y0716(01) OJ C179 16/07/82: 1 and as amended by Resolution 495Y0804(01) (OJ C200 4/8/95: 1).
4 Arguing that the treatment of 'aliens' is an area falling within their sovereign jurisdiction, national governments also blocked Community measures affording effective protection of racial and ethnic minorities by outlawing racial discrimination throughout the Member States. The 1986 *Joint Declaration against Racism and Xenophobia* was viewed as a mere 'declaration of principle'.
5 The Draft Treaty proposed the transformation of the Parliament into a genuine legislative organ which would share with the Commission the power of legislative initiative, ended the Luxembourg Accord and established a comprehensive foreign policy. The Draft Treaty represented a direct challenge to Council and consequently was not endorsed. For an assessment of the SEA, see Pinder (1991); Ward (1996). Pescatore (1987: 10–18) has also criticised the SEA for being 'a fundamentally deceptive statute, designed to convey the appearance of reform, whilst entrenching the particularistic powers of the MS'.
6 There was a convergence towards restrictive immigration policies and tighter deportation legislation in early 1970s in almost all northern European countries: Castles and Kosack (1973); Hammar (1985); Cohen (1987); Collinson (1993a, 1993b). But compare Hollifield (1992); Freeman (1995). Freeman argues that the structural properties of liberal democracies prompt expansive and inclusionary immigration policies.
7 The Dublin Convention aimed at the harmonisation of procedural rules concerning asylum – and not the harmonisation of the substantive law of asylum. It established the so-called 'one-stop rule' – that is, a single Member State is responsible for considering applications for asylum; rejection of the application for asylum by that state precludes entry to another EC country. It came into force on 1 September 1997 (OJ 1997 L281/1). On this, see Wallace (1996, 28); Hailbronner and Thiery (1997).
8 The draft External Frontiers Convention applies to persons who are not entitled under EC law to cross an external border for a short visit to a Member State. It entailed measures on entry controls, visa requirements (such as carriers' responsibility), measures relating to the illegal crossing of external frontiers and the recovery of expenses incurred by expulsion.
9 According to the Spanish Memorandum, European citizenship is 'a personal and inalienable status of citizens of the Member States, which, by virtue of their membership in the Union, shall have special rights and special tasks, inherent in the framework of the Union, which are exercised and protected specifically within

   the borders of the Community, without this prejudicing the possibility of taking advantage of the same quality of European citizen also outside the said borders': *Europe*, 1653, 6/10/90.

10 Prior to the adoption of this directive, local voting rights were granted to non-national residents in Ireland, Denmark, the Netherlands, Sweden, Finland, Spain and the UK. With the exception of Ireland, the exercise of these rights was subject to residency periods or reciprocity agreements.

11 Belgium has been found in breach of its obligations under Article 14(1) of that Directive for failing to implement the Directive within the prescribed time limit: Case C-323/97 *Commission v Belgium*, Judgement of the Court, 9 July 1998.

12 This means that asylum seekers arriving in the Union through countries deemed to be safe may be returned to that country without substantive examination of their application for asylum. Re-admission agreements were signed with neighbouring countries, designed to guarantee the return of persons rejected or expelled after travelling from there to a Member State.

13 Compare the Commission's proposals on a draft decision on the External Frontiers Convention and the draft Visa Regulation with the already existing provisions of Schengen (*Commission Communication to the Council and the EP on Immigration and Asylum policies*, COM(93) 684 Final, 10 December 1994). The draft Convention on the Crossing of the External Frontiers contains provisions on the implementation of a common visa policy, controls on third-country nationals, a list of persons to whom entry may be refused and the combating of illegal immigration. The Convention has not been signed yet, owing to a dispute between the UK and Spain over Gibraltar and disagreements about the competence of the ECJ. Regulation 2317/95 on a common visa list has been adopted and annulled (see Case C-392/95 *Parliament v Council* [1997] ECR I-3213), and common provisions on a uniform format for visas have been laid down (see Council Regulation 1683/95, OJ L164/1, 14 July 1995).

14 The increase in racist violence and xenophobia, coupled with pressure from non-governmental organisations (NGO), migrant groups and the Parliament prompted a generalised awareness of the need to combat racism and xenophobia. See *Council Resolution on the response of educational systems to the problems of racism and xenophobia*, OJ C312, 23/11/95; *Council Resolution on the fight against racism and xenophobia in the fields of employment and social affairs*, OJ C296, 10/11/1995; A4-0135/96 EP *Resolution on the communication from the Commission on racism, xenophobia and anti-Semitism* (COM 995) 0653-C4-0250/96); *EP resolution on racism, xenophobia and anti-Semitism*, OJ C308, 20/11/95.

3

New horizons, old constraints and the Amsterdam compromise

The discussion in Chapter 2 has shown that many of the paradoxes and limitations of the process of European identity-building cannot be accounted for on the basis of structural/institutional constraints alone (i.e. time constraints, conditions of uncertainty, competing interests, conflicting claims, domestic political exigencies, the distribution of costs and benefits and so on). Background understandings, beliefs and assumptions place limits on what is possible and appropriate. In addition, the tendency to deploy old conceptual tools, past practices and past solutions in designing new institutions and in addressing a different set of concerns generates as many problems as it purports to resolve. Institutional design and policy implementation in the fields of identity, citizenship and immigration has thus taken place under conditions of 'fog over the battlefield' of decision-making – that is, under a veil of limited and selective perception, and with the aid of existing conceptual modes which do not correspond to the radical potential of new structures. The basic argument of this book is that there are good reasons for thinking about things differently and for considering alternative institutional designs which are both normatively justified and feasible. And although empirical problems and institutional constraints cannot always be anticipated by conceptual thinking alone, different conceptual frames can often generate solutions by simply changing the ways in which we think about the problem (divergent thinking).

In seeking to construct an identity and community in Europe on the basis of a 'consciousness of attachment' (the Euro-nationalist mode) and performance-related criteria (the functional mode), European decision-makers failed to see that community in the European Union will not arise through people having feelings for each other. Rather, it will emerge out of their co-operative interaction and participation in a variety of associative relations, and through their living in relation to institutions which promote reflexive forms of co-operation and democratic participation (see below, pp. 66–7; see also Chapter 5). Governmental elites, on the other hand, have underestimated the extent of the reciprocal interaction between the national and supranational level (see below, pp. 69–74). Finally, in both pre-Amsterdam and post-Amsterdam Europe, European decision-makers have paid insufficient attention to the potential and the complexity inherent in the new structures.

European citizenship as a new form of citizenship

It is certainly the case that European citizenship is, at present, a weak institution; a pale shadow of its national counterpart (O'Keeffe, 1994; d'Oliveira, 1995; O'Leary, 1996a). Union citizenship may have 'constitutionalised' the Community law rights of free movement, but it has not added much that is substantially new to existing Community law. The European Court of Justice (ECJ), on the other hand, has yet to transform this concept into a prominent building block of the evolving EU legal order.[1] But the constitutional significance of European citizenship does not lie in what this institution is at present, but in what it might be or should be. As Advocate General Leger has stated, in his opinion in *Boukhalfa*:

> Admittedly the concept embraces aspects which have already largely been established in the development of Community law and in this respect it represents a consolidation of existing Community law. However, it is for the Court to ensure that its full scope is attained. If all the conclusions inherent in the concept are drawn, every citizen of the Union must, whatever his nationality, enjoy exactly the same rights and be subject to the same obligations (Case C-214/94 *Boukhalfa v Federal Republic of Germany* [1996] 3 CMLR 22, 38).

The fact that rights and obligations, however limited these may be at present, are granted by the supranational level shows that citizenship can no longer be confined within the framework of national–statist communities. In this respect, Meehan (1997: 73) is correct to say that 'it is perhaps less important that the innovations are small than that they are breaches in normal conventions'. Citizenship features centrally in the quest for new transnational structures which turn 'aliens' into associates in a common venture aiming at ensuring peace, prosperity and the effective protection of rights. True, this process is riddled with fundamental ambiguities, contradictions and tensions and, as we have seen, egalitarian processes co-exist with processes of exclusion. However, for all the shortcomings of European institutions, it is difficult not to be impressed by the extent to which Community rights' jurisprudence has transformed immigration law and practice in the Member States. Nor must we lose sight of the possibility that the demands of European integration may induce further relaxation of established nationality law principles (Evans, 1991: 214–17; Closa, 1994).

Multiple citizenship therefore does not simply allow for multiple standards of citizenship and institutional pluralism. It also segments and divides sovereignty and renders the various citizenships more complex. In other words, citizenships do not merely overlap, but are nested within each other and interlock. This 'nesting' facilitates reciprocal interaction and transformation as much as it increases tensions and ambiguities. Interestingly, even forces which are antagonistic to this interaction are themselves shaped by it and evolve. In examining the impact that the Community rights of free movement have had upon the ways in which states view and treat nationals of other Member States, for example, one observes that notions such as 'immigrant', 'resident alien' or 'temporary guest' have been replaced by that of 'Union citizen' (Plender, 1976, cit. in Wilkinson, 1995). Furthermore, Union citizens are encouraged to participate in various types of associative relations beyond national borders and choose their 'civic home' (Poiares-Maduro, 1998). In this respect, the novelty of European citizenship may lie in its capacity to change our understanding of citizenship and community and to prompt a rethinking of membership with a view to opening up new forms of political community. But if this is the case, are not national elites justified in regarding Union citizenship as a potentially 'dangerous supplement'?

'That dangerous supplement …?'

If European citizenship impacts upon traditional conceptions of citizenship and community, then arguably national fears that it may lead to a parallel Euro-nationality and/or question the very foundations of national citizenship are not misguided (see Chapter 1). Community institutions, for their part, have sought to alleviate such worries – albeit at the expense of European integration itself. Community law upholds the international law maxim that determination of nationality falls within the state's reserved domain of exclusive jurisdiction, despite anomalies that this may create in the field of application of EC law.

In *Micheletti*, the Court upheld that determination of nationality falls within the exclusive competence of the Member States, but it added that this competence must be exercised with due regard to the requirements of Community law (Case C-369/90 *M. V. Michelleti and Others v Delegacion del Gobierno en Catanbria* [1992] ECR I-4329). Michelletti, an orthodontist of dual Argentinian and Italian nationality, was not allowed to establish himself in Spain because he was deemed to be a national of Argentina. According to Articles 9(9) and (10) of the Spanish Civil Code, dual nationals were deemed to be nationals of the country in which they had habitually resided prior to their arrival in Spain.[2] Although it was not Michelletti's Italian nationality which was denied by Spain but its implications in terms of the exercise of Community rights and freedoms, the ECJ made it clear that Article 43 EC cannot be interpreted as permitting national legislation to impose supplementary conditions such as a residence test as a precondition for giving effect to his nationality of a Member State. Far from impinging upon the Member States' discretionary power in this area,[3] the ECJ sought to apply the principle of mutual recognition in their power of ascertainment of nationality so that persons who are legally recognised as nationals of one Member State should be able to exercise their right to free movement without impediments imposed by additional regulations adopted by other Member States (see also Case C-122/96 *Saldanha* [1997] ECR I-5325).

In any case, the Declaration on Nationality of a Member State annexed to the Final Act of the Treaty on European Union (TEU) expressly stated that 'the question whether an individual possesses the nationality of a member state shall be settled solely by reference to the national law of the member state concerned'. Similar declarations were adopted by the European Council at Edinburgh (OJ C348/2 of December 1992) and Birmingham. The Birmingham Declaration stated clearly that Union citizenship constitutes an additional tier of rights and protection which is not intended to replace national citizenship (Bull. EC, 10-1992 1. 8.9). This has been reaffirmed by the Amsterdam Treaty, signed on 2 October 1997, which has added to Article 17(1) EC the statement that 'Union citizenship shall complement national citizenships'. The choice of the term 'complement' is not accidental, for 'complements' normally add, they do not substitute.

Notwithstanding the Amsterdam concession to national sensitivities, national elites continue to be haunted by the spectre of European citizenship as a supplement to national citizenship. They fear that European citizenship, however immature and weak it may be at present, is not simply a mercantile citizenship designed to make the internal market work. It has the capacity to challenge the basic nature of statist citizenship and has implications for citizens' identities. It is perhaps this fear of the 'dangerous supplement' that led the Danish representation to declare, in its instrument of ratification of the TEU, that Union citizenship as a juridico–political concept is entirely different from the Danish concept of national citizenship. As the Danish opt-out Declaration states: 'nothing in the TEU implies or foresees an undertaking to create a citizenship of the Union in the sense of citizenship of the nation-state. The question of Denmark participating in such a development does, therefore, not arise (OJ C348/4, 31/12/94).

The Danish reservations reveal a rather dogmatic adherence to the idea that national citizenship should remain the foundation of political legitimacy and the source of social bonds (see Chapter 1). This line of reasoning, however, 'freezes' national citizenship in time. It overlooks the diachronic as well as synchronic connectedness between old and new citizenships. It is worth mentioning here that the British government entered into discussions with the Community concerning the formulation of its second declaration on nationality following the enactment of the 1981 British Nationality Act (Official Report Standing Committee, British Nationality Bill 20th Sitting, 26 March 1981 C810). And, generally speaking, in reforming their nationality laws, the member states have to take into account the requirements of Community law.[4] On a synchronic level, too, the Danish reservations downplay the processes of transformative interaction between the national and Community levels in the domain of citizenship.

National citizenship is not some integral whole which forms itself out of itself and develops irrespective of developments in the Union and elsewhere. The Community rights of free movement and European citizenship have subtly transformed national citizenship – albeit not without resistance – by eroding the link between citizenship and state membership on the one hand and national identity on the other (see below). In this respect, it may be argued that the relationship between the 'new' (European Union) and 'old' (national) citizenships is not merely complementary, that is, a relationship in which the complement as a super-added element is neutral to and different from what it complements. Nor is it a relationship of substitution. It is, instead, a relationship of ambivalence whereby each element relates back to the other, reverses itself and passes into the other. But would not this make European citizenship, that 'dangerous' supplement, constitutive in part of national citizenships?

The incremental adaptation of national citizenship

As the ultimate gatekeepers, states have had the sovereign power to determine who shall enter their territory, who shall 'belong' once admitted and under what conditions when this is deemed to be conducive to the national interest. The threshold of compelling state interest with regard to admission, residence and treatment of 'aliens' has been significantly lowered in the Union. Long before the Maastricht Treaty, the physical presence of Community nationals in the territory of a Member State and their engagement in economic activities there had ceased to be a matter of state permission and tolerance (Case 159/79 *R v Pieck* [1980] ECR 2171; [1980] 3 CMLR 220). Instead, it has been a matter of fundamental rights. Qualified Community nationals, be they workers, work seekers (Case C-292/89 *R. v Immigration Appeal Tribunal, ex parte Antonissen* [1991] ECR I-745; [1991] 2 CMLR 373), self-employed persons, providers and recipients of services – including tourists (Cases 286/92 and 26/83 *Luisi and Carbone v Ministero del Tesoro* [1984] ECR 377; [1985] 3 CMLR 52), their family members and EEA nationals are entitled to enter the UK and to reside without requiring leave to remain.[5] However, entitlement to reside depends upon continued qualification and, with respect to spouses who are nationals of third countries, the continuing subsistence of marriage. Free-movement rights have been granted also to non-active economic actors such as students, pensioners, persons not otherwise covered by Community legislation and their families provided that they are economically self-sufficient and are covered by health insurance.[6] Finally, Union citizenship has led to a conceptual 'metamorphosis' of the Community rights of free movement and residence 'by enshrining them in the Treaties themselves' (Commission Report *on the Citizenship of the Union*, COM(93) 702 Final, 21/12/93; see also Case C-378/97 *Wijsenbeek*).

Community nationals and EEA nationals have thus the right to be on the territory of a Member State. What is interesting in such a process is not the 'opening' of national citizenship 'from within' which allow nationals of other Member States to obtain citizenship by naturalisation, but the shifting of boundaries 'from outside' through the conferral of rights which are enforceable before national courts.[7] Member States are not allowed, for example, to impose restrictions on the residence of Community migrant workers and can terminate their right of residence only on certain, expressly stated grounds.[8] That said, it must be noted here that the work seekers' right of residence is more qualified: failure to secure employment within a 'reasonable' time limit (six months in the UK and three months in the other Member States) can lead to 'removal under Art. 15(2) of the Immigration (EEA) Order 1994, SI, 1994/1895, unless of course the person concerned provides evidence that (s)he actively seeks employment and has genuine chances of being engaged in the future [*Antonissen*]'. National provisions which provide for automatic termination of the residence period at the end of three months with no opportunity of extending it are unlawful (Case C-344/95 *Commission v Belgium (Re Treatment of Migrant Workers)* [1997] ECR I-1035; [1997] 2 CMLR 187).

Member States are permitted to derogate from the provisions relating to freedom of movement for people on the grounds of public policy, public security or public health (Articles 39(3), 46(1) and 55 EC and Council Directive 64/221 (1964) OJ Special Edition 850/64: 117). However, these exceptions must be strictly interpreted and cannot be invoked to service economic ends (Article 2(2) of Council Directive 64/221). Such measures can be based only on the 'personal conduct of the individual concerned', which must constitute 'a genuine and sufficiently serious threat to the requirements of public policy affecting one of the fundamental interests of society' (Case 30/77 *R v Bouchereau* [1977] ECR 1999; [1977] 2 CMLR 800). Clearly, a Member State cannot order the expulsion of a Community national as a deterrent or a general preventive action.[9] Previous criminal convictions cannot in themselves constitute grounds for deportation, but past conduct may constitute evidence of a present threat to public policy, particularly if the individual concerned is likely to reoffend.[10] It follows that an expulsion order which automatically follows a criminal conviction does not meet the requirements of Article 3 of Directive 64/221 since no account is being taken of the personal conduct of the offender or of the danger which that person represents for the requirements of public policy (Case C-348/96 *Donatella Calfa*, Judgement of 19 January 1999). By insisting on such a strict interpretation of the public policy derogations, the ECJ has circumscribed the Member States' discretionary power in this field, thereby diminishing the risk of possible 'scapegoating' of 'foreigners' in order to satisfy public opinion. In addition, Articles 8 and 9 of Directive 64/221 provide for procedural guarantees and remedies, such as disclosure of the grounds on which any restrictive measures have been adopted and a right of appeal. Although the system of judicial protection entailed by Directive 64/221 is far from perfect, it has, nevertheless, led to the transformation of immigration law and practice in the Member States.

Community workers enjoy a wide range of substantive rights: to move freely within the territory of other Member States and stay there for the purpose of employment; equal access to any form of employment, even that requiring official authorisation; to enjoy equality of treatment in respect of conditions of employment, remuneration and dismissal; to enjoy all benefits accorded to national workers such as social and tax advantages, housing, participation in trade unions and staff associations. The exercise of these rights does not depend on any transfer of loyalty to the host state. Nor is the length of residence or length of employment a prerequisite for qualifying for a social advantage in the host state, as this depends on an individual's status as worker or resident in the national territory.[11] Spouses and dependent relatives in both the ascending and descending line have the right to install themselves with the primary beneficiary and to take up employment themselves. The children of migrant workers are also entitled to receive education, to choose and be assisted to attend the educational course of their choice under the same conditions as nationals of host state,[12] even though this may result in the provision of financial assistance for a course taken outside the national territory (Case C-308/89 *Di Leo v Land Berlin* [1990] ECR I-4185). All this suggests that the Community views the integration of the worker and her or his family into the social fabric of the host state as the end product of equalisation,[13] and not of assimilation to the values and culture of that state.

National governments are not permitted to introduce arbitrary distinctions or other conditions which, although applicable irrespective of nationality, are liable to affect essentially Community migrant workers, thereby placing them at a particular disadvantage.[14] Conflicting national legislation must be repealed or amended, and it is not sufficient that Community law is applied in practice, but not *de jure*, for this may give rise to uncertainty for those subject to it (Case 167/73 *Commission v France* [1974] ECR 359). Differential treatment has to be objectively justified and must be proportionate. Even non-discriminatory measures, that is, measures which are generally applicable, may be in breach of the Treaty if they are liable to prohibit or otherwise impede the exercise of the fundamental freedoms.[15]

Employment in the public service is yet another example of the 'Europeanisation' of national citizenship. Despite claims made by national governments that 'freedom of movement was not meant to alter the legal situation existing before the Communities were established as regards the organisation of the state and in particular access for foreigners to the public service'(Case 149/79 *Commission v Belgium* [1980] ECR 3883, at 3895; [1982] 3 CMLR 539), the Court has diluted the traditional state prerogative of identifying the boundaries of its public sector and determining who may have access to it. Employment in the public sector can no longer be reserved for nationals, who have 'a relationship of special allegiance to the state and can identify with the interests of the state'(*Re Colgan and Others* (Queen's Bench Division) [1997] 1 CMLR 53, at 72), unless, of course, the post in question involves direct or indirect participation in the exercise of powers conferred by public law and duties designed to safeguard the interests of the state or other public authorities. In other words, the public service exception does not apply to posts which are too remote from the specific activities of the public service, even though they might come under the state or other organisations governed by public law (Case 290/94 *Commission v Greece* [1997] 2 CMLR 999). This case law, coupled with the Commission's notice (OJ C72/2, March 1988) which specifies the sectors of employment which do not meet the two cumulative conditions mentioned above, has triggered the amendment of constitutional provisions and national legislation in the Member States. The amendment of the provisions of section 1 of the 1955 Aliens Employment Act in the UK by the European Communities (Employment in the Public service) Order 1991, for example, has led to the opening of a wide range of civil service posts to Community nationals. Finally, *de facto* membership of Community nationals in the civil society of the host Member State results in *de jure* membership in the political community – that is, the conferral of rights of political participation at local government and European parliamentary elections (Article 19 EC).

Community law has not only diluted the link between the possession of state nationality and the enjoyment of citizenship rights, but has also changed the ways in which individuals citizens view their own governments. Internal institutions and practices and policies are increasingly looked at with a multifocal gaze, and citizens are eager to use what ever opportunities may exist at the Community level in order to induce constitutional developments at the national and subnational ones. In addition, the invention of state liability for breach of Community law has enabled individual citizens to achieve a better judicial protection of the rights they derive from Community law.[16] Under this principle, governments are obligated, when certain conditions are met, to make good any damage caused to individuals for infringement of Community law for which they are responsible. The fact that this judicial remedy is enforceable before national courts and that claims for damages against the state are made in accordance with national rules and procedures applicable to actions in tort or delict indicate that citizens have stakes in multiple and mutually interacting publics.

In addition, citizens or undertakings may invoke their rights under Community law not only against the host Member State, but against their state of origin, too. Citizens returning to their home state after having been employed elsewhere in the Community, for example, may wish to invoke Community family rights, if these are more generous than national provisions (Case C-370/90 *R v Immigration Appeal Tribunal and Surinder Singh*, *ex parte Secretary of State for the Home Department* [1992] ECR I-4265; [1992] 3 CMLR 358).

Although the discussion hitherto has focused on the empowering and equalising impact of Community law upon national citizenship, it would be a mistake to assume away the nationality model of citizenship. The legal framework of intra-EU migration may have given precedence to equality of treatment over nationality and to rights over territorial sovereignty but, as argued in Chapter 2, the EU migration regime has reinforced the traditional prerogatives of the European nation-state and revived the traditional dichotomy between citizen and 'foreigner' (i.e. non-EU national). Europeanisation and democratisation of national citizenship are not equivalent in all respects.

Whereas Community nationals have become right bearers and civic participants in the common European venture, long-term resident third-country nationals are deprived of civic standing. As noted in Chapter 2, the only citizenship rights they enjoy are the right to petition the Parliament and apply to the Ombudsman. They may also enjoy 'derived' rights as family members of Union citizens or employees of undertakings providing services in another Member State (*Rush Portuguesa* and *Vander Elst* cases). Third-country nationals could also be beneficiaries of agreements concluded under Articles 300 and 310 EC by the Community with third states. These agreements form an integral part of Community law, but confer only limited rights on specific classes of third-country nationals (the citizens of the contracting state) (Alexander, 1992; Guild, 1996; Peers, 1996). Most long-term resident third-country nationals do not enjoy the benefits of free movement, residence, family reunion and, generally speaking, the protection against discrimination that EC law affords to Community nationals and EEA nationals (there is Community competence over conditions of employment of legally residing third-country nationals). This exclusion is difficult to justify from a normative point of view given that these people have been living their whole lives within the territory of the Member State and have made this territory the centre of their socio-economic life (see also La Torre, 1998; Monar, 1998b; Rubio-Marin, 1998). As both interested and affected parties therefore, third-country nationals should not be silenced by *a priori* definitions of what properly constitutes the legitimate denotation of citizenship or assumptions about where the boundaries of the supranational political community should be.

Broadly speaking, there are two ways of remedying the civic inclusiveness deficit in the Union; namely, through reforms at the national level aiming at facilitating third-country nationals' acquisition of national citizenship or by extending the personal scope of Union citizenship. The former could involve either a deregulatory form of liberalisation of naturalisation rules along the lines suggested by Evans (1994) and Hansen (1998), or a Community-induced harmonisation of the national laws governing acquisition and loss of citizenship. Legislative harmonisation could take the form of minimum harmonisation where a Community measure lays down a minimum set of criteria and requirements for citizenship acquisition, thereby 'acting as a floor'. The problem with this mechanism is that it leads to downward harmonisation. Alternatively, uniform Community provisions could supplement existing national arrangements. In this respect, a directive or regulation applying uniformly to all the Member States could form the foundation of a code of European nationality and of Euro-naturalization procedures. The distinct disadvantage of this, however, is that it would replicate the nationality model of citizenship at the European level and project the European adventure as a quest for statehood. It is also doubtful whether the position of third-country nationals would improve by conditioning their admission on the satisfaction of certain criteria, modelled upon those required by national laws, such a lawful entry and residence, age, employment status, good character, loyalty to the aims of the Union, assimilation and so on (O'Keeffe, 1994: 105). A third possibility might be a multilateral convention drawn up on the basis of Article 293 EC along the lines of the European Convention on Nationality adopted by the Council of Europe in 1997.

Whereas deregulatory liberalisation of naturalisation laws would not put an end to the varying rules and conditions for acquisition of citizenship throughout the Member States, EC-wide harmonisation is bound to be resisted on the grounds that the Community lacks competence in this area. Bearing in mind how jealously the Member States guard their exclusive competence in the determination of nationality, the European Union Migrants' Forum, in its proposals for the revision of the TEU at the 1996 IGC, suggested another institutional mechanism, namely, the acquisition of Union citizenship by reason of lawful residence in the Union for a period of five years or more. This could be achieved through an amendment to Article 19(1) EC. The absence of political will may be a pragmatic constraint on such a reform, but reforms almost never emerge naturally: they are the product of processes of negotiation and political activism.

The Amsterdam compromise

The 1996 IGC which culminated in the Treaty of Amsterdam (signed on 2 October 1997, coming into force on 1 May 1999) did not extend the personal scope of Union citizenship to long-term resident third-country nationals. It merely conferred on them the right to visa-free travel throughout the Member States for three months (Articles 62(3) and 63(4) EC). Nor did the Treaty introduce any significant changes to the material scope of the institution. It merely adjusted Article 18(2) EC by involving the co-decision procedure and added a new subparagraph to Article 21 EC stating that 'every citizen of the Union may write to the institutions or bodies referred to in this Article or in article 4 in one of the languages mentioned in Article 248(1) and have an answer in the same language'. And in symbolic recognition of national concerns, the Amsterdam Treaty has also inserted in Article 17(1) EC the statement that Union citizenship shall complement and not replace national citizenship.

The absence of institutional reforms to Articles 17 *et seq.* EC was disappointing given the prominence of the issue of citizenship in various reports by the Community institutions on the functioning of the TEU; NGO's had also campaigned for a new constitutional dynamic in the domain of citizenship both prior to and during the IGC. Indeed, despite the Commission's inertia and the absence of consensus on the legal status of third-country nationals even within the Parliament, pressure groups such as the Migrants' Forum, the Starting Line Group, the European Anti-Poverty Network and the European Women's Lobby had called for the extension of European citizenship to these individuals. These proposals demonstrated that creating a heterogeneous and inclusive citizenship in the Union is not a policy problem provided one reflects normatively on the issue of exclusion. The nationality model of citizenship may be the condition of possibility of European citizenship (Article 17(1) EC), but it is simultaneously the condition of its impossibility. The transcription of statements and assumptions derived from national citizenship into the discourse and practice of European citizenship constrains the maturation of the supranational model of citizenship and frustrates its potential to create an inclusive European public. In this respect, the Amsterdam negotiations represented a missed opportunity for sorting out the opposing political dynamics operating within the monadic totality of Union citizenship and for developing a coherent conceptual framework.

It is perhaps owing to the intense and skilful lobbying done by NGOs that a new anti-discrimination clause was inserted into the Treaty. Article 13 EC enables the Council, acting unanimously on a proposal from the Commission and after consulting the Parliament, to 'take appropriate action to combat discrimination based on sex, racial or ethnic origin, religion and belief, disability, age or sexual orientation'. The insertion of this clause into the Treaty was a significant breakthrough in that it placed discriminatory behaviour within the remit of the Treaty and the Community's legislative competence. But the new clause suffers from some important limitations, too. First, its optional character (i.e. the Council … may) means that the provision will not give rise to individual rights that can be relied upon in national courts, and that the Court will not adjudicate on actions against the Member States until Directives have been issued. Second, the requirement of unanimity is likely to undermine the effectiveness of this article as some governments object to any EU intervention in this sphere. Third, the marginal role that the Parliament will play coupled with the fact that the application of this article will be limited to measures that already fall within the Community competence makes the clause quite restrictive.

The incorporation of the Social Agreement into the Treaty was also a positive development. It has laid the foundations for the design of a coherent European social policy, and compensated for the absence of a reference to European social citizenship in the new Treaty. Although the provisions in this chapter have been strengthened to ensure equal opportunities and equal treatment for men and women in the workplace and the fight against social exclusion is now enshrined in the Treaty, the new common social policy is still limited. Important issues, such as social security, redundancies and worker representation, still require unanimity. In addition, the common social policy needs to incorporate the right to work and rights in employment (e.g. provisions on minimum wage, the rights of association and strike and so on) as well as to provide effective protection for the elderly, children and adolescents, the unemployed and unpaid workers (i.e. women engaging in family and caring work). The institutionalisation of such aspects of social citizenship would help transform Union citizenship from a 'virtual quality' to a status which is meaningful even to those citizens who do not avail themselves of the free-movement rights. A similar effect, but of a more symbolic nature, might be the emphasis that the Treaty gives to the protection of fundamental rights. Accession by the European Union to the European Convention of Human Rights (ECHR) was not achieved, but the Amsterdam Treaty strengthened the provisions on human rights and established a new sanctions procedure, which provides for the suspension of certain rights for Member States who seriously and persistently breach these principles (Articles 6(2) and 7 TEU).

The extension of the powers of the European Parliament at Amsterdam might also contribute to the flourishing of a European civil society: the extension of the scope of the co-decision procedure as well as its simplification (i.e. through the removal of the third reading) puts the Parliament on a more equal footing with the Council in the legislative process. As such, this is likely to encourage the participation of Union citizens in the European enterprise. With regard to the procedure for the election of the European Parliament by direct universal suffrage, the Amsterdam Treaty provides for the Community's power to adopt common principles (Article 190 EC), and a legal provision has been inserted into the same article to permit the adoption of a single statute for Members of the European Parliament (MEPs). In addition, the Amsterdam Treaty introduced closer ties with national parliaments via a new *scrutiny reserve*. Under a protocol annexed to the Treaty, national parliaments will have a six-week period to scrutinise and debate legislative proposals or proposals for measures falling within the ambit of the third pillar before these are placed on the Council's agenda. Although this provision is primarily designed to enhance the powers of scrutiny of national parliaments in EU matters, it may lead to creation of institutional links between the European Parliament and national parliaments, and of fora of deliberation among parliaments themselves.

Although these provisions enhance the supranational model of European citizenship, they do not efface the inherent traces of the nationality model. Indeed, the Amsterdam Treaty has not only reinforced the duality of Union citizenship, but has also swayed the balance on the part of the nationality model of citizenship through the introduction of Title IV on 'Visas, asylum, immigration and other policies related to free movement of persons'. There, national executives succeeded in transplanting their definition of immigration as a security threat and, generally speaking, the logic of exclusion and the intergovernmental procedures which have characterised the third pillar of the Maastricht Treaty within the body of Community law (the implications of this are discussed in Chapter 6).

More specifically, the Amsterdam Treaty has transferred from the intergovernmental pillar to the Community measures in the areas of immigration and asylum, matters pertaining to third-country nationals, external border controls, visas, administrative co-operation in these fields and judicial co-operation in civil matters. This means that the principles, legislative instruments (i.e. Directives and Regulations) and institutional rules of the Community legal order will apply to these areas. Police co-operation and judicial co-operation in criminal matters remain in the third pillar, whose remit has now been extended to include action against racism and xenophobia, and offences against children.

By adopting a 'phased' approach, the new title set out a five-year transitional period from the entry of the new Treaty into force during which the Council will take decisions by unanimity and the Commission will share the right of initiative with the Member States. At the end of this period, the Commission's right of initiative will become exclusive (Article 67(2)1) and it will have to examine requests for submission of proposals made by the Member States. The Council, acting unanimously, may also decide that qualified majority voting and co-decision with the European Parliament will apply to some or to all of the Communitarised areas. Notably, the transitional period does not apply to measures concerning the list of third countries whose nationals require visas and a uniform format for visas, as these have been subject to qualified majority voting (QMV) since Maastricht. After the transitional period, the remainder of visa policy will be subject to qualified majority voting and co-decision. The Amsterdam Treaty also provided for the incorporation of the much-criticised Schengen *acquis* into the EC/EU institutional framework, a process which was completed in May 1999.[17]

Although the Communitarisation of immigration and asylum policy could be seen as a sign of state retreat in the face of vocal and concerted opposition, the validity of this observation must be judged in light of the relevant provisions of the new title. One observes, for example, that the new system shares many of the intergovernmental features of the Justice and Home Affairs I framework, at least during the transitional period (e.g. unanimity and the Commission's shared right of initiative). Further support for this may be derived from the instances of differentiated integration found in the new Title: the opt out protocols negotiated by Britain, Ireland and Denmark and the Schengen Protocol. Britain and Ireland have also negotiated special arrangements which allow them to maintain a 'common travel area' and to exercise frontier controls on persons at their borders (*Protocol on the Application of Certain Aspects of Article 7a EC*). Interestingly, although Britain and Ireland have opted out from the provisions of the Title, Articles 3 and 4 of the *Protocol on the Position of the UK and Ireland* provide for the possibility of *opting in* during or after decision-making in the Council, should they so decide. All that is required is for these states to notify their intention to participate in the adoption and application of a proposed measure within three months of a proposal being presented to the Council or to accept already adopted measures.[18] Apart from rules on visas, similar provisions apply to Denmark which has dogmatically resisted any possibility of *opting in*. As a party to the Schengen Convention, Denmark may decide to implement Council decisions that build upon the Schengen *acquis* in its national law, but this will create only international law obligations, not Community law ones.

Although it is a truly remarkable achievement that all matters relating to free movement of persons are placed in the first pillar, the new framework entails several risks and problems: the democratic deficit has been reduced, but not removed (Monar, 1998a: 335), and the role of the ECJ has been heavily circumscribed. In particular, the ECJ has no jurisdiction to review measures and decisions relating to the maintenance of law and order and the safeguarding of national security with respect to a Member State's unilateral decision to reinstate border controls (Article 68(2) EC). Although the ECJ will have jurisdiction to interpret this restrictive provision, it is true to say that it contradicts the principle of respect for the rule of law underpinning the Union. In addition, requests for preliminary rulings are confined to national courts and tribunals against whose decisions there is no remedy under national law and these requests will be discretionary – not mandatory (Article 68(1) EC). This adjustment of the preliminary rulings procedure (Article 234 EC) is bound to undermine legal certainty and the consistent interpretation of Community law across the Member States. This is because the ECJ may not have the opportunity to rule on important questions of Community law either because cases may not reach courts of last instance, or because the latter may hesitate to refer questions to the ECJ. This limitation of preliminary rulings is likely to yield undesirable implications, such as expense, delay and ultimately lack of effective protection, for individuals, too, who have now to pursue their cases through successive tiers of national jurisdiction. Important as the concern not to overburden the ECJ with asylum and immigration questions may be, it has been convincingly argued that the ECJ's present jurisdiction could be extended to the new Title while 'conferring on the Court itself the power to determine, at a later stage, that requests shall be filtered if the number of references should be great' (Plender and Arnull

1997: 10). Finally, Article 68(3) EC states that rulings given by the ECJ in response to requests by the Council, the Commission or a Member State shall not apply to judgements of courts and tribunals of the Member States which have become *res judicata*. This will prevent individuals from benefiting retroactively from the ECJ's rulings under this provision (Monar, 1998a).

In addition to these procedural weaknesses, the objective 'to maintain and develop the Union as an area of Freedom, Security and Justice' instils in Community law the logic of the 'securitisation' of migration and the Member States' identification of the sources of insecurity (see Chapter 6). Immigration and asylum continued to be portrayed as security threats and the boundaries between the citizens and the 'others', be they long-term resident third country nationals, third-country nationals or refugees, have become reinforced. In this respect, the new Title's contribution towards enhancing the democratic quality of citizenship and developing the Union not only as a common market but as a system of values seems to be highly debatable. The balance has been shifted in favour of the nationality dimension of Union citizenship. But, surely, European citizenship cannot live in this form: if it is to develop to a genuine form of citizenship beyond the nation-state and 'mature' as an institution, then the normative foundations and boundaries of membership in the Euro-polity must be rethought. Similarly, conceiving of immigration and asylum policy as indispensable flanking measures to the abolition of internal border controls will not suffice. The substantive merits of the current restrictive and law-enforcement policy on immigration, third-country nationals and asylum seekers must be re-examined, and the political implications of the 'Schengenland' vision for the Union addressed. However, this would require a new conceptual frame of reference and a critical reflection on the EU's normative goals.

Conclusion

In light of the discussion thus far it can be argued that the European Union is at a crossroads. Its institutional rules and policies on European identity, citizenship and immigration, as amended by the Amsterdam Treaty, appear to have reached the limit of their cognitive expansion. Any move forward, be it in the sense of articulating a consistent policy on European identity which encompasses the vision of creating a civic and inclusive identity in the EU (Chapter 1), or of analytically separating the distinct models of citizenship underlying Union citizenship and shifting the centre of gravity from the national to the supranational one, or of articulating a coherent conceptual framework for Union citizenship (Chapter 2), or of supplementing the structural shift from the JHA framework to a gradual democratisation of the decision-making processes in immigration matters with an alternative vision of immigration (Chapter 2; see p. 77 above), requires a critical reflection on the EU's internal and external membership rules and the meaning of

European citizenship. However, this task can be undertaken only through a fundamental rethinking of central theoretical presuppositions and the development of distinct theoretical paradigms which can bring about institutional innovations. It is to this task that the rest of the book is devoted. Chapters 4 and 5 focus on the articulation of a new theoretical schema for European citizenship, while Chapter 6 discusses a set of normative ideas which may serve as the building blocks for an alternative design in immigration policy.

Notes

1 The ECJ so far has adopted a 'consolidating', rather than 'constitutionalising' approach to Union citizenship; that is to say, it has used it in order to reaffirm existing Community law. In *Uecker and Jacquet*, the Court ruled that Article 8 is not intended to alter the scope *ratione materiae* of the Treaty so as to cover internal situations: Cases C-64 and 65/96 *Kari Uecker* and *Vera Jacquet v Land Nordrhein-Westfalen* [1997] 3 CMLR 963; [1997] ECR I-317. In *Skanavi*, the question whether holders of driving licences need to exchange their licences for licences in the host Member State within one year of taking up normal residence in order to remain entitled to drive a motor-vehicle there was answered by recourse to Article 52 (Article 43, on renumbering), and not Article 8a (Article 18, on renumbering): Case C-193/94 *Skanavi* and *Chryssanthakopoulos* [1996] 2 CMLR 372; [1996] ECR I-929. Similarly, *in Stöber and Pereira* the Court saw Article 52 coupled with Regulation 1408/71 as the key article in deciding that German legislation which required the children of self-employed workers to reside in Germany in order to qualify for dependent children's allowance was incompatible with the Treaty: Joined Cases 4/95 and 5/95 *Stöber and Pereira v Bundesanstalt Für Arbeit* [1997] 2 CMLR 213; [1997] ECR I-511. In *Martinez Sala*, the Court held that lawful residence of a Community national in another Member State was sufficient to bring her within the scope of *ratione personae* of the provisions of the Treaty on European citizenship (this case is discussed in Chapter 4). In *Bickel and Franz* the Court held that the right to free movement in Article 18 EC would be enhanced if citizens of the Union were able to use a given language to communicate with the administrative and judicial authorities of a state on the same footing as its nationals (C-274/96, 24 November 1998).

2 The provisions of the Spanish Civil Code embraced the ideal of monopatride, thereby treating dual/multiple nationality as an anomaly. However, international legal norms against dual nationality are gradually changing (see the 1997 European Convention on Nationality (*European Treaty Series*, No. 166 (Strasbourg, Council of Europe)) and, in any case, Community law is indifferent and neutral to the possession of more than one nationality. On the latter, see Nascibene (1996: 5).

3 For the opposite view, see O'Leary, (1992); d'Oliveira's note on *Micheletti* (1993) 30 CMLRev 623–37.

4 According to Hall (1996: 129–43), a national measure which withdraws a person's nationality is said to fall within the scope of Community law and as such could be checked for its consistency with the fundamental rights that Community law protects. See also de Groot (1998: 123–4).

5 Article 3(1) Council Directive 68/360/EEC (1968) OJ (Special Edition) (II), 485 and section 7(1) of the Immigration Act 1988, coming into force on 20 July 1994, Immigration (European Economic Area) Order 1994, SI 1994/1895 made pursuant to section 2(2) of the European Communities Act 1972. Compare also Joined Cases C-65/95 and C-111/95 *R v Secretary of State for the Home Department, ex parte Shingara*; *R v Secretary of State for the Home Department, ex parte Radiom* [1997] All ER (EC) 577 26 November 1996, 17 June 1997; *R v Secretary of State for the Home Department, ex parte Mohammed Zeghraba and Sarabjit Singh Sahota*, Court of Appeal (Civil Division) [1997] 3 CMLR 576.

6 Directives 90/364, 90/365, 90/366 (OJ L180/28 1990). Directive 90/366, that was annulled on the grounds that it had been adopted on an incorrect legal basis, has been readopted as Directive 93/96 OJ L317/59, 1993.

7 Case 2/74 *Reyners v Belgium* [1974] ECR 631; [1974] 2 CMLR 305; Case 33/74 *Van Binsbergen v. Bestuur van de Bedrijfsvereniging voor de Metaalnijverheid* [1974] ECR 1299; [1975] 1 CMLR 289; Case 36/74 *Walgrave and Koch v Association Union Cycliste Internationale* [1974] ECR 1405; [1975] 1CMLR 320; Case C-415/93 *ASBL and Others v Jean-Marc Bosman* [1996] 1 CMLR 645.

8 These are voluntary unemployment, breaks in residence exceeding six consecutive months and on the grounds of public policy, public security and public health (Articles 7(1), 6(2) and 10 of Council Directive 68/360/EEC (OJ, Sp. Ed. 1968, L257/13: 485).

9 Case 67/74 *Carmelo Angelo Bonsignore v Oberstadtdirector der Stadt Koln* [1975] ECR 297; [1980] 1CMLR 472. As Advocate General Mayras stated in his opinion in *Bonsignore*, 'In point of fact, one cannot avoid the impression that the deportation of a foreign worker, even a national of the Common Market, satisfies the feeling of hostility, sometimes verging on xenophobia, which the commission of an offence by an alien generally causes or revives in the indigenous population'.

10 In *Astrid Proll (alias Anna Puttick) v Entry Clearance Officer, Dusseldorf* [1988] 2 CMLR 387, the Immigration Appeal Tribunal ruled that Community nationals may not be excluded from entry into the UK on the basis of the criminal record *per se*, and that paragraph 83 of HC 169 (exclusion if convicted anywhere of an extraditable offence) could not apply to a Community worker. But in *R v Home Secretary, ex parte Marchon* [1993] 2 CMLR 132 (a case which was not referred to the ECJ), it was held that past conduct of a 'serious and horrifying' nature and one which is 'repugnant to the public' was sufficient to justify deportation on the grounds of public policy, even though Marchon was not likely to reoffend. Marchon, a consultant psychiatrist, had been convicted of conspiracy to import heroin. As this decision was not wholly based on Marchon's personal conduct and the likelihood of his future offending, it appears to subvert Article 3 of Directive 62/221.

11 'Social advantages are all those advantages, which whether or not [they] are linked to a contract of employment, are generally granted to national workers, primarily because of their objective status as workers or by virtue of the mere fact of their residence on the national territory and the extension of which to workers who are nationals of other Member States therefore seems suitable to facilitate their mobility' (Case 207/78 *Ministere Public v Even and ONPTS* [1979] ECR 2019; [1980] 2 CMLR 71; Case C-310/91 *Schmid v Belgian State* (C-310/91) [1993] 1 ECR 3011; [1995] 2 CMLR 803; Case C-315/94 *Peter de Vos v Stadt*

Bielefeld [1996] ECR I-1417). Note, however, that social advantages under Article 7(2) of Council Regulation 1612/68 are confined only to workers and to their family members (Case 316/85 *Centre Public d'Aide Sociale de Courcelles v Lebon* [1987] ECR 2811; [1989] 1 CMLR 337). On the rights of families, see Case 32/75 *Fiorini v SNCF* [1975] ECR 1085 [1976]; 1 CMLR 573; Case 63/76 *Inzirillo v Caisse d'Allocations Familiales del'Arrondissement de Lyon* [1976] ECR 2057; [1978] 3 CMLR 596). As work seekers are excluded from the application of Article 7(2), they can claim only benefits available under particular rules governing unemployment in accordance with Article 69(1)(c) of Regulation 1408/71, 14 June 1971. However, under UK law, work seekers were eligible for income support for a period up to six months. Since 1994, a Community national, or an EEA national in order to receive income support, council tax benefit or housing benefit, must show that s/he is ordinarily resident in the UK.

12 The Court has interpreted generously Article 12 Regulation 1612/68 (Case 9/74 *Casagrande* v. *Landeshauptstadt München* [1974] ECR 773 [1974] 2 CMLR 422). On the education of the children of migrant workers see also Directive 77/486 OJ L199/32, 1977.

13 In *Cowan*, the Court held that the condition of nationality contained in a French criminal injuries compensation scheme was incompatible with the general non-discrimination clause contained in ex Article 6 EC (Article 12 EC) (Case 186/87 *Cowan v Trésor Public* [1986] ECR 195; [1990] 2 CMLR 613). In *Gravier*, the Court applied the same principle to access to and participation in courses of vocational training (Case 293/83 *Francoise Gravier v City of Liege* [1985] ECR 593 [1985] 3 CMLR 1) and in *Bickel and Franz* (Case C-274/96, November 24, 1998) considered the use of language in criminal proceedings. On the significance of the former two cases for the creation of Community citizenship, see Weatherill (1989); Shaw (1997).

14 The case law on the prohibition of covert forms of discrimination includes: Case 33/88 *Allué and another v Università Degli Studi di Venezia* [1989] ECR 591; [1991] 1 CMLR 283; Case 41/84 *Pinna v Caisse d'Allocations Familiales de la Savore* [1986] ECR 1; [1988] 1 CMLR 350; C-27/91 *Le Manoir* [1991] ECR I-5531; C-279/89 *EC Commission v UK* [1992] I-5785; [1993] 1 CMLR 564; Case C-272/92 *Spotti v Freistaat Bayern* [1993] ECR I-5185; [1994] 3 CMLR 629; Case C-111/91 *EC Commission v Luxembourg* [1993] ECR I-817; Case C-175/88 *Biehl* [1990] ECR I-1779; [1990] 3 CMLR 143; Case C-419/92 *Scholz v Universitaria di Cagliari* [1994] ECR I-505; [1994] 1 CMLR 873; Case C-15/96 *Kalliope Schöning- Kougebetopoulou v Freie and Hansestadt Hamburg* [1998] 1 CMLR 931.

15 The Court has applied its reasoning pertaining to Article 28 EC to 'indistinctly applicable' national provisions which restrict the exercise of the freedom of establishment of nationals or non-nationals (Case C-275/92 *Kraus* v. *Land Baden-Württemberg* [1993] ECR I-1663), or hinder citizens from being employed in another Member State (*Bosman* above) or hinder intra-Community trade in services (Case C-76/90 *Sager v Société Dennmeyer and Co Ltd* [1991] I-4221; Case C-275/92 *Customs and Excise v. Schindler* [1994] ECR 1039; Case C-384 *Alpine Investments BV v Minister van Financien* [1995] ECR I-1141; [1995] 2 CMLR 209.

16 The states' financial liability *vis-à-vis* individuals for loss or damage caused by leg-

islative action or inaction is designed to ensure effective protection for individuals. The principle of State liability was established by the ECJ in its historic judgement in the joined cases 6 and 9/1990 *Francovich and Bonifaci v Italy* [1991] ECR I-5357. In these joined cases, the ECJ ruled that Italy was liable to compensate the employees of a bankrupt company because it had failed to implement Directive 80/987/EC which sought to establish a scheme for the protection of employees in the event of the insolvency of the employer. For a discussion of the substantive conditions for state liability and the ECJ's evolving jurisprudence in this area, see Steiner (1998: 62–9); Wooldridge and D'Sa (1996: 161–7). See also Craig (1997).

17 The Schengen *acquis* consists of the 1985 Schengen Agreement, the 1990 Schengen Implementing Convention, the Accession Protocols with related Final Acts and Declarations, decisions and declarations adopted by the Schengen Executive Committee, and acts adopted by the organs upon which the Executive Committee has conferred decision-making powers. On this, see Hailbronner and Thiery (1997). The two decisions on integrating the Schengen *acquis* into the European legal order were published in OJ 1999 L176.

18 On 12 March 1999, Jack Straw, the Home Secretary, announced in the House of Commons that Britain was interested in participating in all areas of the Schengen Agreement and the new Title which did not conflict with the British frontier control policy: 'we are, therefore, ready to participate in law enforcement and criminal judicial co-operation derived from the Schengen provisions, including the Schengen Information System ...We are also interested in developing co-operation with the European Union partners on asylum and in the civil judicial co-operation measures of the Free Movement Chapter ... We shall look to participation in immigration policy where it does not conflict with our frontiers-based system of control' (House of Commons, *Hansard*, Written Questions for 12 March 1999, Column: 381)

4

In search of a theory of European citizenship

Citizenship remains a contested and elusive concept despite the prolific out-pouring of monographs and anthologies on this subject. Notwithstanding the conceptual and methodological divergence, all writers have, nevertheless, found themselves engaged in critical reflection on democratic political thought, the constitution of community and the role of the individual within it, and the politics of social change. Believing that this literature still provides an appropriate frame of reference for the discussion of the problems, nature, and future of European citizenship, the present chapter examines the extent to which different analytical frameworks of citizenship can help overcome the limitations of the European Union's policy on European citizenship and identity. This does not imply that the discussion is premised on the assumption that there exists a perfect model of citizenship which should be transplanted to the European level. Rather, the rationale behind the critical review of the literature is to ascertain the extent to which these conceptual schemes, some of which have already been applied to the Union, add something significant to our understanding of the problems in EU institutional design of identity and citizenship – and, more importantly, can offer credible solutions. And although this exercise could be fed back into the existing literature on citizenship to produce more sophisticated analyses, the precise features and results of this channelling fall outside the scope of my discussion.

Seven general questions appear to strike at the heart of any theory of citizenship. Each of these questions is of fundamental importance as a critique of existing frameworks and as a building block for a theory of European citizenship (Chapter 5).

1 By what criteria is it to be determined who is to be *included* and *excluded* from citizenship?
2 The issue of *borders* and *territory*. Citizenship may have been historically wedded to territorial nation-states, but its emergence within the European context which is characterised by 'a growing dissociation between author-itative allocations, territorial constituencies and functional competences'

(Schmitter, 1996: 120–50) raises the question as to whether the organising principles of bounded communities remain an adequate normative reference point.

3 The questions of *identity* and *interest formation*. Do individuals have already constructed and fully settled identities which in turn determine their preferences and interests? Or are they constituted though encounters, narratives and processes of negotiation? And, further, to what extent does their participation in everyday social projects and collective struggles in order to achieve what they believe to be in their interest shape who they are?

4 The problem of *society*. Is society an intelligible totality which can flourish only under conditions of domestic tranquillity provided for by nationality, or by some other principle such as cultural neutrality? Or is it time to consider new conceptions of society which accept the infinitude of the social and recognise that the issue of society can no longer be reduced to the general problem of preserving stability and social order?

5 What should the *extent of political power* be? And what kind of safeguards for channelling and restricting the exercise of political power should be built into political arrangements (i.e. issues of rights – including group rights, political opportunities for participation, the extent of political opposition)?

6 To the *attainment of what ends* should citizenship be directed and what are the criteria for determining this?

7 How can citizenship theory deal with *complexity within the state* (i.e. with increasing social differentiation, multiple intersecting differences, demands for cultural recognition, and the demise of integrating narratives) and *above the state* (i.e. the demands of a globalised political economy, international migration flows, the design of supranational institutions and so on)?

The sociological paradigm

In Chapter 2 we saw that European social citizenship remains underdeveloped and that the European Union's approach to social rights has been fragmentary. In view of this, Marshall's paradigm of citizenship can yield fruitful insights for the Union. For although Marshall's work is firmly rooted within the context of post-war British welfare statism, his recommendations on how to resolve the contradiction between democracy (i.e. formal equality) and capitalism (i.e. social inequality) can be applied to the EC/EU.

Marshall believed that equal citizenship would gradually undermine the inequality of class cleavages (1950: 30): citizenship rights, such as health care, education, unemployment insurance, old-age pension and so on, would contain the contradiction between democracy and capitalist economy, and would contribute to 'a general enrichment of the concrete substance of civilised life, general reduction of risk and insecurity, an equalisation between the more or less fortunate at all levels' (Marshall, 1950: 102–3). Although this account overlooks the social distribution of power (Dahrendorf, 1958),

Marshall argued that modern welfare capitalist societies are 'hyphenated societies' in so far as they have achieved some form of democratic egalitarianism amidst inequalities.[1] Although doubts can be raised concerning the effectiveness of Marshall's 'politics of containment' of capitalist inequalities for combating inequalities in the Union, his argument that social rights are a precondition for full membership in a community merits serious attention.

Marshall distinguished three types of citizenship rights: civil rights, which emerged in the eighteenth century and are associated principally with the institutions of legal justice; political rights which emerged principally in the ninteenth century and are associated with the institution of parliamentary democracy; social rights which emerged in the twentieth century and strike at the heart of the welfare state. This evolutionary account gives a deterministic interpretation of the historical development of citizenship, and tends to portray citizenship rights as beneficent gifts of the liberal state (Giddens, 1986: 73) which are deemed to be irreversible. Calling into question the descriptive plausibility of Marshall's incremental typology of rights,[2] however, does not undermine his basic argument about the empowering effects of social citizenship rights and the importance of full membership in the community. But it does raise a few questions concerning the appropriateness of disassociating welfare (social citizenship) from democracy (political citizenship) – a disassociation whose origins lie in Marshall's belief that social rights are potentially in conflict with democratic values (political rights) and capitalism (civil rights) (Roche, 1992: 34–7).

There is also another reason as to why Marshall's theory of citizenship may not be a wholly appropriate candidate for EU citizenship: citizenship is conceived of as 'a status bestowed on those who are full members of the community' (1950: 84). Such a liberal conception underestimates the importance of citizenship as practice – that is, as active engagement and participation – and tends to bracket structural inequalities and disadvantages. In addition, Marshall tends to assume that political community is an undifferentiated collectivity, whose boundaries are fixed and somehow given (Anthias and Yuval-Davis, 1991: 30). As a consequence, issues such as race, ethnicity and immigration, and the entanglement of citizenship with nationality are overlooked.

Notwithstanding these limitations, it can be argued that what is needed is an updating and refinement of Marshall's paradigm. As Turner has put it, 'the limitations of Marshall's theory lie in its moderate focus' (Turner, 1990: 212). Seeking to transcend Marshall's evolutionary and ethnocentric perspective, Turner has situated the development of citizenship within the context of the nation-state and of the international division of labour, where the 'expansion of English social rights went alongside the decline of the political autonomy of indigenous populations in the British colonial system' (1986, p. 47). By so doing, he dispenses with Marshall's 'Anglophile' perspective and develops a historical sociology of citizenship which takes into account differing conceptions of citizenship as developed within different cultures and traditions. This then enables Turner to draw up a typology of citizenship along the axes of active/passive (i.e. depending on whether citizenship has grown from below (via local participatory institutions) or above (by the state) and private/public.[3]

Although this is a useful typology, it conceals the fact that the terms 'private/public', 'passive/active' are constantly defined and renegotiated in the process of structuration of socio–political life. In addition, the boundaries between private and public, active and passive citizenship are just as likely to arise out of the development and institutionalisation of certain forms of citizenship. Furthermore, it may be submitted that it is one thing to retrieve the historicity of certain patterns of citizenship and quite another to make the historical conditions of emergence of 'patterns' of citizenship the foundation for explaining particular outcomes and contemporary practices of citizenship. Can one explain on the basis of this typology, for instance, how birth control became a constitutional issue in America or why wage regulations ceased to be one in Britain? Finally, Turner's typology does not shed ample light upon the issue of social membership and the politics of exclusion/inclusion which shape the nature and the boundaries of political communities. This theme remains undeveloped in Turner's work- albeit the fact that Turner has more recently included it as a component of a general sociological model of citizenship (1997: 9), but it is salient for the politics of European citizenship and identity.

A status-based v a practice-based conception of European citizenship

Liberal citizenship is based on rights. Deontological liberalism is preoccupied with furnishing a legal framework within which individuals as sovereign and morally autonomous beings are able to pursue their chosen form of life. For this reason, emphasis is put on justice, the rule of law, individual rights and freedoms, and the principles of fairness and equal treatment. Accordingly, citizenship is conceived of as legal 'status'. In contrast, the civic republican tradition views citizenship as practice: that is, as active engagement and participation. Citizens are deliberators, participants in common affairs and responsible for the identity and continuity of the community.[4] On this reading, citizenship is about identity. It is the expression of membership in a community and is interwoven with shared conceptions of good life.

Bearing in mind the idiosyncrasies of the Union and the fact that national citizenship is better suited to accommodate the communitarian conception of citizenship, Union citizenship could be seen as status-based. After all, Union citizenship has a minimalist contest and does not contain any duties (see Chapter 2). However, the fact that citizenship rights can be invoked by those Union citizens who have already left the state of their origin and entered the territory of another in order pursue economic activities or to reunite with a family member enjoying rights under Community law indicates that practice is essential for the activation of the status of European citizen. Far from being antithetical, status and practice are therefore each other's necessary supplement. There is also another reason as to why EU citizenship should be a matter of both status and practice – namely, when 'practice' is not accompanied by recognition of the equal standing of all participants in a community, it becomes precarious and risks being a licence for exclusion. At the same time, status is important as 'a certificate of equal membership in the political community' (Shklar, 1991).

Since the Union lacks a philosophical conception of the citizen as individual,[5] one may develop a liberal theory of EU citizenship based on the metaphysical conception of the self as an essential, unified and coherent entity which is constitutive of and not constituted by socio-political life (i.e. individuals are logically and morally prior to society).[6] The origins of this conception lie in Kantian-inspired moral ideas about an autonomous and voluntaristic personhood which is superior, antecedent and independent from the multiple, competing and contingent wants and ends of human beings. According to Sandel (1982) and other communitarians, however, such a conception overlooks the 'embeddedness' of individuals: their very identities as members of a group, of a family or even of the human species depend on intersubjective meanings and understandings. Individuals cannot be prior to society, for it is only through living in society that individuals develop their rationality and become moral agents capable of making autonomous moral choices (Taylor, 1985: 190–1).

True, liberals would not have much difficulty in conceding at least part of these criticisms: Rawls (1993) has acknowledged that selves are 'encumbered' by history and tradition. But communitarians proceed to argue that the liberal contractarian model of society is a poor model for social relations since it can neither foster nor sustain any spirit of public spiritedness, social solidarity and mutual trust (Taylor, 1992: 161–2, 166, 170). After all, citizens are not just contracting parties and privatists, but also members of a community. Communal bonds and social relations are needed for meaningful life.[7]

This argument could take two forms: the form of liberal communitarianism which praises belonging, loyalty and solidarity in a political community and the form of cultural nationalism which portrays the national community as the supreme form of human association. Whereas the former does not preclude the possibility of creating a community and a 'sense of identity' at the European level through practices of co-operation, the latter reflects the intergovernmentalist tendency of overrating the formative effects of 'culture' (Chapter 1). As such, it overlooks the fact that association and communication – rather than culture (culture is a resource which may facilitate) – foster social trust, promote solidarity and create a sense of belonging. More importantly, these can flourish in a national as well as in a supranational setting. In other words, although the communitarian critique could be successfully deployed to criticise the economic character of the European enterprise and the *ethos* of market integration, it entails the risk of mythologising community. 'Thick constitutive attachments' and cosy forms of *Gemeinschaft* often breed domination and exclusion, and recognition of the 'embeddedness' of individuals should not lead to their subjugation to an overarching totality which commands their unqualified allegiance (see Chapter 1; see also Vincent (1997: 285–9)).

For their part, liberals believe that these risks can effectively be ameliorated by adherence to the idea of rights as individual entitlements. Correct as this may be, liberals tend to take the existence of rights for granted: they tend to view rights as metaphysical attributes or moral properties of human beings, which sustain human dignity and enhance effective agency by 'fencing' individual space off from other individuals' interference and state hindrance. Rights thus act as moral 'side-constraints', that is, they must not be violated by anyone without the consent of the right-holder (Nozick 1974). The problem with such ideas is that they assume the existence of rights, instead of establishing it. That is, liberals cannot support their claims with an adequate philosophical justification of rights. Communitarians, on the other hand, may criticise the liberal preoccupation with rights, but they, too, fail to provide a sophisticated account of rights. Some share the Benthamite condemnation of rights as ghostly articulations. Others put emphasis on the context-specific quality of rights and by so doing reduce the normative language of rights to pure conventionalism. Clearly, both perspectives are inadequate for the Union; a theory of European citizenship needs a narrative about rights which acknowledges the artificiality and historicity of rights as discoursive categories without, at the same time, compromising their normative force (see Chapter 5).

Does this mean that statements about rights should be kept separate from concerns about what forms of life and conceptions of the good we would like to see promoted in the Union? Liberals would argue that a 'thin' conception of the good would allow the flourishing of many different 'thick' conceptions of the good within a single political community of equal citizens. After all, in the same way that almost all liberal republics tend to smuggle in certain substantive values and certain ideas as to how people should live under the guise of neutrality, the Union has not been totally 'agnostic' with respect to the Good. It tends to favour the way of life of mobile, well resourced and well educated Europeans who have participated in ERASMUS exchange programmes and developed a cosmopolitan outlook. What really matters is not so much the repudiation of the Good in favour of the Right, but the recognition that European citizens are attached to a plurality of diverse goods.

But how would a liberal conception of European citizenship deal with difference(s)? Liberalism tends to separate the public domain of disengaged reason from the conflicts of incommensurable differences: it acknowledges that individuals have different identities as members of various groups, but it has always insisted that it is within their capacity as (equal) citizens to take part in the political realm. In other words, political liberalism's response to controversial difference is to turn differences (religious, ethnic, cultural, sexual, etc.) into matters of 'indifference'. This strategy relies on two co-ordinate moves: (i) the depoliticisation of identity, whereby the most controversial aspects of identity are relegated to the private or non-political sphere, thus becoming matters of private belief (McClure, 1990: 361–91); (ii) the drawing of a sharp demarcating line between the public and private domains. But such a strategy presupposes the explanandum (i.e. the distinction between the public identity of the citizen and the personal identity of the private self) and regards difference as something to be overcome.

In the European context, individuals do not have to bracket their particularistic identities and abandon their private interests in order to participate in the realm of European citizenship. Rather, it is their situatedness within national publics that makes them European citizens. Although this has had the result of making national citizenship more valuable, it has also exposed the structural and institutional inequalities which prevent full membership and effective participation for certain groups, such as third-country nationals and immobile Europeans. In addition, because the Union does not aspire to neutralise existing identifications by absorbing them into a deeper unified communal identity (see Chapter 1), individuals can participate in the European political realm as both citizens/residents and as members of particularistic groups (i.e. nationals, members of a region, ethnic group, pressure group and so on). This challenges the liberal assumption that private interest is hard to reconcile with the pursuit of public good. By asserting and defending their 'private' interests individuals, as members of particular groups, often advance the principles upon which the Union is based by inducing the creation of a body of jurisprudence (e.g. in the fields of sex equality, consumer protection, non-discrimination on the grounds of nationality) which then permeates the domestic arenas.

In this respect, it may be argued that civic participation in the multilevel Euro-polity transcends the familiar distinction between liberal private morality on the one hand and communitarian public citizenship on the other. The mobilisation of various actors at all levels of governance seeking to influence the Commission and the various specialist committees surrounding the Directorates sows the seeds for a reinvigorated public life in which citizens and residents do not hesitate to question the state of public life and reflect on the Union's commitment to the realisation of ideals. Civic participation is not simply directed to episodic 'grand bargains' or constitutional moments, but it also accompanies the routine phases of policy-making and implementation. As such, it calls into question Ackerman's idea of 'dualist democracy' – that is, the distinction between a lower law-making track of normal liberal politics managed by professional politicians, and a higher law-making track of constitutional politics. Ackerman has devised this scheme in an attempt to remedy the most serious limitation of private citizenship: namely, its indifference to public good (1984: 1013–72). By envisaging a higher track of constitutional politics which calls irregularly on citizens to commit themselves and participate in changing the constitutive principles of the republic, Ackerman has sought to transcend the limitations of private citizenship without embracing the all-consuming commitment to participation that public citizenship requires. In reality, however, dualist democracy is not an alternative to both private citizenship and virtuous citizenship, but is instead a modified version of private citizenship. This is not only because Ackerman takes for granted the fully inclusive nature of past, present and prospective constitutional politics. It is also because he fails to consider the perspective of actively engaged minorities struggling for equality and inclusion. Indeed, by modelling his account of virtuous citizenship on the experiences and attitudes of white, middle-class Americans, Ackerman overlooks that for minorities and their struggle for equality, regular and assertive political action on the lower law-making track (i.e. in the field of housing, education, jobs, health care and so on) is absolutely essential.

In contrast, the emergence of a more participatory politics in the Union involves a wide range of actors engaging in what might tentatively be called 'associative democratic governance'. According to Bellamy and Warleigh (1998: 460–8), an ethics of participation and neo-republican forms of governance fit well with multilevel governance understandings of the Union. Drawing on proposals suggested by Hirst (1994), Schmitter (1996), and Cohen and Sabel (1997), Bellamy and Warleigh argue for the replacement of the ethic of integration with an ethic of participation inspired by what they call 'cosmopolitan communitarianism' – that is, by communitarian commitments to democratic participation which involve a cosmopolitan regard for fairness. This perspective may provide adequate answers to questions 5 and 6 above about the scope and ends of citizenship, respectively, but, like liberalism and communitarianism, it fails to provide the theoretical tools we need in order to understand the politics of European identity-making and the boundary-producing discourses (questions 1, 2 and 3) and the process of community-building under conditions of radical pluralism, contestation, and asymmetrical relations of power (question 7).

Citizenship on an-'other' register: identity, difference and the logic of community

A political alternative to both liberal pluralism and the politics of the common good has been suggested by feminism, poststructuralism, postcolonial criticism and anti-subordination literature. By addressing the issue of citizenship from the standpoint of membership or what counts as 'full membership' of a community, this literature has shown that 'the problem' of citizenship is not so much a matter of striking a balance between the individual and the community. Nor is it simply a matter of choice between the Right and the Good. It is, instead, a matter of questioning and deconstructing the constructed senses of community and the self underlying these politics. As argued below, this insight is crucial for the politics of European identity and citizenship.

Feminism has criticised the atomistic conception of the self underlying deontological liberalism and has challenged the liberal idea of universal citizenship by exposing the domination and inequality that pertains the private gendered sphere (Pateman, 1988; Okin, 1989; Young 1990; Yeatman 1994). For although citizenship is supposed to be gender-agnostic, in reality, it is underpinned by gender considerations. EU citizenship is no exception: despite its universalist pretensions, it is shaped by gender differentials. Women may have the right to free movement (which is modelled upon male wage-earners), but they often lack the opportunity to exercise it owing to structural constraints. In the same vein, anti-subordination perspectives have exposed the liberal fiction of universality and, thus, the illusion of race equality by focusing on the reality of oppression and the experiences of black people (Gilroy, 1987). By so doing, they have destabilised culturally produced representations and exposed the structures of inequality and injustice.

But in their attempt to theorise and undo relations of domination, some theorists have mistakenly opted for a dialectical synthesis of the Right/Good dichotomy by invoking a higher ideal of community which domesticates all oppositionality (communitarian universalism). Examples of this are the feminist idealisation of motherhood and of relations of intimacy, transparency and spontaneity. By sketching a vision of community in which power relations, conflict and antagonisms will evaporate through the direct exchange of experience, feelings of empathy and face-to-face communication, these theorists tend to view society as a totality (i.e., as a unified and non-contradictory entity). Difference is seen as something to be overcome. Others, for strategic reasons, see gender as an internally undiffererentiated category defined by its opposition to domination by men (Okin; 1989; Flax, 1996: 508). This results in the underscoring of other differences, such as racial, class, ethnic and so on which are constitutive of women's identities. And although some worry that the 'deconstruction' of 'woman' may render this category meaningless, most feminists do not regard the 'death' of the unified woman as an obstacle to political action.

Certain multicultural narratives, too, might invoke notions of origin and authentic self in order to depict the hegemonic majority and minority cultures as homogeneous, static and essentially different (Modood, 1998). Evidently, the European experiment has discredited narratives concerning both the essentialism of the whole (i.e. European civilisation, or essentialist national identities) and of the part (i.e. essentialist ethnic identities). For individual identities, group identities or cultures are not unified, bounded, complete, homogenous and static; they are shifting, interacting entities – and, above all, are subject to processes of adaptation, redefinition and change.

Another perilous path might be the reification of difference and the abandonment of universalism altogether. Here, universalism is condemned for suppressing difference and heterogeneity (Lyotard, 1984; Lyotard and Thebaud, 1985); justice is only local and particular. The paradox in this celebration of particularity is that particularity can be defended only by recourse to universal categories. It also leads to the de-contextualization of difference – that is, to the transformation of differences into categorical oppositions. Young (1997: 64) and others have insisted that recognition of differences does not imply the absence of similarities and possibilities for common action. Nor does it preclude the possibility of collective mobilisation or the suspension of critical judgement.

Indeed, in *Justice and the Politics of Difference*, Young sets out a theoretical framework which appreciates diversity and recognises difference without abandoning normative theorising about justice. The discussion about justice is extended beyond the confines of the distributive paradigm by focusing on the empowering, enabling qualities of a heterogeneous public. The latter is conceived of as a public realm which enables rather than disables the recognition of group differences and the approximation of equality by giving groups a 'voice' in all deliberations (1989: 257–8). According to Young, the public should be an open, accessible, differentiated sphere, which neither threatens to assimilate otherness nor to essentialise it – an ideal which is captured by the 'unoppressive city'. In the unoppressive city, strangers and different groups dwell together; they interact with the space and institutions they all experience themselves as belonging to, but without those interactions dissolving into a 'community of shared final ends' (1986: 21; 1990: 237–8). However, in order to support the conception of community governed by an ethic of 'openness to unassimilated otherness', Young has to rely on a sociology of the city and urban life which is characterised by residential proximity and weak social bonds. This raises the question whether mere 'awareness of each other's presence' can promote respectful relationships: can awareness of others foster mutual respect, as opposed to apathy or indifference and sustain the civic bonds required for redistributive policies? Young's conception of city life as the 'being together of strangers' and the weak, almost minimalist bonds of civility that go with it might not be able to foster solidarity and social trust, or to create a sense of community in the EU context.

Notwithstanding this critical observation, Young's idea of differentiated citizenship contains many fruitful insights which could be utilised in the context of EU citizenship. Differentiated citizenship is designed as a political alternative to universal citizenship (i.e. citizenship as generality and equal treatment) and entails the provision of 'institutionalized means for the explicit recognition and representation of oppressed groups', such as guaranteed representation in political bodies, public funds for advocacy groups, veto rights over specific policies that affect the group directly as well as multicultural rights (i.e. language rights for Hispanics, reproductive rights for women and so on).[8] For many, differentiated citizenship appears to contradict the orthodox conception of citizenship as a matter of isonomia (i.e. legal equality) and equity (i.e. those who are similarly situated be similarly treated). Critics have pointed out that differentiated citizenship inappropriately discriminates among 'similarly situated people' on the basis of irrelevant differences (Miller, 1995). Philips has eloquently responded to some of these criticisms (1997, 57–63), but she has also argued (1993) that group representation entails the dangers of freezing identities, 'group closures' and divisive politics. Frazer (1995) has also criticised Young for paying too much attention to the politics of recognition and for overlooking issues of redistribution. She concludes that both distribution and recognition are required to overcome multifaceted oppressions. I will consider these criticisms in more detail in Chapter 5. What needs to be mentioned here is that critics of differentiated citizenship often overlook that differences which are irrelevant, on moral grounds, are relevant in the socio-political field. After all, if these 'differences' were politically irrelevant, then the race-blind and sex-blind politics of equal citizenship would have reduced discrimination, inequality, racism and sexism. Since social statistics give a very different picture, we cannot but conclude that society systematically disadvantages groups on the basis of their allegedly irrelevant differences. Taking equality seriously may well require difference-conscious strategies aiming at empowering disadvantaged groups and at attending to group specific needs (Young, 1997: 65; Philips, 1997).[9] In other words, groups do not need differential treatment because they are 'essentially' different, but because they live in a discriminatory society which turns differences, which are irrelevant from a moral point of view, into disadvantages. Although critics fear that group-conscious policies could lead to separatism or to 'mutual mistrust and conflict' (Kukathas, 1993: 156), this argument has to be weighed against considerations concerning the impact of systematic discrimination on social relations and the political institutions of a country. Since justice and the 'sense of community' are undermined by oppression and inequality, differentiated citizenship may be capable of restoring the sense of community and creating a richer and more meaningful notion of community membership.

New schemas of citizenship beyond the nation-state

But how can trustworthy social relations be built in an institutional setting which has become simultaneously more global and internally more differentiated? What kind of normative standards should imbue our conceptions of membership, community and equality in contemporary plural and complex environments (questions 1, 2 and 7 above)? Although Young's conception of differentiated citizenship addresses the challenges of cultural pluralism and group equality it, nevertheless, remains confined within the setting of the nation-state. In his quest for a new schema of citizenship which takes into account contemporary global political conditions, Turner has argued for the replacement of the debate about citizenship with a debate about rights (Turner, 1993b 15, 187). According to Turner, a new discourse of human rights and animal rights is needed to transcend the difficulties of contemporary politics. Similarly, Soysal has observed that that post-war developments have undercut the foundational principles of citizenship, thereby diluting the 'natural dichotomy' between citizens and aliens (Soysal, 1994; 1996: 20). The codification and elaboration of human rights principles have led to a redefinition and expansion of rights of migrants in Europe: migrants are entitled to rights and protection by a state which is not 'their own', and are being incorporated into a wide range of rights and privileges which were originally reserved only for nationals.

Despite the attraction of the human rights discourse, it is true to say that citizens do not derive rights from international law instruments on human rights unless nation-states are willing to recognise and enforce them. Additionally, human rights reforms, such as the introduction of dual citizenship[10] or of more relaxed naturalisation procedures for second-generation Turks in Germany (both are seen as manifestations of postnational citizenship by Soysal (1996: 25)) often result in the modernisation, rather than the weakening of national citizenship. In other words, it is debatable whether postnational citizenship challenges the primacy of the state. Indeed, international law instruments have never questioned the nationality principle as a criterion for distributing community membership nor the state's sovereign power in this area. EU citizenship differs from the postnational model in that it confers rights on individuals independently of the will of the Member States, but neither Turner nor Soysal premise their arguments on EU developments. Moreover, Turner and Soysal tend to view citizenship in formalistic terms, that is, as an issue of status and rights. By so doing, they overlook other important dimensions of citizenship, such as political participation, civic obligations and a sense of belonging. In this respect, their accounts could be enriched by incorporating a theory of identity and a discussion about the modes of governance which can enhance citizen participation, promote accountability and ensure rights' compliance.

Held's conception of cosmopolitan democracy is a more convincing alternative since his reflections on the future of democracy in a global world of overlapping and divided authority structures, multiple power centres and criss-crossing loyalties, include concrete institutional recommendations which promote political participation (Held, 1993: 14–15; 1995: 140). Held's discussion contains many similarities with the Union, although it is a far from perfect match. Held envisages the formation of an association of democratic nations – that is, of an international community of democratic states and societies committed to upholding democratic public law both within and across their own boundaries (1995: 201–30). This requires several institutional reforms: a reformed UN Security Council and the creation of an authoritative assembly of all democratic states and societies (a global parliament); the creation of regional parliaments and transnational constituencies; a new economic co-ordinating agency to deliberate the broad balance of public investment priorities, expenditure patterns and emergency situations and to oversee international commerce; enhancement of the democratic accountability of international organisations; entrenchment of human rights and the creation of a new International Human Rights Court (Held, 1993: 40–3; 1995: 286).

Bauböck has called into question the feasibility of the political strategy to transform citizenship rights into human rights and/or international law norms. Bauböck's strategy is to strengthen the intermediary positions between human rights and citizenship, that is, between global society and 'societies with states' (1994a: 19–20). Bauböck argues that international migration and the ensuing interactions between receiving and sending countries expands mobile societies beyond the borders of territorial states without dissolving borders. It also changes the composition of society along with its internal social and cultural structures' (1994b: 217). This extends citizenship into an institutional setting which is beyond the national level but below the international law of human rights (transnational citizenship).

Bauböck defines citizenship as a set of rights, exercised by individuals, and a corresponding set of institutions guaranteeing these rights. These rights are equal for all citizens, and universally distributed within a political community. Such a liberal definition of citizenship could be criticised for paying insufficient attention to socio-economic structures of inequality, identity politics and the issue of community formation – issues which are antecedent to normative considerations about the distribution of rights. Notwithstanding these criticisms, however, the definition is still important, in that it recognises that citizenship rights should be distributed equally within the resident population independently from their status of nominal citizenship (Bauböck, 1994a: 38). Such a reform is necessary because, according to Bauböck, the Western liberal concept of citizenship has been rooted in national closure, in the sense of limited access from outside and internal cultural homogenisation (Bauböck, 1992: 7). But closure and the 'exclusion of immigrants from basic citizen rights jeopardises basic democratic achievements' (Bauböck, 1992: 59). Conversely, if the structure of citizenship became dynamically adjusted and immigrants were included in the polity, external boundaries would become more relaxed. This would facilitate institutional fusions between sending and receiving countries.

Bauböck argues that there are two possible strategies for the admission of migrants to full citizenship: the 'liberal' and the 'egalitarian'. The former leaves the hierarchical structure of the nationality model of citizenship intact, but allows for transition and upward mobility through naturalisation. Naturalisation ensures that new members have the intention to remain in the territory on a long-term basis, recognise the importance of upholding a set of civic values and are willing to declare their loyalty to their host state. Such justifications, however, conceal the fact that restrictive naturalisation conditions, such as knowledge tests, long periods of qualifying residence and expense coupled with discretionary decision-making, are essentially designed to reinforce the fictions of social homogeneity and unitary identities. The gate to full citizenship may be potentially open to 'alien residents', but not too much, for this is seen to weaken the affective link among the existing members of the community. But this contradicts the democratic principle that all those affected by decisions should be able to influence them without unreasonable delays.

The egalitarian strategy views transitions to the higher status of citizenship as rights, thereby reducing the discretionary power of the authorities of the receiving state (Bauböck, 1994a: 73–114). This is Bauböck's favourite strategy, inspired, perhaps, by the fact that in Germany alien residents between the ages of 16 and 23 have the right to naturalise if they renounce their previous citizenship, have resided there for at least eight years, have completed six years' full-time education and do not have criminal convictions (85, 1993 Auslandergesetz [Aus1G] cit. in Hansen, 1998). Residence thus gives rise to a right to naturalisation. Entitlement to citizenship is also given to second-generation immigrants resident in European polities – with the exception of Austria and Greece (Weil and Hansen, 1999).

Although Bauböck's suggestions would improve the position of third-country nationals in the Union, a crucial weakness of transnational citizenship is its failure to address in depth the relationship between nationality and citizenship. Bauböck takes the nationality model of citizenship as a premise and articulates a more liberal and reformed version of it. How else can one explain his preference for optional naturalisation which is available upon request over 'automatic transition' of resident migrants to full citizenship? Bauböck argues that automatic transition would deprive immigrants of choice (i.e. the option of staying in the previous position (Bauböck, 1994a: 98, 1994b: 204): 'a receiving state should not naturalise foreigners without their consent even if their previous citizenship remains unaffected'(Bauböck, 1994b: 225). Notably, the same argument was put forward by the French Commission on Nationality to justify abolition of the automatic right to citizenship of first-generation children by the 1993 reform of French nationality law: immigrant children would be deprived of their right to consent to be part of the republic. However, such an argument fails to convince since domiciled migrants could always demonstrate their consent by deciding not to opt out from citizenship. They could thus be entitled to automatic citizenship but with the option of voluntary repudiation. This is something akin to inheritance: I have a right to inherit as a heir of my deceased relative, but can always repudiate the inheritance. Such a clause in citizenship design would symbolically confirm the equal citizenship status of domiciled persons without depriving them of choice. After all, in some Member States there exists the possibility of renouncing involuntarily acquired additional nationality by virtue of marriage via a declaration.

In sum, transnational citizenship enriches the liberal democratic model of national citizenship by accommodating dual citizenship and genuine denizenship, by respecting the right to family unity and by affirming humanitarian obligations to refugees (Bauböck, 1994b: 217–18). But it does not go beyond it. It is very much entangled with the nation-state and national communities. The boundaries of 'transnational' citizenship are shaped by the existence of separate sovereign states and their right to control admissions.

Conclusion

I began the search for a theoretical framework of European citizenship with theoretical and historical givens, that is, with existing paradigms of citizenship framed within the setting of the nation-state. Although a framework of European citizenship can neither be a derivative of the statist model of citizenship nor an extension of the nationality model of citizenship, several of the problems, concerns, normative standards and theoretical assumptions underpinning otherwise dissimilar theories of citizenship do apply to EU citizenship. This is because they are intrinsic to the very notion of citizenship and entail standards against which concrete institutions can be evaluated. The foregoing discussion examined these theoretical frameworks, evaluated their claims, assessed whether and how they respond to the questions raised in the introduction, drew up the ideas which are crucial for the articulation of a theoretical framework of EU citizenship, changed some of the intellectual proposals, bridged others, abandoned some of the arguments and redefined others. Unavoidably, this process of drawing up and revising involved an examination of the central tensions surrounding citizenship, such as citizenship as status v citizenship as practice; universality v particularity; the politics of solidarity v the politics of cultural pluralism; public v private; identity v community; and cultural pluralism v the politics of social justice. It has also unravelled the tension inherent in the national state – that is, between universalist conception of citizenship anchored on uniform rights and duties, and the particularist conception of 'the people' (the community of citizens). Soysal and Bauböck have sought to reconcile 'the irreconcilable' and to resolve this tension but, as observed above, both 'postnational' and 'transnational' citizenships are still wedded to the territorial nation-state.

In contrast, the supranational institution of Union citizenship rests on a different set of organising principles. The EC/EU does not force the 'opening' of national citizenship from 'within' so as to allow nationals of other

Member States to obtain citizenship by naturalisation. Rather, it 'shifts' the boundaries of citizenship from 'outside' through the conferral of rights which are enforceable before national courts. More importantly, the integration of working EC nationals and of their families into the socio–economic fabric of the host Member State does not depend on their assimilation or willingness to conform – or, indeed, an express declaration of their wish to belong (Chapter 3). Rather, it is seen as the by-product of equalisation. Furthermore, the constructivist mode of European identity does not warrant the continuation of the differential status of resident third-country nationals. It requires, instead, that all those entitled actually accede to European citizenship.[11] How are we, then, to rethink citizenship and membership in the Union in ways that avoid both the institutional limitations discussed in the previous chapters and the theoretical limitations identified in this chapter? This is the question which I must now address.

Notes

1 Turner (1993a: 8) points out that there is an ambiguity in Marshall's work: it is not clear from Marshall's analysis whether citizenship contradicts the market principle of capitalism by requiring some redistribution of wealth or if it actually supports the differentiated social system by integrating the working class into society through welfare provisions.

2 The case of 'aliens' rights' is yet another example of the problematic nature of Marshall's typology; aliens have been given first social rights, then civil rights and, much later, political rights at a local or regional level in certain states (Hammar, 1990: 54).

3 According to Turner's typology, the French conception of citizenship combines active citizenship with an emphasis on public space, while the English conception is passive and public. American liberalism entails an active but private conception of citizenship, and citizenship in the German tradition is passive and private.

4 For a full explication and discussion of the debate, see Kymlicka (1990); Oldfield (1990); Avineri and de Shalit (1992); Mulhall and Swift (1992).

5 For the opposite view, see Everson (1995: 73–90).

6 Rawls (1985) has argued that his theory of justice need not involve questions of philosophical psychology or a metaphysical doctrine of the self, for his project is political, not metaphysical.

7 In Sandel's own words, 'the procedural republic cannot secure the liberty it promises because it cannot sustain the kind of political community and civic engagement that liberty requires': Sandel (1997: 24).

8 Rosenblum (1994: 1) criticises Young for failing to designate which groups qualify as 'constitutive' and whether every constitutive group is entitled to have political rights and representation. She fears that Young's politics of empowerment may lead to the exclusion of dominant groups, privileged social groups and unopposed minority groups.

9 Group rights constitute an essential part of Kymlicka's liberal theory of minority

rights. Kymlicka's main concern is to justify group rights for aboriginal communities striving to protect their heritages (i.e. their societal cultures). In this respect, multicultural citizenship is multinational citizenship. However, it is doubtful whether Kymlicka's theory can be extended to other groups seeking not to defend their rooted territorial origins as a source of their identity, but to be included in a community as respected participants. On this, see Favell (1998). As far as the European Union is concerned, it is inclusion and equality – and not the primacy of a discrete culture as a context of choice for its members – that underpin the politics of citizenship, identity and immigration.

10 Objections against dual/multiple citizenship include conflicting loyalties; the evasion of civic duties (military service and tax evasion) and problems of free-riding; and problems that may arise owing to conflict of laws.

11 According to Bauböck (1997), this reform would devalue Union citizenship in the eyes of citizens of the Member States by reducing it to a generalized citizenship, disconnected from the notion of consensual membership in a political community. Optional access of third-country nationals to Union citizenship via a Euronaturalisation procedure is a more attractive option, but it has also the drawback of reducing the pressure on the Member States to reform their national citizenship laws. For this reason, Bauböck favours a harmonised status of Union denizenship for resident aliens of third countries: this would contain all the present rights of Union citizenship apart from electoral rights at EP elections.

5

Constructive citizenship in the European Union

This chapter suggests an alternative theoretical perspective on Union citizenship based on evolving ideas of community membership and the institutional dynamics of the EC/EU. Constructive citizenship thus has a dual reference. Because delimitations of political units by boundary-drawing are not natural acts but the artificial product of ongoing political processes, constructive citizenship seeks to address the challenges of diversity (i.e. the claims of 'belongers' for recognition) (see Young, 1990; Honneth, 1994; Tully, 1995) and membership (i.e. the claims of non-citizen residents for inclusion in the political community). Secondly, constructive citizenship capitalises on the emergent opportunities for the formation of a European polity beyond the nation-state and for multi-level governance. This duality highlights the need for novel institutional designs.

Any new endeavour in this area is bound to stumble against the fact that citizenship is always embedded in power structures and is entangled with stories: stories about historical communities with distinctive identities, institutions that have been handed down, founding myths and symbolisms, political traditions that may be worth preserving and so on. Although the entwining of citizenship with nationality, immigration and state sovereignty is constraining, it is far from disabling. The reason is that citizenship has always carried within it the 'tradition v. innovation' dilemma – that is, settled institutional forms and delineation of boundaries between members and non-members on the one hand, and a burden of expectation and of responsibility for those who have legitimate claims for inclusion in the political community on the other. Believing that citizenship is not only still a worthwhile project but, in fact, the only project that could address the problem of unjust exclusion, this chapter seeks to articulate a framework for democratic citizenship beyond the nation-state which is inclusive and respectful of 'difference'.

Constructive citizenship: an argument

My discussion of constructive European citizenship as a paradigm of citizenship beyond the nation-state takes the form of an unfolding set of propositions, as follows.

Proposition 1
A theory of citizenship need not depend either on some essentialist conception of individual identity or a foundationalist conception of community. It needs to acknowledge the fact that citizens have multiple identifications, to open up space for 'communities of concern and engagement', and to consider a new paradigm of citizenship based on domicile.

Despite disagreements over the meaning and content of citizenship, both liberals and communitarians take the nationality model of citizenship as given: they fail to problematise the issue of social membership that strikes at the heart of multicultural politics and to reflect critically on the historical construction of exclusion in national states. It is perhaps this oversight that has led feminist and anti-subordination perspectives to argue that the 'problem' of citizenship today is not so much a matter of striking a balance between the individual and the community, but of questioning and deconstructing the constructed sense of the self and of the community underlying these politics (Chapter 4). As regards the former, anti-essentialist critiques of subjectivity have broken up the sovereign, essential self postulated by modernity and shown that individuals have multiple identities as a result of their movement in and out of various subject positions (Laclau and Mouffe, 1986).

The process of European unification has given an unprecedented expression to the pluralisation of attachments and multiplication of political identifications, in spite of the veneer of nationalism. As already argued above, citizens are eager to use opportunities offered on one level in order to force a recognition of their suppressed identities or to accelerate constitutional changes on another. This process, in effect, compromises nation-states' ability to monopolise the terms of collective identity, and calls into question the validity of traditional narratives which link citizenship with cultural conformity. In other words, the 'decentring of the subject' has been accompanied by the 'decentring of the nation-state', that is, the questioning of traditional national–statist narratives which have propounded ethnic or cultural heterogeneity as a 'problem' and multiple identification as an 'unhealthy'. The free-movement provisions of the EC Treaty, coupled with the local electoral rights granted under the Union citizenship provisions, have severed the link between national community and the enjoyment of equality of treatment and rights. Interestingly, the boundaries of national citizenship have not been relaxed 'from within' so as to allow Community nationals to obtain citizenship by naturalisation, but they have been ruptured 'from outside' through the conferral of rights which are enforceable before national courts.

The main task of citizenship theory is to articulate a narrative which takes into account these developments and the complexity of our era, without retreating into a nostalgia for 'a politics of place' or to the romanticism of 'embeddedness' in organic communities. As an alternative conception of community which respects the Other, I suggest the notion of 'community of concern and engagement'. In such a community, all its corporate and individual members – associated by virtue of their differences from one another – share a concern over the nature and the future of the polity and are engaged in collectively shaping that future.

The European Union is a good example of a community of 'concern and engagement', for what unites the various political units together in the European venture is neither some shared conception of Europe's destiny nor a cohesive identity in a communitarian sense. Rather, what binds them in a Union is their commitment to the future of the Union, in the sense of working together towards creating 'an ever closer union among the peoples of Europe' while preserving and respecting the distinctive identities of its members. In this process there is neither consensus nor indeed certainty about the juridico–political shape of the outcome. There is only an active concern and a willingness on behalf of its units to participate in the collective shaping of this process by designing appropriate institutions. Participation is not confined to one privileged site, one unified public, as was previously the level of the state, but takes the form of a complex and multifaceted interrelationship of individuals, groups or even regions with multiple, strategically interacting political communities formed on various levels.

In negotiations over European institutions, for instance, actors bring their own particular agendas and viewpoints about the future of European integration. But there is a common interest in improving things, a shared concern about a better future for the European polity, and this opens up a critical space for debate and negotiations on how, with what speed, and to what effect structures can be improved. Understandably, draft agendas on this often fail to coincide and often even go in opposite directions. Through a process of negotiation, debate and persuasion in which power (i.e. the threat of veto) is involved, compromises are made, draft agendas become rearticulated and modified, final results are reached which are accepted by all as much as they remain contested. Via the process of gradual trial and error, further steps towards greater integration are made. But the outcome can hardly be considered as a resolution of the opposing views or the result of finding a common neutral ground. Differences remain. But the subsequent process of implementation reveals which of them are based simply on doctrinaire attitudes and which are driven by a genuine concern for improvement and better arrangements. Such a conception of community allows for disagreements and conflicts. It also shows that a community can be created among those who have very different views about its nature and its future.

The empirical implementation of this notion of community cannot depend on the subjective standard of state nationality. Instead, it requires a model of citizenship founded on domicile. As already argued in Chapter 3, domicile is based on certain factual conditions from which an intention to make a particular territory the centre of one's interests and life can be deduced. As the legal criterion of membership in the Euro-polity, domicile would thus enable all those (i.e. third-country nationals) who have made the territories of the Union their home and the centre of their economic life to be included as full and respected participants in the Euro-polity without requiring them to possess nationality of an individual Member State. In addition, it could easily be propounded as a Community law concept, thereby ensuring uniformity and fairness in the interpretation of the personal scope of Union citizenship throughout the Union. Moreover, accession of third-country nationals directly to Union citizenship on the basis of domicile would be an attractive policy option since it would not result in loss of their nationality. The merits and demerits of alternative policy options designed to facilitate acquisition of Union citizenship by acquisition of nationality of a Member State, such as possible relaxation of domestic naturalisation laws or the introduction of Community legislative instruments harmonising nationality laws for the purposes of free movement have already been discussed and, therefore, I will not repeat them here. What I would like to do here is to defend the domicile-based mode of Union citizenship against possible objections, and to outline the institutional steps required for its implementation.

A possible objection to this proposal might be that one does not become a citizen by simply inhabiting a place (Miller, 1996, 1998; Schnapper, 1997): there is a shared set of norms, values and cultural practices which form the fabric of a community and give meaning to life projects. This might be threatened by the inclusion of people who do not share these commitments. In response, it may be argued that a sense of community in the Union or in any other polity does not arise through people having feelings for one another, or holding the same or similar values. Rather, a community of citizens emerges thorough their being in mutual relations within one another and through their engagement in reflexive forms of community co-operation (Honneth, 1998). In addition, since the mobility of Community nationals has not given rise to such concerns, it is difficult to justify why the mobility of long-term resident third-country nationals would pose a threat to the survival of these traditions and beliefs and/or to internal stability. True, the inclusion of 'resident aliens' will prompt national communities to redefine themselves in a pluralistic way and, over time, is bound to induce institutional changes. But such processes of redefinition, negotiation and renegotiation are an essential part of political cultures and living traditions.

Another related objection may be that the domicile model of citizenship might encourage a passive attitude and lead to a general devaluation of citizenship, particularly since it is not at all clear that residents living in state for a long period of time have the requisite longer-term view (Bauböck, 1997).

Interestingly, mobile Community nationals are not generally expected to have the requisite longer-term view. Nor is the social fact of their attachment to the host Member State or the Community itself the principal determinant for citizenship capacity in the Union. Instead, what really matters is that a person has left his/her home state and entered the territory of another in order to pursue economic activities as an employed or self-employed actor (and, in the case of non-economic actors, that s/he is self-sufficient). As to the argument concerning the possible devaluation of Union citizenship, it may be argued that the imposition of quasi-nationalist trappings on Union citizenship has not only reduced the significance of this institution, thereby making national citizenship more valuable, but it has also undermined the democratic principle that all those ruled should have an input as to how and by whom are ruled. As O'Leary (1996b: 91) has noted, 'the preservation of Member State sovereignty rather than promotion of individual rights or democratic legitimacy is central to the determination of the scope and content of Union citizenship'.

The impact of the political inclusion of third-country nationals on the welfare regimes of the Member States might also give rise to concern. It is said that intra-EU mobility of workers from third countries is likely to generate burdens on the Member States' social systems and to create tensions on the labour market. But this argument overlooks the fact that granting migrant workers equal rights and opportunities in the workplace and society may be a blessing and not a curse. First, any increase in the workforce could have a beneficial effect on national social security systems which have been affected by negative population growth in the industrialised world. Secondly, the exclusion of third-country nationals from the benefits of free movement and Union citizenship might lead to a sharp increase in undeclared work; as internal border controls are removed, third-country nationals might seek to escape the fluctuations of national labour markets by seeking work elsewhere in the Community. Thirdly, this argument perpetuates a socially constructed representation of migrants as a burden on the social security system and a threat, thereby overlooking the multifarious and valuable contributions migrant workers make to the economic, social, cultural and political development of the Member States and the Community as a whole (see Chapter 6).

A final objection might be that acquisition of Union citizenship by lawful domicile would result in automatic extension of citizenship to all lawful residents without asking for their consent. This argument overlooks the fact that Community nationals are not forced to cross borders: they are free to choose their 'civic home' and the place where they prefer to act. Since Union citizenship does not entail compulsory rights, third-country nationals could well demonstrate their consent by choosing to exercise these rights. Needless to say that if strong objections persist, renunciation of the status of Union citizen via a declaration remains a viable policy option (see Chapter 4).

But what kind of institutional mechanisms could be adopted in the short term in order to end the subjecthood of long-term resident third-country nationals? The new immigration Title of the Amsterdam Treaty creates a Community law competence (albeit not exclusive) in matters relating to the third-country nationals' right to free circulation and the rights and conditions of their residence in another Member State, coupled with the Commission's proposed Migration Convention (COM(97) 387, 30/7/97), indicate that a directive on the legal position of long-term resident third-country nationals is forthcoming. What is not clear is whether this directive will grant third-country nationals free-movement rights on an equal footing with Community nationals. Peers (1998) has commented favourably on the gradual step of granting third-country nationals a form of denizenship, that is, of free movement and residence within the Union. Another, more radical, option might be for the Community to adopt a regulation amending Regulation 1612/68 and a directive amending Directive 68/360, thereby deleting any reference to the nationality of the persons concerned and to categories of persons who are not EU nationals.[1]

Although a domicile paradigm of citizenship would free the emerging European *demos* from the grip of state nationality and lay the foundations for an inclusive European identity, more reforms may be required for the creation of a 'heterogeneous' and democratic European public where individuals can participate as individual citizens and members of communities or groups having equal status in the public sphere. This issue is addressed below.

Proposition 2
Citizenship theory should focus on the issue of social membership and the politics of 'respectful belonging' and 'multifaceted exclusion'. In this respect, constructive citizenship: (i) needs to rethink the meaning of membership in contemporary plural societies and in the European Union; (ii) need not ignore the reality of structures of inequality by an appeal to universalism; (iii) nor should it postulate an abstract, undifferentiated and frictionless collectivity.

Whereas Proposition 1 dealt with the issue of formal inclusion in the personal scope of Union citizenship, Proposition 2 focuses on the reforms needed to maintain inclusiveness in the practice of citizenship by tackling multifaceted exclusion and designing suitable strategies for incorporation of minority constituencies in the European polity.

Instead of making community the precondition for democracy and justice, constructive citizenship makes concern for justice and the willingness to participate in the collective shaping of the future of the European polity the basis for constructing a community in the European Union. This conception of membership is founded on the 'affirmation' of differences – that is, on an appreciation of their enriching and revitalising effect on social life, and the recognition that *heterotis* (i.e. difference) and not *omoiotis* (i.e. identity) is the basis for social relations. The model of civic incorporation suited to such a community is that of 'respected symbiosis' of different communities – not assimilation, integration, exclusion, or expulsion of differences. Obliteration of differences has been the main goal of models of citizenship, such as the French, which seek to assimilate culturally diverse people into the dominant national culture and values. If domestication of nationalism in France has resulted in the succumbing of the state to the nation, in the British civic–territorial state the official commitment to pluralism has always involved inequality and hierachisation – the hegemony of the white 'Anglomorphic' majority over the 'Celtic Fringe' and black settlers (Hechter, 1975; Gilroy, 1987). Differences are tolerated only in so far as they do not challenge the hegemony of the 'Anglo–Saxon majority'. Integrative responses to difference can be contrasted with strategies advocating exclusion or expulsion of the Other under the guise of cultural differentialism (see Chapter 1; Balibar and Wallerstein, 1991): immigrants have to be repatriated, because they are culturally 'other' and thus represent a threat to the alleged ethnic and spiritual homogeneity of the national collectivity.

The formation of a heterogeneous and inclusive European public requires that differences should be taken seriously, be they identity-related (cultural recognition) or disadvantage-related (substantive inequalities). Although scholars tend to distinguish between the cultural politics of difference (i.e. struggles of oppressed groups for parity of esteem) and the social politics of equality (Frazer, 1995, 1997, Philips, 1997), in reality these dimensions are intertwined. Individuals and groups are deprived of recognition when their needs and their expectations are systematically disregarded, and redistribution strengthens the intersubjective recognition of individuals and groups. After all, recognition is not an end in itself; rather, it is a means to economic and political equality (Young, 1997: 148). It is thus important to maintain the connection between recognition and redistribution without conflating them since not all struggles have a material content.

Critics point out that the politics of 'difference' is marked by the difficulty of establishing which groups are entitled to recognition. However, because struggles for recognition stem from experiences of social disrespect, discriminatory institutionalised practices, deep-seated structures of power, oppression and marginalisation, they have a normative appeal and an egalitarian orientation which distinguishes them from uncritical invocations of 'difference' by privileged groups. Another common concern is that the politics of recognition may 'freeze' differences and turn them into oppositional categories. This line of reasoning overlooks the fact that differences do not arise because groups or people are essentially different. Rather, they emerge in the process of challenging structures of inequality and practices of discrimination and therefore are neither given nor fixed in advance. In addition, appeals to group interests or needs should not be taken to imply a homogeneous and unified group (i.e. the danger of group closure). Race, class, gender, disability, age and sexual orientation cut across group categorisations; members of a group can have very different views about the joint reality or differentiated experiences of the same reality. But this neither precludes group mobilisation nor does it deny a wider politics of solidarity and participation in rainbow coalitions (Mouffe, 1992; Yeatman, 1993; Young, 1997). In sum, maintaining inclusiveness in the practice of European citizenship requires a consideration of the intersections of race, gender and class (Anthias and Yuval-Davis, 1992) and the combination of a politics of positive appreciation of diversity with policies designed to promote full and effective inclusion of disadvantaged groups in the political and socio–economic life. Let us now see how this can be empirically implemented.

As regards cultural recognition, Article F(1) TEU stated that 'the Union shall respect the national identities of the Member States'. This provision is retained in the amended Article 6(3) (formerly Article F) of the Treaty of Amsterdam, and the Union's commitment to facilitate the expression and flourishing of individual identities, cultures and traditions is reiterated in Article 151 EC: 'the Community shall contribute to the flowering of the cultures of the Member States, while respecting their national and regional diversity and at the same time bringing the common cultural heritage to the fore.' Similarly, Article 151(4) EC states that the Community shall take cultural aspects into account in its action under other provisions of this Treaty, in particular in order to respect and to promote the diversity of its cultures. Notwithstanding these positive statements, the Treaty provisions fall short of granting concrete rights, such as linguistic rights or linguistic expression in public, respect for minority cultural expression, a right of access to and ownership of media, the right to have minority opinions and beliefs reflected in the mainstream media. Interestingly, Article X6 of the draft text on Union citizenship had recognised a right to cultural expression and emphasised the Union's role in promoting cultural enrichment and dissemination by developing exchanges and encouraging mutual understanding. Future insertion of similar provisions in the body of Union citizenship would highlight the relational and permeable character of cultures and the importance of establishing interconnections among contending, overlapping and interacting forms of life.

Similarly, Article 149(1) EC (formerly Article 126(1) on 'Education, Vocational Training and Youth') mentions the Community's role in developing quality education 'while fully respecting the responsibility of the Member States for the content of teaching and the organization of educational systems and their cultural and linguistic diversity'. But it fails to mention that planning and implementation of national educational policies and programmes must take into consideration the legitimate interests of subcommunities and ensure that persons belonging to minority constituencies are taught in the minority language and learn about the history, traditions and culture of their community. Such measures are important for the creation of a pluralist culture which makes citizenship rights meaningful and effective.

A pluralist culture can be inclusive and empowering only if it tackles the inequality that lies behind the polity's formal adherence to universalist principles (redistribution). Although Union citizenship has been presented as 'de-gendered', 'de-raced' and 'classless', in reality, its scope reflects gender, race and class differentials. It excludes long-term resident third-country nationals and non-active economic actors who are not self-sufficient, be they women engaging in domestic work or care for children and dependent relatives, unemployed people, or persons who have not acquired the necessary skills owing to institutionalised discrimination in education and the labour market. True, the right to free movement 'is now regarded as a fundamental and personal right within the EC and which may be exercised outside the context of an economic activity'(COM(97) 230, 27 May 1997: 14). But British courts have held that the rights contained in Article 18 EC are neither free-standing nor absolute; they are expressly subject to the limitations and conditions laid down in this Treaty and secondary legislation.[2] This conclusion derives further support from the fact that all Community initiatives on the right of residence so far have linked the right of residence with economic self-sufficiency.[3] Interestingly, in *Martinez Sala*, the ECJ left for the referring court to decide whether Sala, a Spanish national living in Germany who, with various interruptions was employed until 1986 and apart from a short period of employment in 1989 later received social assistance under Federal Social Welfare Law, was still a worker within the meaning of Article 7(2) of Regulation 1612/68 or an employed person within the meaning of Article 2 in conjunction with Article 1 of Regulation 1408/71. And by skating over the important issue concerning the legal basis of Martinez Sala's right to reside in Germany given her reliance on social assistance, it went on to reaffirm that Article 12 EC (formerly Article 6 EC) remains an alternative route to Council Regulation 1612.[4] Since Sala had already been authorised to reside in German territory, the Court held that the requirement of the 1985 Federal Law that a national of another Member State should produce a formal residence permit in order to receive a child-raising allowance, when that state's own nationals are not required to produce any document of that kind, amounts to unequal treatment prohibited by Article 12 EC.

Admittedly, the entanglement of the right of residence with economic activity sits uncomfortably with the alleged 'constitutional status' of the right to free movement. In addition, the principle of equal treatment does not warrant the creation of two-tier citizenship – that is, for favoured and 'non-favoured' (i.e. economically inactive) citizens respectively. Theoretically speaking, there exist three options for reform. First, the right of residence could be freed from economic qualifications, but residence in the host Member State could continue to be unconnected with equality of treatment in matters of social assistance. Under this option, all Union citizens would be free to move and reside in the territory of other Member States, but would not be able to receive social assistance there. Although this option would have the advantage of not imposing economic costs on the welfare budget of the Member States, its main disadvantage is that it maintains the link between equality of treatment and worker status. A more radical option would be to combine an unconditional right to reside with entitlement to receive equal treatment in social assistance. A person exercising her/his right to free movement, but lacking sufficient resources, would be entitled to seek public assistance from the Member State of her residence. This would result in transforming the right to equality of treatment from a right attached to the worker and her family to one which is available to Union citizens by reason of lawful residence. Although many would regard this proposal 'a political and economic dynamite'(O'Leary, 1996b: 92) given the disparities among the Member States in extent and scope of social security, nothing in this scheme stipulates that the host state must meet the financial cost alone. Member States could negotiate the sharing of the cost or agree on possible reimbursements of the amounts of benefit paid by the state of origin.

Alternatively, the present conditions attached to the right of residence (i.e. sufficient means of subsistence and health insurance) could still apply, but subsequent reliance on social assistance would not affect the right of residence. Under this scheme, beneficiaries of the right of residence and the members of their families would continue to enjoy this right even if they happened to rely on welfare assistance. Similarly, work seekers would be entitled to be treated by the host state in the same way as work seekers who are nationals of that state. Once again, the financial burden could be shared or met exclusively by the state of origin. Whereas all three policy options would strengthen the supranational character of Union citizenship, the second and third options would make membership in the European polity more inclusive and meaningful.

Another important limitation is that the rights of family members are parasitic on the workers' rights, that is, the workers' families do not have an independent right of residence under Articles 10 and 11 of Council Regulation 1612/68. This causes substantial hardship to family members since their right of residence may cease on the event of death of the primary beneficiary who has not acquired the right to remain in the host Member State under the provisions of Regulation 1251/70 and, on divorce, spouses who are nationals of third countries are deprived of their right of residence. Undoubtedly, expulsion of those who have established an 'effective family life' would contravene Article 8 of the European Convention on Human Rights, but this does not guarantee security of residence. In its proposals for a Regulation amending Regulation 1612/68 (COM (1998) 394 Final, OJ C344/9, 1998) and for a Directive amending Directive 68/360 (COM (1998) 394 Final, OJ C344/12, 1998), the Commission recommended the grant of an autonomous right of residence to members of the family who have lived in the host Member State for a period of three consecutive years and by which time they can be considered to be sufficiently integrated into the host State. Commissioner Vitorino also presented to the Council a proposal for a Directive on the right to family reunification of third-country nationals (December 1999), but several Member states expressed concerns about the rights to family reunification of unmarried partners, including same-sex partners. A theory of citizenship which takes equal and dignified membership seriously would thus provide for automatic acquisition of separate status for family members after a period of legal residence.

Distinctions on grounds of sex which have the effect of imposing burdens and disadvantages on women or withholding or limiting their access to opportunities also have a detrimental effect on equal and full membership in a community. Non-discrimination on the grounds of sex has been recognised as a fundamental right under Community law. But although EC sex equality law has been quite significant in combating individual cases of sex discrimination and in forcing the Member States to enact or amend existing legislation on equal pay, equal treatment, pregnancy, maternity and so on, it has, nonetheless, been individualistic in its orientation. By focusing somewhat exclusively on measures designed to hinder discrimination in the decision-making process, it has overlooked the wider structure of gender discrimination. Addressing the latter may well require a group-oriented approach and measures designed to bring about equality of outcome.

Mazey (1988: 63, 71–3, 76–7) has pointed out that the Equality Directives have been confined to the employment context and have had very little impact on tackling the structural causes of sex discrimination which very often lie beyond the workplace -in the educational system, the family and the unequal division of responsibility between parents. As Mazey (1988: 77) has put it, 'for women who cannot enter the labour market on the same footing as men, because they lack the necessary educational and employment qualifications or because they have family responsibilities, the Equality Directives have little to offer'. In this respect, accompanying the equal opportunities policy with more group-oriented measures may be more effective in tackling discrimination against women. The Council Recommendation of 13 December 1984 on *The promotion of positive action for women* (Recommendation 84/635, OJ L331/34, 1983) has no legally binding force. A form of positive action has been promoted by Community projects, such as the Community Action Programme on the Promotion of Equal Opportunity for Women 1982–85 (adopted by the Council of Ministers in 1982) and the Community Programme 1986–90 (adopted in July 1986). These programmes have focused on issues, such as education and vocational training for women, in-service training for women, women's cooperatives, 'confidence-building' courses for women, the appointment of equal opportunities counsellors, public awareness campaigns intended to change attitudes towards sex discrimination and the complex employment problems facing handicapped and immigrant women. More importantly, having noticed the inflexibility of the procedures of means of redress provided by national laws as well as the difficulty of assembling evidence of discrimination, the Commission has suggested the establishment of special bodies offering advice and assistance. But these initiatives hardly amount to a wholehearted acceptance of a group-oriented model.

Article 2(4) of Directive 76/207 offers scope for affirmative action by allowing for measures designed to promote equal opportunities for men and women, in particular by removing existing inequalities which affect women's opportunities in certain restricted areas. However, it is true to say that the Community has been more interested in promoting formal legal equality between the sexes than tackling in a more direct way the structural causes of sex discrimination. For instance, in *Hofmann v Barmer Ersatzkasse* (Case 184/83, [1984] ECR 3047) the Court ruled that the equal treatment Directive is not designed to settle questions concerned with the organisation of family or to alter the distribution of parental responsibility. By postulating that there shall be no discrimination in obligation to contribute to benefits, the Directive has been criticised for treating the equality principle as an end in itself, rather than as a mechanism for correcting disadvantage (Friedman, 1989; Sohrab, 1994: 13). It may be interesting to note here that this interpretation of the equality principle was invoked in *Caisse d'Assurances Sociales pour travailleurs Indépendents 'Integrity' v Rouvroy* (Case C-373/89, [1990] ECR I-4243) in order to challenge affirmative action provisions. Similarly, the ECJ has held that the French system of special rights for women, such as additional days leave for mothers, shorter working hours for women over 59 or obtaining leave when a child was ill, was contrary to Article 2 of the Directive (Case 312/86 *Commission v France* [1988] ECR 6315). In another controversial decision, the ECJ struck down a rule that guaranteed absolute and unconditional priority to female candidates, equally qualified for the post as male candidates, but where women make up less than 50 per cent of a particular category of employment (Case C-450/93 *Kalanke v Freie Hansestadt Bremen*, Case C-450/93 [1995] ECR I-3051). The incorporation of the Agreement on Social Policy into the Treaty at the Amsterdam summit resulted in a new paragraph 4 of Article 141 EC which allows the Member States to 'maintain or adopt measures providing for specific advantages in order to make it easier for the underrepresented sex to pursue a vocational activity or to prevent or compensate for disadvantages in professional careers'. This has prompted the ECJ to soften its approach to quotas (Case C-409/95 *Hellmut Marschall v Land Nordrhein-Westfalen* [1997] All ER (EC) 865) by striking a delicate compromise with its previous jurisprudence (i.e. *Commission v France*; *Kalanke*). That said, one must also recognise that the ECJ has been instrumental in enhancing the rights of pregnant and birthing mothers (-another example of group rights) (Case C-394/96 *Brown v Rentokil Ltd* [1998] 2 CMLR 1049; Case C-411/96 *Boyle v Equal Opportunities Commission* [1998] ECR I-6401; Case C-136/95 *Caisse Nationale d'Assurance Vieillesse des Travailleurs Salaries v Thibault*, Judgement of 30 April 1998; Case C-66/96 *Handels-og Konturfunktionærenes Forbund i Danmark*, Judgement of the Court of 19 November 1998). In addition, the Commission, backed by the European Parliament, has introduced positive Action Programmes aiming at, among other things, eliminating sex discrimination beyond the workplace and promoting equal opportunity for women. A crucial feature of these programmes is the acknowledgement that women's educational and employment opportunities are closely linked to the sharing of family responsibilities. However, further reforms are needed in order to promote full and effective equality and to extend equal treatment beyond the workplace by addressing issues such equal participation of men and women in political decision-making.

In the field of social security, the Community Directive on equal treatment in social security has been fashioned following male employment patterns, thereby resulting in penalising women who follow different employment patterns (Sohrab, 1994). By confining its personal scope to workers whose employment activity is interrupted by illness, accident, involuntary unemployment and persons seeking employment, the Social Security Directive overlooks other 'income-loss' risks, such as family care obligations (Directive 79/7). As a result, women's access to social security is limited. Whereas in *Drake v Chief Adjudication Officer* (Case 150/85, [1986] ECR 1995, [1986] 3 CMLR 43), the Court ruled in favour of a broad definition of the term 'working population', so as to include persons who have been working, but whose work has been interrupted in order to look after sick or invalid relatives, in *Achterberg-te Riele and Others v Sociale Verzekeringsbank* (Cases 48, 106, 107/88, [1989] ECR 1963, [1990] 3 CMLR 323) it was decided that Article 2 cannot be invoked by persons whose work has not been interrupted by any of the above-mentioned risks referred to in Article 3 (1). A possible explanation, according to Ellis (1994: 75), for the Court's rather more conservative line in social security cases than in employment cases may be its fear of the possibility of wide-scale financial disruption as a result of implementing sex equality or its fear of disobedience of its rulings. Irrespective of possible explanations for the ECJ's approach, however, the crux of the matter is that equality of opportunity between men and women cannot be furthered unless women's different employment patterns are addressed and different measures for achieving some form of equality of outcome are considered. In addition, faced with overburdened social security budgets, Member States may embark upon a process of levelling down drawing on the ECJ's jurisprudence regarding equalisation of pensions and retirement ages (Case 152/84 *Marshall v Southampton and South-West Hampshire Area Health Authority* [1986] ECR 723; Case C-262/88 *Barber v Guardian Royal Exchange Assurance Group* [1990] ECR I-1889, [1990] 2 CMLR 513).

The disparate treatment of members of different ethnic groups within the Community has also prompted calls for the introduction of Community-based anti-discrimination legislation. In 1993, the Migrants' Forum took the initiative of preparing a proposal for a draft Council Directive concerning the elimination of Racial Discrimination along the patterns set by Directive 76/207/EEC, arguing that equal treatment between persons of different racial/ethnic origins constitutes an objective of the Community. In Article

1(1), the text defined the term 'equal treatment' as the absence of any discrimination, direct or indirect, on grounds of race, colour, descent, nationality, national or ethnic origin in the economic, social and cultural fields. The
draft proposal obligated Member States to ensure that laws, regulations and
administrative provisions related to the above-mentioned areas conformed
to the principle of equal treatment (Article 2(1)). In addition, it supported
the outlawing of racist and xenophobic propaganda, insult, incitement to
racial discrimination, hatred and violence, and of 'organizations which promote such propaganda together with membership of those organizations and
aid, financial or otherwise given to them' (Article 3(1)b, c).

Although the anti-discrimination clause introduced by the Amsterdam
Treaty placed racial discrimination within the competence of the Community,
it did not create directly effective rights. The ECJ will not be able to adjudicate on actions against Member States until directives have been adopted, and
the effectiveness of the article is further undermined by the requirement of
unanimity, since any Member State can block future proposals. Although the
insertion of a directly effective anti-discrimination clause into the Union
citizenship provisions would have been a more radical reform, in the medium
term the adoption of a directive on non-discrimination and equal treatment
covering all of the prohibited grounds of discrimination would offer more
effective protection by combining a corrective approach which targets
discrimination with a pro-active approach designed to promote active and
full participation.

Proposition 3
*Constructive citizenship needs a language of rights which is not wedded to
either essentialism or social subjectivism, and conceives of rights as meaningful tools for individual empowerment.*

Since rights are important for inclusion and respectful participation in the
polity, constructive citizenship needs to provide an adequate philosophical
justification of rights. Understanding the philosophical credentials of rights
is not only important for political theory but also for rights' practice. For one
can adequately defend rights only by providing arguments that are grounded
in a coherent and rigorous rights theory (Freeman, 1994: 491–5).

In Chapter 4 we saw that, notwithstanding its attention to rights as individual entitlements, liberalism tends to assume the existence of rights instead
of establishing it. Similarly, communitarians have failed to develop a sophisticated account of rights. What is needed is a way of thinking about rights
which relies on the normative language of rights without giving them a foundational status; that is, it rejects metaphysics and essentialism (i.e. the liberal
invocation of human nature or its essential attributes) without lapsing into
social subjectivism. After all, rights are not the 'property' of individuals or
groups (Donnelly, 1985; Young, 1990), but are discursive categories grown
out of historically specific social contexts and encapsulating a normative

ordering of social relations and practices. Such a normative ordering is essential for the flourishing of both the individual and the society.

Asserting the historicity of rights does not in any way compromise their universality. For although rights have emerged within a historically specific context, they simultaneously exceed this context by setting standards that can be followed by others. In this way, rights supersede the realm of 'is' (the actualities of specific communities) and set critical normative standards which transcend particular cultural understandings. On this view, rights do not constitute a fixed code. European unification has given rise to the 'new' rights of free movement, residence, establishment and non-discrimination on the grounds of nationality which, in the process of their concrete application, may be conceptually refined, further extended (e.g. to third-country nationals) and enriched (e.g. statutory prohibition of discrimination on racial grounds). Unanticipated problems often accompany their concrete application, or further injustices might occur which would give rise, in turn, to new moral claims and prompt a wider application of normative principles.

An example of this is the way in which the ECJ has used the principle of non-discrimination on the grounds of sex enshrined in Article 2(1) of Directive 76/207 as a springboard in order to extend the principle of equal treatment between men and women to transsexuals. In *P v S* and *Cornwall County Council* (Case C-13/94 [1996] ECR I-2143), where P was dismissed by the Chief Executive of the Council after undergoing gender reassignment surgery, the Court held that the scope of the Directive could not be confined simply to discrimination based on the fact that a person is of one sex or another (paras 18–19). The unfavourable treatment suffered by transsexuals is based on a negative image or a moral judgement which has nothing to do with their abilities in the sphere of employment. That said, the Court in *Grant v South West Trains* (Case C-249/96 [1998] ECR I-621) was not prepared to extend the principle of non-discrimination to lesbians and gay men. It ruled that the defendants were not in breach of the plaintiff's contract of employment by refusing to grant to her lesbian partner the travel concessions to which she would have been entitled as a partner or a spouse of the opposite sex. On the grounds that there exists no Europe-wide law against discrimination on the grounds of sexual orientation, and that there are various definitions of the family across the Community, it preferred to place the matter in the hands of the legislature which is now empowered to act under the new anti-discrimination clause introduced by the Amsterdam Treaty (Articles 13 and 137 EC). Another illuminating example is Clapham's argument for the 'privatisation' of human rights, that is, the extension of international human rights law to the private sphere. Clapham favours such an extension of the protection of human dignity 'from all bodies whether they are public or private', because 'inhuman and degrading treatment can be just as damaging whether meted out by a Securicor guard or an officer in the police force' (Clapham, 1996: 29). There is also a strong argument for making marital rape, child abuse and domestic violence international human rights issues. As Clapham (1996: 31) puts it, 'putting a woman who is beaten up by her husband on an equal footing with a political detainee who is beaten up by his interrogators does not trivialise human rights; rather it enriches the whole question of human rights'. So rights may be a product of human adventure, but they are also statements of 'ought'. As such, they enjoy a quasi-transcendental status (Cornell, 1988: 1587–628; Squires, 1993) which is the very source of their strategic force. Clearly, this is a dynamic conception of universality[5] since it neither points towards a final end, an accessible *telos*, nor does it prescribe a particular form of life. Instead, it opens up and sustains a critical space which makes any final answer to the question of what is objectively Right simply inappropriate.

This critical space has been opened in the Union by the ECJ. Despite the absence of any Treaty references to fundamental human rights, the Court has succeeded in making human rights part of the general principles of EC law, and in requiring the Community institutions to respect fundamental rights. The Amsterdam Treaty has proclaimed that the Union is founded on the principles of liberty, democracy, human rights and the rule of law, and has introduced the possibility of suspending the rights of a Member State for 'serious and persistent' breaches. Many believe that these provisions fall short of the development of a fully fledged Community human rights policy and further developments concerning the drawing of an EU charter of rights are forthcoming. Interestingly, the Committee des Sage (1998) in its report, which is entitled 'Leading by Example: a Human Rights Agenda for the European Union for the Year 2000', has invited the Court to revisit its jurisprudence on Article 230 EC with a view to facilitating the standing of individuals and public interest groups alleging violation of fundamental human rights. Intervention by non-governmental organisations and public interest groups would make access to judicial remedies effective since the present rules on *locus standi* are very restrictive. Effective access to justice also requires a variety of policies which would empower individuals to vindicate the judicially enforceable rights given to them. This is crucial from the point of view of citizenship since the latter must transcend the language of vulnerability underlying human rights issues and embrace a pro-active approach centred around individual empowerment and equal membership in all spheres of socio-economic life.

Consumer rights are a good case in point. Given the risks for consumer abuse across national frontiers, greater attention needs to be paid to the quality of services and goods, in particular as regards foodstuffs, to cross-border purchases, to misleading advertising and unfair commercial practices. Promoting the interests of consumers in all areas throughout the Union is envisaged to transform consumers resident there into active and confident participants in the European venture. True, Article 129(a), made consumer protection a policy of the Community, and the Amsterdam Treaty has improved the provisions concerning consumer protection by extending and clarifying the objectives of Community action in this field and integrating consumer protection into the Union's other policies (Article 153 EC). The European Consumers' Organisation had called for the development of a pro-active consumer policy which would entail the inclusion of the promotion of consumer interests as an EU objective in the principles of the Treaty, explicit references to enforcement and the strengthening of sanction possibilities, promotion of easier access to courts and references to consumers' rights (The 1996 IGC-Revision of the Treaty: observations by BEUC, 27/6/95). But in the end reference was made only to the consumers' right to information and education and to organise themselves to protect their interests. Union citizenship could promote the position of consumers by providing for consumer rights, such as: the right to health and safety (this could cover toy safety and thus, protection of children); the right to protection of economic interests of consumers (e.g. protection against the unfair exclusion of essential rights in contracts, regulation of credit agreements); the right to information and the right to redress for injury or damage; and the right of consumers to be consulted and represented through their organisations (see Proposition 5).

Similarly, references to the rights and obligations of the European residents in the field of environment within the context of Union citizenship provisions will be welcome. Syngellakis (1996) has commented on the need to connect environmental rights and values with citizenship, and has noted that the provision of procedural environmental rights has not yet been accompanied by a substantive environmental right. Interestingly, the draft text on Union citizenship had stated that 'citizens should have a right to enjoy a healthy environment coupled with an obligation to preserve and protect it'. In political terms, the incorporation of such a right within the ambit of Union citizenship would give added value to this institution. In legal terms, the adoption of such a provision would facilitate civil liability for damage caused by pollution and waste, since, at the present, it is the Member States who are responsible for the implementation and enforcement of the policy, and not corporations or individuals.

Proposition 4
Constructive citizenship needs to take democracy seriously by fostering processes of democratic decision-making and encouraging participation in public discussion by all those who 'express a will to share actively in a common experience rather than in a common life' (Wolin, 1993: 472).

Given that the aim of the European project is not to 'abolish states or to replace old states by new states, but to devise levels of co-ordinate government' (Koopmans, 1992: 1050), constructive citizenship has to address the issues of decentralisation of power within states and of constitutional federalism in the European Union. Since democracy is closer to divided powers or concurrent competences than to unitary arrangements, principled diffusion of power among different levels of government is likely to enhance political participation. Although distribution of power underpins the principles of decentralization and federalism, the latter cannot provide much guidance as to how competences can be distributed among different layers of government or how to resolve disputes that might arise from such distribution.

The principle of subsidiarity is a useful guide: it requires that decisions should be taken as closely as possible to the citizens, and that higher authorities may intervene only when lower authorities are unable to fulfil a given task. As already argued in Chapters 1 and 2, the genuine decentralist meaning of subsidiarity has been compromised because competence belongs in principle to the Member States, and there is no reference to distribution of competences between the national and subnational levels. The Amsterdam Treaty incorporated the Interinstitutional Agreement of 25 October 1993 and the main points of the Birmingham and Edinburgh Conclusions on the application of the principle of subsidiarity into a Protocol thereby conferring on them a legal status which they did not previously enjoy. The Protocol clarifies the role of each institutional actor and espouses a dynamic view of subsidiarity in that it 'allows Community action within the limits of its powers to be expanded where the circumstances so require, and conversely, to be restricted or discontinued where it is no longer justified' (para. 3 of the Protocol). Although this confounds the minimalist interpretation of subsidiarity, conceived of as possible repatriation of competences at the national level, it nevertheless falls short of satisfying regional demands for incorporating explicit references to local and regional authorities.

The Amsterdam Treaty also strengthened the Community's democratic legitimacy by extending the powers of the Parliament. More specifically, the extension of the scope of the co-decision procedure as well as its simplification (i.e., through the removal of the third reading) has put the Parliament on a more equal footing with the Council in the legislative process. As such, the reforms are likely to encourage the participation of Union citizens in the European enterprise. With regard to the procedure for the election of the Parliament by direct universal suffrage, the Amsterdam Treaty provides for the Community's power to adopt common principles (Article 190 EC), and a legal provision has been inserted into the same article to permit the adoption of a single statute for MEPs.

In addition, because lack of transparency impairs the exercise of political rights and affects the quality of citizens as political beings, the Amsterdam Treaty institutionalised a right to access to Council, Parliament and Commission documents (Article 255 EC). A new clause in the former Article 8d EC also provides for the right of every citizen writing to one of the institutions or bodies of the Union to receive a reply in the same language. Although it is doubtful whether such provisions will bring about openness and more political accountability they, nonetheless, mark the beginning of an active Community policy on transparency.

Notwithstanding the Union's commitment to transparency, the political dimension of Union citizenship continues to remain deficient. Union citizens continue to enjoy only partial franchise in the Member State in which they reside (Article 19 EC), despite the fact that it is at the national level that most decisions which are directed relevant to the work of the Community are taken. Many believe that admission of Union citizens to the 'national community of citizens' would undermine the distinction between nationals and 'aliens', would dilute the 'nationalness' of parliamentary elections and jeopardise national interests. Although such objections are deeply embedded within national cultures, they need to be reassessed in light of the co-ordinated efforts to devise a common European security policy, and the marginal position of defence and security issues in normal parliamentary business. After all, commitment to democracy requires the strengthening of the instruments for democratic participation by Union citizens at all levels of governance. Critics might argue here that Union citizens would be deprived of their right to consent to be part of national publics if they were automatically allowed to vote at national elections. However, this argument appears to overlook the fact that Union citizens are free to choose whether or not to exercise their rights in the Member State in which they reside. Union citizens could thus always demonstrate their consent by choosing to exercise their electoral rights in their place of residence. This could affect their voting rights in their Member State of origin, but considering that several Member States do not permit their own nationals to vote or to stand as candidates if they reside outside their territory, many Union citizens might not hesitate to take this risk.

Equally important for the development of the supranational model of European political citizenship is the development of European political parties operating on a transnational level. Although Article 191 EC establishes a clear link between the formation of political parties and the expression of political will at the supranational level and European integration, it leaves the matter of the possible setting up and operation of European political parties to the discretion of civil society. In this respect, a framework regulation on the legal status of European political parties coupled with a regulation on their financial circumstances would give greater substance to European political citizenship. A similar effect might arise from the recognition of the rights of association and assembly within the context of Union citizenship provisions. This could be achieved in the future by the insertion of a new subparagraph in Article 19 EC stating that 'every resident of the Union shall have the right to associate with other residents of the Union in order to represent their interests and defend their rights'. In the same vein, an explicit recognition of the residents' right to set up foundations, associations and organisations, coupled with a commitment on behalf of the Union to support those organisations which promote co-operation in certain policy areas and are active at the transnational level, would contribute to the flourishing of a democratic European public.

Proposition 5
Political democracy has to be accompanied by social justice. Constructive citizenship must devise more egalitarian principles of distribution of socio–economic benefits, thereby enabling citizens to take advantage of opportunities for participation.

The discussion above has suggested that willingness to tackle the social inequalities that belie the liberal ideal of formal equality is essential for inclusion and democratic participation. In the Union, the 'long-term growth' of poverty, the increase in the ranks of homeless and hungry (particularly among the young), the increase in poverty among the elderly and the female-headed households and the persisting poverty of the inner cities are all major causes for concern. New Right politicians who, following Friedman (1962; Friedman and Friedman 1980) and Hayek (1973, 1986) praise unregulated private market economies, have failed to consider seriously the quality of economic life for all these affected. Questions such as who might suffer, how much and how long in such an economy have been sidelined: the New Right has never considered inequality and social exclusion has never been perceived as a problem or a cost. Instead, the orthodox paradigm of social citizenship has been attacked, and the welfare state has been blamed for encouraging a dependency culture and promoting welfare clientism (King, 1987; Mead, 1986). Citizenship theory must take into account the fact that people are forced into the welfare system because there are no real job opportunities: the prospect of full-time employment is no longer a certainty and part-time jobs do not pay enough. Although there are also large macroeconomic issues at work here, and in the Union the risk of 'social dumping'[6] is a major concern, the development of a form of European social citizenship has remained firmly on the Commission's policy agenda. The Community has recognised that unemployed people, women, old people, ethnic communities, religious minorities, people with disabilities, young people, informal carers, the homeless and travellers are at great risk of social exclusion. True, a strategy for growth and job creation is vital. But vital, too, is the acknowledgment that the problem of unemployment will not be automatically solved by economic growth. A 'Europe of solidarity' cannot be built on commitment to enhance economic competitiveness alone. The Commission's White Paper on *Growth, Competitiveness and Employment* (COM(94) 333 Final) noted that the future of European integration depends on the reduction of unemployment, and the Parliament has emphasised that economic prosperity, competitiveness, increased productivity and social progress must not be seen as conflicting ideals.

Against this background, it is not surprising that employment was an important item on the agenda of the 1996 IGC. The objective of promoting a 'high level of employment' has been added to the objectives of the Community, which now possesses the power to draw up a coordinated employment strategy (see the new Title VIII on Employment). This mirrors the co-ordination arrangements for economic policies and is conditioned on their compatibility with the broad economic policy guidelines referred to in Article 99(2) EC. The employment guidelines are not the usual Community legal instruments, but are a range of 'soft law' measures. An Employment Committee will promote co-ordination between the Member States on employment and labour market policies (Article 130 EC). Finally, provision is made for the Council, acting by qualified majority and the co-decision procedure, to adopt incentive measures (these are not designed to harmonise national employment policies) (Article 129 EC). Clearly, the new Title falls short of introducing a European social approach to employment and does not undermine the primacy of national policies which 'shall be respected' (Article 127 EC (formerly Article 109p)).

In contrast, the incorporation of the Social Protocol into the Treaty restores coherence in Community social policy and strengthens the social dimension in Community legislation. Although the incorporation of the Social Protocol was not accompanied by a fundamental revision of its content (Chapter 2), certain provisions have been strengthened: the new legal basis for the adoption of measures in the sphere of equal opportunities and equal treatment of men and women in matters of employment and occupation (Article 141(3) EC). However, further reforms are also needed: the incorporation of employment rights, such as the right to work, and rights in employment, the right to a fair wage, provisions on the rights of association and the right to strike, night-work for women and young people – in accordance with international labour standards (i.e. ILO Conventions and the Council of Europe's European Social Charter (1961)) and the jurisprudence of the European Court of Human Rights; and provisions which provide better protection for the elderly, the unemployed, children and adolescents. Such an extension would transform workers' rights into citizens' rights.

Apart from extending and strengthening the cluster of social rights, a coherent and well designed social action programme to combat poverty and homelessness is also needed. 'Poverty programmes' have been a successful pilot scheme which, in the Commission's opinion, has helped disseminate information about poverty and stimulate debate (COM(93) 435, cit. in Spicker, 1997: 134). The Commission has also acknowledged that effective action may well depend on the forging of a partnership among all those involved in the fight against poverty, in both public and private sectors. In addition to this principle of partnership, the Community's action programmes (1989–94 and 1994–99) espouse the principles of multidimensionality and participation. Multidimensionality reflects two things: first, the realisation that social exclusion has been the result of structural weaknesses in more than one policy area, and as such, can be tackled only by multiobjective policies and strategies. The principle of participation, on the other hand, aims at encouraging effective participation by the least privileged groups, promoting solidarity and active citizenship. An agenda for social reform in the Union would have to incorporate these principles into a clear and effective anti-poverty strategy. Such a strategy should aim primarily at bringing people above the poverty line or helping them to avoid poverty – and not just at reducing some of the hardships of poverty. This means targeting the following four main areas. First, the area of employment rights and childcare provision, by devising policies aiming at ensuring that jobs pay enough to keep families above the poverty line and at providing affordable childcare to low-income working parents. Second, in the context of welfare provisions, prime targets must be healthcare coverage, investment in housing, education and training. Third, in the area of labour market policies, welfare policy must be linked to job opportunity policy. Clearly, putting back people to work must be the prime target, to be achieved via the stimulation of training programmes and jobs in the private sector as well as by public investment and EU finance. To this end, the articulation of a European workforce development policy may be essential. Finally, anti-discrimination legislation and policies must accompany these measures.

The pursuit of these policies goes against the grain of the neo-liberal agenda of strong anti-inflationary policies and deregulated labour markets. But economists do not preclude the possibility of combining tactical interventions in the labour market with a monetary and exchange policy aiming at maintaining price stability. Reducing poverty goes hand in hand with including people into the active economic sphere by giving them the opportunity to work, to earn a decent income which keeps them above the poverty line and to make contributions as both workers and consumers. Given the determination on behalf of most EU Members to develop a European social citizenship, efforts should be made to ensure that citizenship is not denuded of meaning as a result of poverty.

Proposition 6
Constructive citizenship should not expect people to be total citizens. Nor should it aspire to offer a all-consuming fulfilment of their lives, for individuals have multiple commitments and shifting loyalties. However, constructive citizenship requires citizens to be responsible (to be concerned with justice), to show respect and sensitivity for others, and to be ready to question rather than to accept things on the basis of trust (critical citizenship).

What underpins the above theoretical agenda on constructive citizenship, and what supports the proposed institutional reforms, is the cultivation of those citizenship qualities mostly associated with critical and responsible citizenship. The debate concerning citizenship virtues tend to be confined almost exclusively to the issue of political participation. Though political participation is important and should be encouraged (see Proposition 5), it cannot in itself provide solutions to all problems of citizenship or be an antidote to the growing racism and rising xenophobia in the countries of the European Union. So – apart from the debate whether political participation is an occasional and burdensome activity, or whether it requires an all-consuming commitment by citizens – the issue of responsible citizenship has to be addressed. For citizens could always use their rights of participation irresponsibly, by supporting exclusionary citizenship laws, pushing for tougher immigration controls or even deportation of undocumented immigrants.

Inclusion and respectful belonging depend on the cultivation of an ethos of responsibility and respect. The latter would obligate officials in public authoritative bodies, educators, legislators and persons working in the mass media to ensure that policies, laws, provisions and so on respect the equal dignity of all residents and abstain from discriminatory, racist and xenophobic speech. Future insertion of a directly effective anti-discrimination clause in Union citizenship could aid the institutionalisation of such an ethos.

Such an ethos, if cultivated, would also obligate citizens on three levels. On a first level, it would require citizens to ask questions, to criticise official discourses and policies and to engage in rational discourse. On a second level, in the realm of commitment, it would prompt citizens to display solidarity and an active sense of fellowship towards the vulnerable and oppressed. Third, on the level of political intervention, it would obligate citizens to support policies aiming at combating discrimination and injustice as well as resisting unjust policies.

Much also depends on the institutionalisation of a civic culture of anti-discrimination and anti-racism within which moral obligations can be discursively established and civic obligations can be actualised. Such a civic culture is more likely to foster what Young has called a 'spirit of openness to unassimilated otherness', or Heller and Feher's idea of radical tolerance (1988: 82-5). Unlike the liberal attitude of 'letting be' of difference in the private realm, Heller and Feher's idea of radical tolerance entails the positive recognition of other forms of life – the experience of the other as other. In addition, it is more relational and concerned, in that it recognises the relation of interdependence between identities as well as extending concern to the well-being of our neighbour whose particular form of life we may or may not share.

The idea of virtuous citizenship based on an ethic of the Other does not amount to total citizenship since it does not call citizens to abandon their private selves in order to engage in the public realm of citizenship. Nor does it demand that citizens invest all their energy in citizenship, that is, to spend all their afternoons discussing the fate of the polity and to be compelled to participate in public meetings. Rather, it requires their reflecting on and criticising governmental policies and discourses (e.g. on immigration and asylum[7]); displaying an active sense of solidarity towards the vulnerable and oppressed (e.g. a gay neighbour who is systematically harassed by other neighbours); responding to racist and sexist comments at work, public transport, schools and universities; instituting support groups for victims of violence and discrimination; disseminating information against racism and xenophobia; and so on. All these are forms of personal involvement which do not involve a great sacrifice of one's 'personal' interests. This is particularly pertinent for practical politics in the European Union today. The increase in racially motivated attacks, xenophobic speech, and the extent of institutional discrimination, show that responsible citizenship cannot appropriately be confined to the gesture, 'this is none of my business'. It should rather imply the gesture, 'I do care' (Heller and Feher, 1988: 83).

Union citizenship could include references to citizens' duties. It could, for instance, incorporate a solidarity clause stating that 'any acts adopted for the purpose of applying this Treaty should reflect every Union citizen's obligation to display solidarity with other Union citizens and with nationals of non-member countries resident in the Union; this obligation entails respect for each person's dignity and the rejection of any form of social marginalization'. It could also institutionalise other special obligations, such as the obligation to join a voluntary European 'peace-corps' engaging in humanitarian missions. Needless to say, the Community legal order has made an important contribution towards the promotion of responsible and critical citizenship. As already noted, certain provisions which meet the criteria for direct effect – that is, they are sufficiently clear and precise, unconditional and legally perfect – are fruitful sources of individual rights which can be invoked against public authorities and private persons or undertakings (the horizontal direct effect). This means that national governments as well as their own private citizens or undertakings should not discriminate against Community nationals on the grounds of nationality or on the grounds of sex, should refrain from conduct in the workplace or in other zones of commercial activity which breaches the provisions concerning free movement of workers, the right of establishment and the right to provide services and so on. The development of this jurisprudence, which has resulted in the transformation of directly effective provisions of the Treaty into fundamental rights to be enjoyed by Community citizens, has converted the traditional international law-based right of the individual against the public authority into a citizen duty towards other individuals (Mancini and Keeling, 1994: 183).

Proposition 7
Constructive citizenship must avoid the temptation of positing a complete, settled and non-contestable interpretation of political life. It should resist closure and be more at ease with the infinitude of the social that accompanies institutionalised projects.

In sketching this outline, I have tried to affirm an openness to the ambiguity and indeterminacy of social life – both in the sense of awareness of the conditionality of my arguments, and in the sense of allowing space for political actors themselves to test its claims, to criticise them and to redefine them. Instead of postulating the necessity of an overlapping consensus or pledging such consensus on values, I have sought to articulate a conception of citizenship which 'teaches dissensus'. The reason is that in contemporary differentiated and fragmented polities, the theory and politics of citizenship need not be embarrassed by conflict, contradictions and fundamental disagreements. Instead it should make a community out of them. Of course, this presupposes among other things the abandonment of dogmas, a willingness on behalf of the parties concerned to engage in a process of constructive negotiation of differences and, more importantly, a commitment to protest against inequality and exclusion. But such a process also promises to affirm the openness of the future.

Having said that, I must note that the argument presented here would be incomplete if I did not consider its implications for migration law and policy. Since immigration rules affect and are being affected by citizenship, constructive citizenship relies on and requires a re-articulation of the existing immigration discourse and policy. Admittedly, this task is surrounded by further conceptual and empirical difficulties which will be highlighted in Chapter 6. Notwithstanding the difficulties, however, the subsequent discussion will show that the realisation of constructive citizenship ultimately depends on how Europe defines itself with respect to the outside world, and on whether Europeans will realise what it means to dwell concernfully among co-dwellers in a world that is meant to share.

Notes

1   The Commission has already submitted a proposal for a Council Regulation amending Regulation 1408/71, based on Articles 51 and 235 EC, which extends Community co-ordination of social security schemes, as laid down by this regulation, to employed persons and self-employed persons who are insured in a Member State and who are not Community nationals; OJ C6, 10/1/1998: 15).

2   This argument was first suggested by Hall (1995: 191), and was submitted by Peter Duffy QC in *R v Secretary of State for the Home Department, ex parte Vittorio Vitale*, Court of Appeal [1996] 2 CMLR 587; *R v Secretary of State for the Home Department ex parte Vittorio Vitale and Do Amaral*, Queen's Bench Division [1995] All ER (EC) 946; *R v Secretary of State for the Home Department, ex parte Vittorio Vitale and Another*, the High Court, Leicester [1995] 3 CMLR 605, 619). Since Vitale was neither employed nor seeking work with genuine prospects of obtaining it, he did not have the right to reside in Britain after the end of the six-month period. In *Kuchlenz-Winter* the Court of First Instance argued that 'limitations and conditions' in Article 18 EC includes Directives 90/364/EEC and 90/365/EEC: Case T-66/95 [1997] ECR II-637.

3   The Commission's proposal for a Directive on the right of residence for nationals of the Member States in the territory of another Member State (COM(89) 275, Final, OJ C207, 17/8/1979) granted a permanent right of residence to all Community nationals and their families who are economically self-sufficient.

4   Case C-85/96 *Maria Martinez Sala v Freistaat Bayern*, Judgement of the Court of 12 May 1998. See Fries and Shaw's reflections (1998) on the contribution of this judgement to a universal non-discrimination right, including access to all manner

of welfare benefits, which has now taken root in Community law as a consequence of the creation of the figure of the 'Union citizen'.

5 Amy Gutmann's (1993) 'deliberative universalism' is intended to apply to issues of decision-making in cases of fundamental moral conflict; it does not offer an account of the philosophical credentials of principles.

6 Member States with high unemployment and low social welfare provision may export their unemployed to Member States with lower unemployment and higher welfare provision. Similarly, firms might choose to operate in countries where social wages are low, thereby driving high-cost firms out of business or forcing them to relocate elsewhere.

7 Compare, however, Dagger's (1997) perspective of republican liberalism which allows for 'qualified moral parochialism' in which citizens are treated more favourably than non-citizens.

6

Schengenland and its alternative

Whereas Chapter 5 put forward an argument for an analytical framework for European citizenship, this chapter examines the possibilities for an alternative design of immigration policy. Though this is a useful division, there are several points of overlap between the two chapters. First, what happens 'at the door' is shaped by – and, in turn, shapes – internal conceptions of membership and community and the practice of democracy 'on the floor'. As argued above, admissions policies have an important bearing on the integration of settled migrants and their access to citizenship. At the same time immigration provisions mirror cultural understandings and the prevailing conceptions of membership. This begs the question whether the alternative conception of community put forward in Chapter 5 will yield a different vision of immigration policy. Second, European citizenship and immigration are central to the formation of European identity and the building of the European polity. Third, both chapters draw on the importance of normative political theory in expanding the notion of 'us' internally, embracing pluralism and diversity, and in reflecting on how open or restrictive EU immigration policy should be.

This chapter suggests a principled and non-restrictive paradigm for immigration policy in the European Union, based on a different way of thinking about immigration which questions the states' or democratic communities' 'right' to exclude. I argue that democracy in the Union does not only require flexible membership and a constructive model of citizenship, but also porous boundaries and a more liberal immigration policy. By the latter, I do not mean one which simply complies with international law norms by: admitting all those having rights of admission under bilateral agreements concluded by the Member States and third states or by the Community and third states; refraining from introducing arbitrary distinctions; respecting the right to family life; defending the humanitarian admission of displaced persons and refugees as an integral part of its constitutional tradition and culture[1]; providing a system of effective appellate remedies and procedural safeguards against arbitrary expulsions. Although the Member States' record of compliance with these norms is far from perfect and there is much scope for drawing on them in order to improve the design and implementation of European immigration policy, these standards are, nonetheless, well established in international law and academic literature.

What is more difficult to establish is how the vast majority of applicants, who have no *prima facie* right to be admitted into a country because they do not belong in any of the above categories, should be treated. I argue that the EU and European polities have a positive obligation to admit these migrants, but not out of a universal right to immigration, or international distributive justice, or even charity. They have a duty to admit out of concern about the 'costs of restriction', that is, about the profound effects that closure and the current law-enforcement immigration regime have upon admission applicants, the principles on which they profess to be based and upon the identity of their citizens. After all, admission and·belonging are issues relating to 'what kind of polity we wish to have' and 'who we choose to become'- not simple correlatives of the state's power to exclude.

In such a schema, the goals, interests and aspirations of non-members are neither disregarded nor superseded by the needs of insiders and/or the relevant duties towards one's community. For any damage or hardship inflicted upon outsiders owing to the restrictive and law-enforcement character of immigration policy is a cost since it impacts negatively upon the scope and nature of the principles underpinning a polity. And when this happens, one's status as 'alien' or 'outsider' becomes morally irrelevant. For instance, a racially discriminatory immigration policy does not only injure admission applicants; it injures citizens and 'alien' residents too. Discrimination on the basis of alien status may also be a pretext for discrimination against a particular insider group. By reducing the welfare value for admission applicants, such an immigration policy undermines the future of democracy for all.

An obligation upon states to admit migrants does not give rise to a corollary right to be admitted. Breaking the correlation between rights and duties is significant for European immigration politics. First, unlike the proposed human right to transborder movement (Carens, 1987; Dummett, 1992), it establishes a 'morality of duty' and not a 'morality of aspiration'.[2] Second, by shifting the focus from the immigrant to the host, it shows that alienage is produced only in relation to what constitutes membership. Such a shift may be necessary for the politicisation and 'securitisation' of this issue in the European Union indicates that the 'problem' of immigration has much to do with the 'host' Member States - not with migration flows *per se*. Before elaborating on this design, however, it may be useful to remind the reader why an alternative is needed despite the Communitarisation of migration-related areas by the Treaty of Amsterdam.

The 'protective' Union, the mutating state and the evolving doctrine of immigration control

In Chapters 2 and 3 we saw that the institutional pattern of intergovernmental co-operation from which the Union has moved has not been lean. Rather, it has been culturally and structurally 'thick'; that is, the outcome and the medium of policies and practices rooted in prevailing societal assumptions about the problem of immigration and the presumption of the existence of a security deficit within a borderless Europe. On a macro level, this presumption caused the Member States, in exchange for their consent for the removal of controls at the internal frontiers, to demand compensatory powers of control at the external frontiers. On a meso level, the requirement of stringent policing of external frontiers and internal police surveillance has also given police and customs agencies the opportunity to construct a new role for themselves within an enlarged Europe. These agencies have been endowed with the task of identifying specific categories of security risk at the borders and dealing efficiently with them by developing European-based law-enforcement structures.

From the outset, the main security risks were identified as immigration, drug-trafficking and international crime. The inclusion of immigration and asylum in this trilogy did not give rise to concerns as it coincided with domestic systems of cultural representation which had framed immigration as a problem and a 'law and order' issue (Chapter 2). Since immigrants are seen 'to challenge the basis of "national" social and political cohesion upon which the integrity of the nation-state ostensibly depends' (Collinson, 1993b: 14), restricting immigration is often portrayed as an exercise of the right to self-defence. So whereas policy towards intra-EU migration has been liberal and expansionist due to the ECJ's judicial activism and the Community's rights-based approach to free movement (Chapters 2, 3 and 5), policy towards extra-EC migration has become increasingly controlled and restrictive.

In pre-Amsterdam Europe, these parallel albeit contradictory trends were kept apart. In theory, both are designed to serve the same purpose, that is, to create an area without internal frontiers within which the free movement of goods, persons, capital and services is ensured (Article 14 EC). However, the general approach and philosophy underpinning them are very different. The Amsterdam Summit ruptured the membrane separating the two migration policies and general approaches. The amended Article 2 TEU states that the Union shall set itself the objective to develop and maintain an area of Freedom, Security and Justice. The latter is defined as an area in which the free movement of persons is to be assured in conjunction with appropriate measures with respect to external border controls, immigration, asylum and the prevention and combating of crime. The mutual interdependence among the different aspects of this overall objective is confirmed by Article 61 EC which mentions Article 31(e) TEU. In addition, official discourses emphasise that the full benefits of an area of freedom will never be enjoyed unless they are exercised in an area where people can feel safe and secure, as the Action plan of the Council and the Commission (1988: 1–2) *on how best to implement these provisions of the Amsterdam Treaty establishing an area of Freedom, Security and Justice* states:

Freedom loses much of its meaning if it cannot be enjoyed in a secure environment and with the full backing of a system of justice in which all Union citizens and residents can have confidence. These three inseparable concepts have one common denominator - people - and one cannot be achieved in full without the other two. Maintaining the right balance between them must be the guiding thread for Union action. It should be noted in this context that the treaty instituting the European Communities (Article 61, formerly Article 73Ia), makes a direct link between measures establishing freedom of movement of persons and the specific measures seeking to combat and prevent crime (Article 31 (e) TEU), thus creating a conditional link between the two areas.

The concept of security underpinning the notion of an area of Freedom, Security and Justice refers to measures designed to ensure that the citizens of Europe are free from risk or danger as well as from anxiety or fear (Bull. EU, 5, 1995: 92). The notion of 'security' has an individual dimension: the Community worries about Union citizens who are vulnerable and thus in need of security. In this sense, 'the term security has undergone an expansion of applications in the EU, where it has until now been used in reference to defence and international security matters under the Common Foreign and Security Policy' (Van Selm-Thorburn, 1998: 635). By contending that there exists a security problem in the EU,[3] the Community has inherited the Member States' discourse on the 'securitisation' of migration and asylum policy (Huysmans, 1995) and the concomitant identification of possible sources of insecurity. The notion of Freedom, Security and Justice is based on the assumption that migration is a security threat that must be effectively controlled and reduced.[4] The significance of this should not be underestimated, for the symbolic framing of an issue defines and confines the terrain within which institutional actors forge preferences, devise policy strategies and act to maintain or to reform the law.

Communitarisation has not only left the conceptual parameters of the security paradigm which characterised the third pillar intact, but the latter has now come to define the terms of the free movement of persons in Community law. The Community has welcome the Schengen project of creating a unified European migration area surrounded by a uniformly controlled border, and the Member States' evolving security agenda has gained a legitimate foothold in the debate. Consequently, security is no longer an interaction effect between the third and first pillars. It becomes, instead, a categorical endogenous value of the Community. This is likely to impact negatively on the production of social identities and the formation of a European identity.

Instead of giving a coherent normative response to the problems of membership and citizenship in the Union and adopting an enlightened approach to migration flows (Chapter 5), the Community seems to have uncritically adopted the Member States' definition of 'who the Europeans are'. In this respect, Title IV may not only help create narratives which are insulated from principled judgements, but it may also contribute to the institutionalisation of a civic but exclusive mode of European identity. Interestingly, in Community official discourses the logic of exclusion is being presented as security-enhancing: enforcement of the law against migrants is said to have been dictated by the need on the part of the Union to fulfil its obligations to Union citizens. But such a 'protective' Union may well be a defective Union.

It is unlikely that the existing restrictive and law enforcement approach to migration flows will be reversed - unless, of course, the ECJ's involvement profoundly affects the nature of the migration regime. Support for this may be derived from the fact that although states are losing their ability to control their borders and to provide security they, nevertheless, continue to be the chief interpreters of security. Security continues to mean simply what the rulers say it means, and our earlier discussion on the Community concept of Freedom, Security and Justice has demonstrated this. In other words, the vocabulary may change, the discourse of security may evolve, but states, acting individually or collectively, still remain in control of this discourse. In addition, the Member States' commitment to stringent border controls leads them beyond the outer frontier of the Union into a virtual outward projection of borders. The outward shift of borders and the corresponding shift in operational strategies can be seen in the following three key aspects of the Union's migration policy. First, an idea which is gaining increasing momentum is that more effective management of migration requires activities to counter migration pressure at source.[5] This does not only entail the elimination of the economic causes of migration from the Third World through economic schemes of co-operation and development aid, but also policies of prevention of crises and intervention in order to contain conflicts and restore normality. Immigration is no longer a home affairs issue, but it gradually becomes a foreign policy priority. The need for such interventions was discussed in the Commission's Communication on Immigration and Asylum Policy (1994). The Strategy paper on Immigration and Asylum policy submitted by the Austrian Presidency (1998) elaborated on this theme, and called for the development of a co-ordinated approach to reduce migratory pressure that extends beyond the narrow field of policy on aliens, asylum, immigration and border controls by incorporating international relations and development aid, too (paras 51–7). As the Strategy paper put it, 'all the EU's bilateral agreements with third States must incorporate the migration aspect. For instance, economic aid will have to be made dependent on visa questions, greater border-crossing facility on guarantees of readmission, air connections on border control standards, and the willingness to provide economic co-operation on effective measures to reduce push factors' (para 59). This clearly represents a major adjustment of traditional migration policy management patterns since it involves interconnections and parallel policy design with Common Foreign Security Policy (CFSP) and development aid. The crux of the point, however, is that prevention and restriction is the rationale of the 'root causes' approach.

A second (linked) feature is the new emphasis on a comprehensive migration policy which tackles anticipatory migration. In this respect, the notion of 'fortress Europe', which has underpinned most policy initiatives in this area, is gradually being replaced by a model of 'concentric circles of migration'. According to this model, the Schengen EU members constitute the first circle, and are surrounded by a second circle consisting of prospective members and associated states. These states are required to bring their migration policies in line with the first circle's standards, particularly with respect to visa, border control and readmission policies. They may be persuaded to meet the Schengen standards or may be forced to do so if they are made a precondition for EU membership (paras 60–61). A third circle of states in the CIS area and North Africa would focus on transit checks and on combating illegal immigration networks. The co-operation of these states could be achieved by linking migration policy objectives with the priorities of the Union's funding programmes. Finally, a fourth circle of states in the Middle East, China and Africa would co-operate with the Union on eliminating the push factors of migration. Once again, co-operation in this area would determine the extent of the development aid that these countries would receive. It is interesting to note here that a priority of the Council's (and the Commission's) work programme in migration policy is the development of the 'model of concentric migration policy circles' through a comprehensive assessment of third states in the framework of that model and the formulation of a medium-term plan for each circle (para 134 et seq).

The third aspect of the EU's future migration law and policy involves the concept of control of legal entry. The Strategy paper called for the formulation of an overall concept of control of legal entry which shifts the focus from illegal apprehension after entry to deterrence before entry. According to this document, an effective entry control concept is not based simply on controls at the border but centres around increased legal regulation and effective preventative strategies. It begins in the country of departure at the time of granting the visa, and covers every step taken by a third-country national from the commence of the journey to arrival at destination: in transit by checks on transport undertakings, involving the transit states from which migrants reach the Union territory in a control system, EU external border controls, security nets at the internal borders and so on (paras 41, 85–92).

In the light of this discussion, it would be hasty to argue that the Communitarisation of immigration policy weakens the Member States. States may lose sovereignty over migration-related issues but their power increases.

Communitarisation offers them the opportunity to expand the logic of control and law enforcement which underpinned the intergovernmental framework of co-operation, and to construct new forms of power which do not only increase the regulatory capacity of states within a geographically contained structure, but also enable them to impose their security agenda beyond the narrow confines of the Union. In this respect, Title IV represents a new and more effective management of immigration control, and not the end or the beginning of the end of an era.

Rethinking immigration

In the previous section we saw that institutionalising forms of better – in the sense of more democratic and efficient – management of (limited) migration may not undercut the prevailing definition of immigration as a security threat and a problem. Nor does it question the legitimacy of the Schengen Convention as the model for the development of a European immigration policy. What is needed is a new conceptual framework which challenges the securitisation of immigration and reflects critically on the meaning and terms of membership in the Union. This is not an easy task for liberal democratic perspectives accommodate restrictive immigration policies. This may be due to the fact that liberal theories of justice have been elaborated against the background of bounded communities with given membership and assumed borders. The question which has escaped attention is whether porous boundaries and liberal admission policies can be defended on the basis of democracy itself.

Making the states' right to admit and exclude aliens an issue of democratic self-determination has probably been the most credible justification of the states' right to exclude. Walzer (1983: 31) addresses the question of immigration from the standpoint of membership in a political community: 'the primary good that we distribute to one another is membership in some human community.' Accordingly, Walzer's defence of the right of a sovereign state or a political community to restrict the entry of foreigners ('legitimate' closure) is that democracy entails the right of the community to determine its membership and to maintain its distinct identity and the integrity of 'shared understandings'. Like clubs, democratic communities are marked by the present members' power to control admission of new members. Unlike private clubs, however, democracies must, on the grounds of justice, grant full membership (citizenship), irrespective of nationality, to resident participants in the local economy and refrain from expelling existing inhabitants.[6]

Walzer's analogies of political community with clubs, neighbourhoods and families have received much critical attention, and I will not repeat them here. What I draw attention to is the discrepancy between internal membership decisions, which are subjected to principled constraints, and admissions decisions, in which the present citizens' alleged power of control appears unconditional. What has escaped Walzer's notice here is that commitment to democratic ideals may require subjecting a community's competence on immigration to principled thinking and to the same constitutional constraints that limit the exercise of other political competences.

This discrepancy may be accounted for on the basis of three assumptions which underpin, but are by no means unique to, Walzer's theory. First, membership in a community is taken as 'given', and community is not only assumed (i.e. 'natural') but it is also a value in itself. Because Walzer's conception of community is a cohesive and transparent one, discretionary power at the gate seems essential. The latter ensures the 'filtering of movement', thereby guaranteeing the conformity of new 'applicants' to the shared meanings, values and way of life of the community. Interestingly, Walzer does not question the meaning of membership itself, nor its terms and conditions – albeit the fact that these are subjected to an ongoing redefinition and significantly affects the distribution of membership. This is because abandoning the idea of fixed membership and placing the formal meaning of membership in modern territorial democracies under the normative test would require an approach which transcends the particularistic standpoint to which Walzer is committed. To put it differently, the particularism of 'history, membership and culture' can hardly furnish any strong external principles guiding the distribution of membership, thereby leaving Walzer no other option except to justify the state's discretionary power to admit and exclude.

Second, conceiving community in terms of the nation-state projects boundaries as barriers (stopping points) - not as permeable membranes (meeting points). Freedom of movement internally is seen to depend on some form of external closure: neighbourhoods can take shape as 'indifferent' associations and have open membership only because they are part of the sovereign nation-state with legally enforceable admissions policies, and that in the absence of a larger protective unit neighbourhoods would turn into 'little states' (petty fortresses) (Walzer, 1983: 38–9). Empirical evidence drawn by French municipal councils, however, suggests otherwise. Encouraged by restrictive national immigration policies, French Councils in the 1980s introduced the quota or 'threshold of tolerance' system which denied migrant children education and housing if their number surpassed a certain threshold somewhere between 10 and 30 per cent of the local population (Silverman, 1991: 338). It is also assumed that closure, partial or otherwise, is needed in order to protect the distinctiveness of cultures and groups. To tear down the fortresses would create 'a world of radically deracinated men and women without cohesion' (Walzer, 1983: 39).

The projection of boundaries as barriers contradicts the reality of global systems of communication and the constant perforation of boundaries by messages, cultural images, money and people (Goodin, 1992). There is no reason to suppose that the physical presence of immigrants has a more far-reaching effect in 'eroding the distinctiveness of a culture of a group' than all the above. Moreover, in a world of fluid, overlapping and interwoven cultures, distinctiveness and vitality in cultures and societies is the product of contact, communication, the flow of ideas, cultural exchanges and cultural collisions.

Theorists could still defend cultural interchange to the extent that it does not threaten the survival of a culturally distinct society. Kymlicka (1995), for example, argues that changes in the character of a culture must be the result of the choices of its members, and must not threaten the existence of a culture 'as an intelligible context of choice'.[7] While it is true that individuals' pursuit of worthwhile life plans take place only within a cultural–societal context, Kymlicka fails to show that the narratives and resources needed for making meaningful choices must come from a single, unified, fully constituted and secure cultural matrix. Nor is the congruence between society and culture so unproblematic as Kymlicka himself assumes.

Perspectives which take membership and community as 'given' have not examined whether restrictive immigration policies may compromise democratic ideals by perpetuating fictions of internal homogeneity and promoting nativist narratives of belonging. It has been assumed that polities are empowered to restrict immigration without compromising their internal process of democracy. This brings me to the last, latent, assumption found in Walzer's schema and others: namely, that exclusionary immigration policies have no significant bearing upon the nature of the polity ('the no-effect assumption').

But is it possible to separate the 'outside' from the 'inside'? As already noted, restrictions on family reunification have a detrimental effect on community relations. The way ethnic members are perceived and treated also depends on how immigrants are perceived. Accordingly, immigration cannot be disentangled from its internal ideological or cultural definition; strangers are perceived as a 'threat' for the liberty, welfare or the culture of the host group only in relation to certain ideological conceptions as to what constitutes a member. Immigration is inextricably linked with how political communities respond to diversity itself. Admittedly, one of the most important yardsticks by which to judge the quality of democracy is how the Other is treated. Adherence to supposedly unified, single and homogeneous nation-states or cultural frameworks impairs the cultivation of an ethic of the Other. It precludes a deeper understanding of the 'dynamics of distancing and relating' in contemporary societies – that is, the possibility of togetherness in apartness (the creation of border-transcending communities) and apartness in togetherness (the various forms of diversity existing even within the most supposedly homogeneous group). Immigration may be a 'blessing', precisely because it forces a rethinking of community itself and exposes the artificiality of binary oppositions between 'us' and 'them'.

Walzer concedes that the principle of mutual aid may require political communities to provide aid to necessitous strangers either by admitting those who have no other place to go, or by exporting some of their superfluous wealth without excessive cost to themselves (Walzer, 1983: 44–5, 47–8). But such obligations can easily be overridden by communal fears about the survival of the community. Walzer also mentions two other constraints on states' right to exclude which do not apply to immigration: namely, justice requires states to grant citizenship to all those admitted as residents and participants in the local economy, irrespective of their nationality, and states must not expel existing inhabitants even if they are regarded as aliens by the rest of the population. As far as immigration is concerned, however, the essence of Walzer's argument is that the right to restrict migratory flows derives from the right to collective self-determination. But such a line of reasoning hardly allows for an argument that can override exclusionary policies and ideologically-led action in this area and for putting 'a particular community's understanding of itself' to a critical test.

Critics may object here that the right to democratic self-determination entails the nation's right to preserve its specific political culture. Immigrants should accept the political culture of their new home as it has been interpreted by the majority culture. By confining critical exchanges within the culture of the constitutional state, this argument insulates constitutional principles from the very forces and challenges that could allow them to operate in a more universalist context. After all, a strong democracy needs a strong critique. There is also another reason why one should hesitate to make protection of political culture a ground for imposing 'legitimate' closure. American history has shown that 'distrust and fear of persons with different cultural backgrounds usually finds expression in language emphasising a conflict of values' (Karst, 1989: 29). EC-wide discourses on fundamentalist cultures and the 'inassimilability' of 'Arabs' attest this. But what if admission of non-liberal entrants is likely to endanger liberal democratic institutions? Liberal theorists who favour free movement either as an expression of individual rights or as a vehicle for realising equality of opportunity allow for the imposition of restrictions on the admission of migrants in order to protect the ongoing process of liberal conversation itself (Ackerman, 1980). But as Parekh has observed, it is not entirely clear what Ackerman means by 'liberal conversation' and whether this would exclude people who do not share secular rationalist values but are otherwise law-abiding (Parekh, 1995: 95). In addition, it is not entirely clear why non-liberal non-members would pose a much greater threat to liberal democratic institutions than non-liberal members, thereby justifying substantial differences in their treatment. Because the above protectionist argument is underpinned by the requirement of conformity to an integrated society characterised by a set of clear and incontestable values and the protection of the 'common culture' from unwanted change, it overlooks the fact that commitment to democratic ideals does not merely entail an obligation to preserve democratic achievements. It requires also a reflexive attitude towards these achievements and a commitment to make society better. On that view, only a few committed terrorists and subversives would have to be excluded. In any case, the protectionist argument would never justify the exclusion of individuals as a class. Bearing in mind the scope for ideologically-led action in this area, one should not discount the possibility that the real threat to liberal democratic values may not come from a Muslim migrant whose dream of a better life urges him/her to cross borders, or the presumed cumulative impact of non-liberals on institutions but, instead, from the host society's unreasonable fears of 'being swamped by alien cultures'. After all, arguments about the absorptive or assimilative capacity of a country reveal a way of thinking which unavoidably slips back to essential national identities, unified cultures and communities, fear of difference and change (Chapters 1, 4 and 5).

This is why Carens insists that the threat to liberal institutions must not be a hypothetical possibility; it must be supported by 'evidence and ways of reasoning acceptable to all'. The difficulty in establishing this distinction in reality forces Carens to concede that 'non-ideal theory provides more grounds for restricting immigration than ideal theory' (1987: 259–60).[8] Similarly, Scanlan and Kent (1988: 65) recognise that the moral basis for a restrictive immigration ceiling is problematic. But they also admit that any morally just position has to take into account political constraints.

One such constraint may be the imposition of restrictions on the grounds of public order. Whereas hardly anybody would disagree with Rawlsian-inspired restrictions on immigration for the sake of protecting another important liberty, or to strengthen the overall system of liberties, it is true to say that the public order argument gives authorities wide discretionary power. For this reason, the scope and terms of the public order constraint must be defined strictly. Carens argues that disruptions to public order posed by immigration should not be a hypothetical possibility (1987: 259). But he fails (Carens, 1992) to place the 'serious threat to national security' justification under qualifications, such as: the decision to exclude must be based on the individual conduct of the person concerned; past membership of associations should not in itself be a reason to exclude; previous criminal convictions should not in themselves constitute grounds for refusal of entry and so on. Carens also considers legitimate the exclusion of those 'who come from non-liberal societies even though they have no subversive intent', on the basis of the 'presumed cumulative effect of their presence' on liberal institutions (Carens, 1992: 28–9). But this could serve as a pretext for discriminating against larger groups and, in many respects, contravenes the principle of equal respect by improperly penalising individuals for where they belong, and not for their personal deeds.

Perhaps the most important objection to non-restrictive immigration policies, and which is implicit in the public order argument, is the 'numbers issue': if Europe were to open its borders the number of those coming might overwhelm the capacity to cope, leading to a breakdown of public order. This argument is based on the presumption that most people would not hesitate to move if they could. However, it may be observed here that despite the lifting of internal restrictions to free movement in the Union and the incentives given for intra-EU migration, there has been no mass-scale migration from the poorer Mediterranean countries to the richer North. This suggests that uprooting oneself is not as painless as the above argument suggests. But even if one admitted that admissions applicants are rational actors seeking to maximise their welfare, adherents of the 'numbers argument' would have to demonstrate that: (i) restrictive immigration policies are responses to large-scale migration, and (ii) the nature of immigration policy (i.e. its restrictive or liberal nature) correlates positively with variations in the number of admission applicants.

As regards the former hypothesis, we saw in Chapter 2 that mass-scale immigration did not cause the EU-wide co-ordination of migration policies. As Lu (1999: 3–4) states, 'the mass influx of entrants only became a prominent issue after a number of revolutionary plans for intensive co-operation regarding border control had already been launched' (i.e. circa 1988). In this respect, Lu argues that the inflow of great numbers of arrivals should be viewed as the intervening variable: 'it did not cause the harmonisation to take place, it only contributed to the restrictive nature of the harmonisation' (1999: 29). As regards the latter hypothesis, it may be observed that since sudden increases in the number of asylum applications are period-specific (e.g. the wars in Bosnia and Kosovo) one would expect that European policy-makers would refrain from treating these contingencies as the basic platform upon which to build a general model of immigration policy. Since this has not been the case so far in the Union, we are led to believe that there is something to be gained by identifying the massive influx of immigrants and asylum seekers as a problem to be tackled by tighter immigration controls and asylum legislation – namely, political and electoral capital gain for national executives and an increase in the Union's social legitimacy.

But does the fact that European electorates perceive 'foreigners to be too many' (see *Eurobarometer*, 48, Autumn 1997: 71) render my proposal for a liberal immigration policy impractical? In answering this question, it can be argued that current levels of political support for firm immigration policies are the outcome and not the cause of a restrictive policy regime. Restrictive appeals and negative 'folkloric' representations of immigrants (Freeman, 1995) have been made by the far right as well as mainstream European parties for at least twenty years (Brubaker, 1995: 907) and immigration politics has become chronically populist in a number of West European countries. In this respect, instead of taking public opposition to a more relaxed immigration policy as given, we should view it as a conjunctural feature of a particular discursive regime. As already argued, immigration is entangled in discursive articulations of the dichotomy between 'us' and 'them' and immigration policy-making is essentially a story about changes in the shape and boundaries of these discursive fields (Brubaker, 1995).

And yet it may be objected here that this argument offers little practical guidance as to how open EU immigration policies should be. In other words, how much is 'fair' and why? Answering this question would unavoidably involve an assessment of current immigration levels. But any attempt to identify the 'correct' number is bound to reinforce the view that immigration impacts negatively on society since there must be a threshold point, a 'safety valve' to admissions. In addition, one discerns that debates concerning immigration are caught into the dualism of upholding the state's sovereign prerogative to control admissions and exclude on the one hand and advocating open borders and universal free movement on the other. But the either/or dualism is quite misleading since it forecloses various possibilities for in-between positions. It also reinforces the traditional view of upholding the state's right to exclude since, in the absence of a realistic alternative, theorists are persuaded to turn their attention to the ethics of restricting migratory flows[9] or to articulate standards of decision-making in local contexts that are fair from the perspective of society members only (Adelman et al., 1994). Given that the present European migration regime is about letting a few in, but keeping most out, a principled and non-restrictive immigration policy which circumscribes admissions decisions within definite legal bounds and extends the obligations that polities may have to individuals beyond the confines of national borders would entail a much more generous intake of applicants. That is, the Union should accept, as a matter of official policy, many more people in all categories of admission: family reunification, humanitarian admissions and employment-based migration.

Having discussed the constraints posed by public order and the 'numbers issue' let me now address the thornier question about the possible effect of immigration upon a community's heritage, culture and way of life. Preservation of a community's distinctive way of life is yet another 'legitimate' restriction on immigration conceded by many theorists, including Carens. Cherishing a distinctive way of life, seeking to passing it on to one's children as unchanged as possible are seen as legitimate concerns – a multicultural Japan, for example, would be a very different place (Carens, 1992: 37–8). What is striking in this argument is the monistic and rather oversimplified conception of 'culture' underpinning it.

A closer inspection of the dynamics of any specific culture, however, reveals that cultures are crossed by the most diverse and contradictory currents. There may be 'many Japans' within Japan, in the same way that there are many 'Europes' within Europe. By questioning the 'authoritative' interpretation of Japanese culture, one may unravel the selectiveness of the featured characteristics, and unearth the existence of other, marginalised, accounts of what Japanese culture is or what it should be. In opposition to the idea of monocultural Japan, for instance, one could invoke the image of the fifteenth and sixteenth century Japan shaped by the merchants of Kyoto and of other towns, or the writings of Confucian scholars in order to question the former narrative and ground a different immigration policy.

Arguments that justify legitimate closure in order to preserve a collective identity are also underpinned by a static conception of identity. They tend to locate identity in some existing, inherent attributes of an entity, thereby overlooking the fact that identities (both personal and collective) are complex entities in process. Identities evolve, develop, become negotiated and renegotiated within a context and in response to that context. Events, policies, laws and practices have a significant bearing upon identity formation.

While identities are not possible without processes of differentiation, the way we relate to the Other becomes part of our identity. It defines who we are. Similarly, the kind of immigration policies a polity articulates at time t will bear a significant mark upon both its collective identity and citizens' identities in $t+1$. A law-enforcement and restrictive regime that institutionalises exclusion and discrimination, as the present immigration framework does, cannot but affect citizens' identities negatively. White hegemonic identities are forged in a racist society. Ethnic identities are also forged in such a juridico-political context. By pursuing illiberal admissions policies, polities risk fostering an ugly identity and place democratic achievements in jeopardy.

Membership rules thus convey important messages for the nature and quality of the polity and, in turn, affect perceptions about membership and shape attitudes toward democratic citizenship. Because many problems stem from overreliance upon executive discretion in this field, constitutionalisation of immigration is likely to enhance democratic legitimacy, and the shift of official discourse and policy from law enforcement and control to a liberalisation ethos could help fashion a public ethic of the Other. This is essential for combating racism and xenophobia.

But would a non-restrictive immigration policy clash with other principles, particularly those underpinning the welfare system? Many believe that any redistributive system cannot keep unrestricted access to its benefits; free migration is seen to contradict social citizenship rights (Bauböck, 1992, 1994a, 1995). A major weakness of this social rights–protectionist argument, in its various forms, is that it overlooks the fact that immigrants are not merely poor. Similarly, refugees are not just scarred people and vulnerable dependants. They are people with talents, skills, energy and determination to build a better life and contribute to economic growth. Many migrants are entrepreneurs, ready to start their businesses. And although the effect of immigration on entrepreneurship in the host country has not been the focus of systematic research so far, most studies confirm that migrants are more likely to be self-employed or employers than non-immigrants. In addition, all are consumers creating a greater demand for manufactured goods and investors. As actual or potential participants in socio-economic life, they are entitled to welfare, and trade unions could well be strengthened by taking up their case. True, migrants often have access only to contributory benefits and they risk non-renewal of their permits if they rely on state resources. Borjas admits that immigrants pay more in taxes than they receive in welfare benefits (1990; 1991). Smith and Edmonston (1998), too, consider the economic and fiscal consequences of immigration as net gain for the USA. Overall, it is argued that the contribution immigrants make to the federal budget outweighs the financial burden imposed upon the state and local government in areas that receive large number of immigrants. Similarly, Kurthen (1997) has noted that the public debate in Germany and the USA about the undue cost of immigrants' welfare is not warranted by empirical data. In the light of this, it may be argued that claims concerning alleged non-entitlement seem to rest on the national boundedness of welfare systems, rather than upon principles of redistribution *per se* (but compare Miller, 1993, 1996; Tamir, 1993).

The positive economic contributions made by migrant labour have gone largely unrecognised in Western Europe. Migrants are often accused of drawing more from public funds as recipients of public services (housing, education, social insurance, job training and language courses) than they contribute in taxes. But most studies confirm that both documented and undocumented migrants pay more in taxes than they receive in social security. This is to be expected since the great majority of them are working and do not have elderly parents receiving Social Security. Research conducted by the Rhein-ishe-Westfälische Institute (RWI) in 1991 found that refugees, economic migrants and family members contributed substantially to Germany's affluence: the RWI also calculated an increase in economic growth of between 0.5 per cent and 1.0 per cent per annum which was attributed to the increase in foreign labour (Findlay, 1994: 186, 200–1). Economists also seem to agree that supply of cheap labour not only reduces costs, promotes lower prices, stimulates growth and boosts productivity, but may be crucial to the survival of certain businesses (Simon, 1989).

Other 'undesirable' effects attributed to the use of migrant labour are its alleged effects on wages, labour standards and the employment of domestic labour. Butcher and Card (1991: 292–6), however, have found no statistically significant effect of immigration on the rate of increase of wages for the least skilled workers. Similarly, Dawkins et al. (1992) argue that 'although immigration may cause some decrease in employment and wages among low-skilled non-immigrants, depending very much on the region or industry examined, the effects are small. Immigrants (and illegals) tend towards only weak substitutability or complementarity with non-immigrant groups, with the overall result being essentially benign' (Freeman and Jupp, 1992: 118). It is certainly the case that the non-immigrant job displacement claim is predicated on the incorrect assumption that labour markets are highly homogeneous and that domestic labour can fill all occurring vacancies. However, most markets are highly segmented, meaning that gaps and labour shortages always appear on various levels (i.e. on both lower unskilled and higher skilled) irrespective of the existing levels of unemployment. In fact, unfilled job vacancies can co-exist with high unemployment (Harris, 1996: 172).

Given that fears of job displacement and claims about other migration-related risks tend to be either exaggerated or misperceived, it seems to me that there is no pragmatic reason as to why European polities and the Union should not re-evaluate their immigration policies. After all, a willingness on the part of a political community to put its self-understanding and definition of membership to a normative test, as far as the admission of 'aliens' is concerned, is an integral part of democracy. Considering the profound effects of the current immigration regime upon democratic principles and citizens' identities, a positive commitment to inclusiveness in the Union is thus needed. Immigration should no longer be seen as an anomaly or a threat but, instead, as an opportunity. An opportunity for internal reflection and self-assessment; for rethinking what belonging in community means in European polities and the Union, and whether this is all it ought to be; to acknowledge weaknesses in the implementation of principles and to devise procedures to improve them; to fashion a new democratic political sensibility in the Union which respects the Other and responds positively to their plight. But to what extent does this reasoning also apply to undocumented migration?

Undocumented migration

It is generally assumed that states have very few responsibilities towards unauthorised entrants and residents, and that their decision to exclude or deport undocumented migrants carries the presumption of legality since the persons concerned has no *prima facie* right to be there. However, the line separating legal from illegal immigration is quite thin: both are merely different parts of the same process and, in many respects, a political unit's response to both challenges has a crucial impact upon the principles underpinning it. In addition, restrictive immigration rules and stringent administrative procedures tend to produce more 'illegals'. Moreover, there exist several policy options designed to bring as much undocumented immigration as possible into the legal domain: the adoption of a liberal admissions policy which eases the procedural requirements for obtaining residence permits; legalisation of those who have entered without authorisation; facilitating family reunification; and granting citizenship to children of undocumented migrants who are born in the host country. Although such policies are seen to create incentives for immigrants to avoid the regular channels for legal immigration and employment, it can be plausibly argued that their cumulative pursuit would decrease incentives for irregular entry by increasing the probabilities of success in admission applications. Naturally, this will yield an increase in the level of immigration, but this would be a problem only if one subscribed to the 'immigration control thesis' – that is, if it was accepted that control of undocumented migration aims at the prevention of entry altogether, not of illegal entry.

The construct of illegality in immigration law refers primarily to illegal residents – that is, to persons who have entered surreptitiously or have overstayed the period permitted as visitors or their temporary residence permits (students, temporary workers and trainees and exchange visitors). Illegal employment is connected with undocumented immigration in so far as it functions as a pull factor. Whereas stringent border controls can reduce illegal entry, illegal entry is only one source of illegal residence. The other most important source is overstaying. The latter is not affected by border controls or governmental rhetoric about the need for effective control over the flow of undocumented migrants. However, because perceptions in this area seem to matter more than reality, governments are led to adopt a 'get-tough' and law-enforcement approach against those who 'are seen to make a mockery of the selection system' (Birrell, 1992, cit. in Freeman and Jupp, 1992: 25). This approach relies heavily on the expansion of measures of internal control aiming at identifying illegal residents, detaining them and subsequently deporting them. Measures of internal control entail the stepping up of identity checks, the exclusion of immigrants from social rights, the imposition of an obligation on employers to check the employment eligibility of new hires and imposition of sanctions (criminal and/or administrative) on those who hire unauthorised workers. A typical example of the latter is the Council Recommendation *On harmonising means of combating illegal immigration and illegal employment and improving the relevant means of control* ([1996] OJ C5/1, 22/12/95). This soft law instrument encourages employers to check the residence and work permits of job applicants and they could also be compelled to vet every application with immigration authorities. The Recommendation calls for the imposition of employer sanctions, the creation of a central file on all residence foreign nationals and the 'criminalization' of foreign nationals 'who have deliberately brought about their illegal position'. Along similar lines, the Strategy paper (1998, para. 133) stated that,

> there is a need for a concerted effort to ensure that illegal entrants are consistently and efficiently repatriated and to see if the return of illegal migrants to the country of origin is enforced. This requires a consistent policy on the part of the states of entry as well as their co-operation in carrying out deportations and a comprehensive system of rules on admission and transit both within the European Union and in relation to the applicant countries and to problem states.

This means that 'states with a particularly high potential of illegal emigrants must be induced to set up effective fingerprint files' (para. 69) and that 'an international exchange of date of facilitators, rejected asylum-seekers and illegal immigrants is necessary' (para. 70).

This law-enforcement approach to undocumented migration is underpinned by the doctrine of control and of prevention of migratory flows: by making the conditions in the country of settlement as undesirable as possible recent entrants are induced to go home and prospective entrants are deterred from coming. This assumption, however, reflects more the wishes of politicians than empirical reality.

In addition, it is often argued that undocumented migration exacerbates social tensions by pushing domestic labourers out of labour and by threatening labour standards. But such fears are exaggerated, given that unauthorised migrants engage in economic activities for which there is a scarce supply of domestic labour and, by entering the labour market at lower skill levels, pave the way for domestic labour to ascend to higher-skilled and higher-paying jobs as the economy expands.

Undocumented migration tends to complement existing employment rates. Economists agree that the supply of cheap labour also reduces costs, promotes lower prices, stimulates growth and boosts productive and wages (Findlay, 1994: 185). deWind (1982: 12 cit. in Cohen, 1988: 173) has showed that undocumented migration was crucial to the survival of New York's manufacturing industries which faced stiff competition from cheap imports. In addition, in California, the state where the anti-immigration campaign has reached its climax, the Senate Office of Research (July 1993) reported that the majority of economists (74 per cent) agreed on the overall positive economic effects of undocumented migration (cit. in Lacey, 1993: 20). In this respect, arguments which tend to scapegoat undocumented persons for competing for scarce jobs overlook the structural conditions of undocumented migration – that is, the high demand for low-skilled, flexible and wage-competitive labour in agriculture, construction, the tourist industry, domestic services and in secondary labour markets dominated by small firms.

The 'immigration as a threat to labour standards' argument underscores that undocumented migrants are very vulnerable to exploitation; they are forced to work more hours for less pay and without social security in establishments that often harbour security risks. They are unable to achieve protection of their rights through legitimate channels without risking discovery and subsequent deportation. Provision of legal services independently of immigration status may be a solution, but possible imposition of a legal obligation on these agencies to relinquish information concerning their clients to immigration services will weaken rights' protection.

Whereas few would object to the combating of the smuggling of undocumented migrants in the Union and their recruitment as cheap labour, law-enforcement policies aimed at reducing the size of the resident undocumented population (i.e. overstayers) carry important costs. Detection, detention and removal of overstayers tends to reinforce ascriptive definitions of membership and to undermine democratic commitments. Indeed, the insertion of undocumented migrants into the social fabric of a community owing their economic engagement and/or familial obligations calls for a shift of approach from a model of governmental restraint to a participation model. If a migration system does not have the necessary flexibility to do this, then the destruction of the various webs of social interaction and the shattering of expectations may well increase the power of the state, but it will impact negatively on democratic principles. As argued above, democracy does not necessarily pressupose nationality as the qualifying criterion for participation in the decision-making process, and individuals' interests as homeowners, parents, employees, tax-payers, neighbours, local participants and consumers do not differ fundamentally in accordance with their 'citizen', 'resident alien' or 'undocumented alien' status. More importantly, such policies undermine the dignity of undocumented migrants by making them objects of policy and of governmental power against which they have very little protection since their illegal status prevents them from voicing claims as to how they should be treated. Instead of fostering an apprenticeship of democracy, apprehension and removal of undocumented migrants after entry thus sends signals to the public that these people are undesirable, thereby fuelling intolerance and xenophobia.

An unintended (albeit foreseen) consequence of the expansion of internal control measures aiming at identifying overstayers is that they may lead to an increase in racial discrimination. The police is equipped with a 'probable cause' for stopping and searching individuals without distinction. Similarly, worksite enforcement and employer sanctions have been found to lead to widespread discrimination against members of ethnic minority groups (Bean and Fix, 1992, cit. in Freeman and Jupp, 1992: 47–8). Employers tend to comply with such legal provisions by hiring only persons born in the country – or, worse still, by not hiring persons because of their appearance or accent. This cost is compounded by the fact that data on the impact of employer sanctions on undocumented flows shows that sanctions do not have a lasting effect in reducing undocumented immigration. Limiting the eligibility of undocumented aliens for any publicly funded assistance except those available on emergency basis, on the other hand, can also lead to the diminution of the long-term lawfully resident aliens' access to welfare benefits.[10]

All this suggests that prevention of illegal entry is more sensible than apprehension after entry. But whereas under the present security paradigm prevention of illegal entry is associated with better and firmer control and management of borders, increased inspections of border-crossers and 'operations to hold the line', a desecuritised approach would seek to prevent illegal entry by facilitating legal entry and by making boundaries more porous. A distinct advantage of the latter approach is that it refuses to subjugate critical moral and legal principles and humanitarian concerns to ideological construals of national interest and ascriptive conceptions of membership. In addition, it recognises that the struggle to affirm the rights of migrants and to change the ways in which they are perceived in the Union is intimately connected with the struggle to realise the ideals of the European project. In this respect, the real question and biggest challenge on immigration agendas is not so much whether an alternative approach is needed in the Union, but whether it is required by the universalist norms underpinning both the European Union's legal order and the Member States' constitutional traditions.

An alternative framework for a European migration policy

A point of departure for an alternative framework for European migration policy would be the transfer of migration-related issues into the full competence of the Community. This would involve decision-making by co-decision and the exercise of full judicial supervision by the ECJ. The transfer would have to be accompanied by the 'desecuritisation' of immigration, that is, its removal from the conceptual realm of security and sovereignty and its designation as a 'normal' issue to be dealt with through political processes (Wæver et al., 1993: 8; Wæver et al., 1998).

A Charter on European migration and refugee policy containing the basic principles and the main objectives of a common migration policy could be drawn up and adopted either as a trilateral institutional agreement concluded by the Parliament, the Commission and the Council or through Treaty amendment. An advantage of ad hoc interinstitutional negotiations is that the cumbersome process of Treaty amendment is avoided. Although such negotiations do not normally result in a legally binding document (i.e. a 'soft law' Inter-Institutional Agreement (IIA)), the Charter could, nonetheless, be more than a simple political declaration if it created an obligation on the part of Community institutions to translate these political commitments into 'hard' legal obligations. At a later stage, the content of the Charter could be transposed into primary Community law though Treaty amendment - even though it is always possible that the ECJ might wish to accord its 'soft law' version binding legal effect.

Bringing the various strands of the argument presented so far together, the charter would be underpinned by the following considerations:

- Immigration is a long-standing phenomenon which must be understood with reference to its *structural causes and its global character*. This necessitates transfrontier co-operation and intra-EU partnership arrangements among the Union, national political units and subnational units, be they local and regional government, NGOs and churches.
- All the Member States are *de facto* countries of immigration and, as such, they should create the right conditions for the respectful symbiosis of all residents (Chapter 6) and the promotion of cultural diversity as a *factor for enrichment*, and not as a problem or a factor for division.
- Policy responses to migration flows mirror the *political and cultural values* of a society and, in turn, impact upon *democratic values*.
- European migration policy must observe *human rights standards and international law norms*.

- The decision to immigrate has a huge impact on the life of an individual and the motives behind it are wide-ranging. Migrants are not merely sellers of their labour power moving from country A to country B. What is thus needed is a *multidimensional view* which affirms the potentialities of the human spirit by viewing migrants as creative beings, endowed with skills, knowledge, experience, organisational competences, personal virtues and courage, and takes into account their position of vulnerability in the state of residence or employment.
- Irregular immigration is an *economic and human reality*. While efforts should be made to combat trafficking in human beings, the Member States should be encouraged to prevent clandestine movements by relaxing the doctrine of control and by facilitating legal entry and residence. The fact that an individual has evaded immigration control is not *per se* a sufficient ground for removal, and his/her rights to private and family life set out in Article 8 (2) of the ECHR must be respected;
- Appropriate action must be taken against the dissemination of misleading information about immigration and socio–political consequences, and to combat *racism and xenophobia*.

In more specific terms, the Charter would spell out the Union's/Member States' duty to allow the entry, residence and employment of migrant workers into their territory. Entry-clearance requirements could be waived for both short-term visitors (i.e. tourists, short-term business travellers, researchers and representatives of cultural life) and mid-/long-term migrants without discrimination as to the country of origin.[11] Alternatively, there should be a clear obligation on the part of authorities to issue visas to admission applicants within a reasonable time.

The charter would stipulate that a person may be refused admission on the grounds of inadequate travel documents and, in the case of non-active economic actors, because s/he lacks sufficient funds to provide for the stay (compare Chapters 3 and 5). However, applicants must have a right of appeal against a refusal to issue entry clearance. An entry or stay prohibition may also be ordered against a non-member who has been deported from the territory because s/he is involved in activities contrary to the constitution, or s/he is a member of a terrorist organisation, or an agent, member of organisations dealing illegally with arms, explosives, drug-trafficking, or assists the illegal production of materials and equipment for mass destruction, or engages in the smuggling of people or s/he is a government official convicted of human rights' violations.

The Charter would also affirm the migrants workers' right to liberty and security of a person. Any verification of the identity of their family members by law-enforcement officials should be carried out in accordance with procedures established by law, and not by using techniques pertaining to serious criminal investigations. The Member States should facilitate the admission of family members of third-country nationals residing in the Union (i.e. spouses, descendants and relatives in the ascending line who live with the worker: C-179/98 *Belgian State v Fatna Mesbah*, Judgement of the Court 11 November 1999) and should refrain from intruding into the private life of the parties (in order to test the genuineness of the marriage or parenthood). Provision could also be made for the conferral of legal status on spouses independently of that of the breadwinner after a probationary year (i.e. independent residence rights). Members of the family should also have the right to engage in gainful activities.

.Migrant workers and their families should have the right to equality before the law and of equal protection of the law. This entails, among other things, a right of appeal and procedural safeguards against expulsion decisions taken on the grounds of public security or public order. Mid- and long-term residents should not be liable to expulsion (save in very exceptional circumstances), and deportation decisions should conform to international obligations concerning the protection of private and family life. Expulsion decisions should be communicated to the person concerned in writing and should state the reasons for the taking of such a decision. The person concerned should have the right to have his/her case reviewed before a competent authority and pending such a review, the person should have the right to remain in the territory. If a decision of expulsion that has already been executed is subsequently annulled, the person concerned should have the right to seek compensation according to law and the earlier decision should not be used to prevent him/her from re-entering the state concerned. Migrant workers should also have the same rights and duties as the rest of the population. As argued above, social benefits, medical assistance, work permits, political rights and eventually citizenship are guaranteed consequences of domicile. Finally, the Member States should encourage intercultural dialogue, rebuild the bonds of solidarity which have been damaged by years of negative portrayal of immigrants and promote mutual respect and understanding among all persons living in the territory of the Union.

Furthermore, the charter would enshrine the Union's commitment to protect *de jure* refugees, *de facto* refugees and persons deserting from combat. Broadening the definition of 'refugee' to include political refugees (according to the UN Geneva Convention on the status of Refugees, 28 July 1951) and those fleeing for other reasons, such as internal conflicts, aggression, occupation, generalised violence, natural disasters and other events seriously disturbing public order, will solve the problems surrounding the distinction between *de jure* and *de facto* refugees. In addition, given the variation in asylum determination procedures in the various Member States, the charter would set out the basic principles underlying the development of an effective and fair refugee-determination process which is consistent with international commitments and respects human dignity. Such a framework would provide any asylum seeker with an equal chance of being recognised as a refugee irrespective of the Member State in which the claim was submitted.[12] This requires official recognition of basic standards in asylum procedures, such as giving asylum seekers and refugees automatic and unfettered access to a procedure for examining his/her request for refugee status or for other form of protection; the right to a fair hearing during the initial admissibility procedure and during the subsequent examination of the asylum application by the relevant authority; the right to appeal against a negative decision which must have suspensive effect (i.e. the applicant shall not be expelled before hearing the outcome of the appeal), and respect for the principle of non-refoulement. The implementation of these principles would prompt a rethinking of carrier sanctions (except in cases of serious negligence which could constitute assisting illegal immigration, having regard to Standard 3.36 of Annex 9 of the Chicago Treaty of 1944 on international aviation). It also presupposes the existence of a clearly identifiable authority endowed with the responsibility for examining requests for refugee status which would hear and determine refugee claims in accordance with the law and in a manner that meets the standards of international protection (i.e. decisions should not be made by border officials; applicants have the right to full participation in the hearing, to be represented by counsel and to the services of an interpreter, if necessary). Decisions concerning refugee status should be made on the basis of the individual circumstances of the person concerned and independently of any other consideration (including domestic political pressures and foreign policy). Decisions should be communicated to the applicants in writing and should state the grounds for a negative decision and the appeal procedure available to them. Rejection of an asylum request may be the likely outcome in cases where the claimant has been convicted of serious crimes in the Union or abroad and is considered to be a threat to public order, or where he or she is found to be a terrorist or subversive war criminal or a senior government official engaged in gross human rights violations. However, asylum applications should not be rejected as inadmissible or 'manifestly unfounded' on the sole ground that asylum seekers have travelled via a safe third country or come from a safe country of origin without an examination of the substantive merits of the asylum claim, and an objective assessment of a country's risk factor for the applicant concerned: the number of asylum seekers from a particular country during the previous year is not a reliable indicator of a country's risk factor. In addition, clear, common criteria for identifying 'safe countries of origin' should be formulated. The wishes of refugees in the choice of their preferred country of asylum should be respected, and special consideration should be given to the needs of unaccompanied children. Family reunification must be facilitated for all categories accepted for asylum or residence on humanitarian grounds. Finally, there must be provision for policies of reception which guarantee the liberty, safety and health of asylum seekers in partnership with local authorities and NGOs involved in refugee work and foster their integration in the host countries.

This list of principles is not meant to be exhaustive. The European Parliament and other bodies, such as UNHCR, Amnesty International and other NGOs have made policy recommendations in the past, and their input in the process of drafting the charter would certainly improve the design of immigration and asylum policy. The crux of my argument is that the articulation of a legally binding, constitutional framework for immigration would free immigration from the whims and prejudices of transient majorities, and promote a fairer understanding of migration movements.

A new institution called 'European Committee on Immigration and Asylum Affairs', consisting of representatives of the Parliament, the judiciary, migrant communities and NGOs, in conjunction with the Council of Ministers, would be in a position to propose amendments, give opinions to the Commission and provide feedback concerning the administration of the relevant agreements. The role of national parliaments could also be enhanced by bridging national and Community agendas on immigration, setting up Immigration Boards and linking them institutionally with the Parliament and strengthening the accountability of national ministers and civil servants. European committees could scrutinise and debate all substantial Community proposals, and 'summon national ministers, national civil servants and Commission members and staff to give evidence' (Williams, 1990: 315–17).

Municipalities wishing to revitalise their drained agricultural sector or their declining industrial plants, could put forward proposals to Immigration Boards concerning settlement and accommodation of immigrants. Ethnic communities, having special ethnic, religious or cultural ties with prospective newcomers, could also have a say in the immigration process and facilitate the admission of such persons. Similar initiatives could be taken up by interest groups, the Church, or even ad hoc relief committees with or without an established inter-European or international network, which possesses funds and has the organising capacity of accommodating and supporting migrants and refugees.

Such a multivocal design of immigration policy has a twofold attraction. First, it gives a fair chance to all those legitimately affected by admissions policies to have a say and influence the design of such policies. Second, it is likely to yield a more positive approach to immigration, measured in human rights' fulfilment and more liberal admission policies. This is because checks and balances could be provided among the units involved, thereby ensuring the constitutional compatibility of their acts with the guidelines set at the European level. Institutional guarantees could also be provided at the national level in order to block exclusionary policies and decisions taken by subnational units. Judicial review of local official acts would hinder abuses of authority by local politicians and administrators. This would alleviate fears that greater involvement of subnational political units might actually yield more restrictive admissions policies.

True, NGOs and voluntary associations, organised on a local, ethnic or religious basis, have proven to be more eager than politicians and administrative officials to ensure protection of migrants and refugees, to raise awareness about particular situations and to implement assistance programmes. One may recall the initiatives taken by the Jewish community in Britain in 1933 in order to secure refuge, settlement, accommodation and employment for Jewish people fleeing Nazi Germany, despite the government's invocation of the powers under the 1905 Aliens Act in order to 'protect this country from the undesirable flux' of Jewish people (Dummett and Nicol, 1990: 155). Church groups in England and the Society of Friends had also established similar funds. Generally speaking, churches have been particularly active in welcoming migrants and refugees, providing effective assistance, resettlement and training, as well as in building bridges between communities of newcomers and established communities (Ferris, 1993).

The sharing of responsibility over immigration and its constitutionalisation would act as an important counterbalance to the 'fortress logic' and the 'invasion syndrome' which lie at the heart of the present regime. By undercutting the logic of securitisation of migration and the potential for ideologically-led action to immigration, the proposed immigration design complements the conception of 'political community' as a community of concern and engagement which underpins constructive citizenship and furnishes a vision of a more relaxed and inclusive democratic community in the European Union.

Notes

1 See the 1951 Convention Relating to the Status of Refugees (189 UNTS 2545) and the 1967 Protocol on the Convention Definition (606 UNTS 8791).
2 The terms are taken from Fuller (1964).
3 As Kate Hoey, MP, Parliamentary Under-Secretary of State at the Home Office submitted to the Select Committee on European Communities (Seventh Report) 'systematic controls at the frontiers of the United Kingdom are important not only for immigration control purposes, but also to help with law enforcement (Q 327) <http://www.publications.parliament.uk/pa/Id199899/Idselct/Ideucom/37/3702.htm>.
4 Similarly, the creation of an area of 'justice' is underpinned by the ambition to create a European judicial area from which Union citizens could derive benefits, particularly with respect to access to justice and the reinforcement of judicial co-operation in civil matters.
5 The idea of 'root causes' emerged in early 1980s in the context of refugee flows. In the EU context, the idea was adopted circa 1989. Although the need for political involvement and for action to address the causes which force people to leave is a worthwhile goal, its instrumental deployment in the context of migration policy is reactive. This is because action to tackle the root causes does not stem from a sustained commitment to international distributive justice, to peace and democracy. Rather, it is used in order to keep 'foreigners out'. Hathaway (1995), Harvey (1998) and others have pointed out that the rationale for the new-found concern for the enforcement of human rights is the desire on the part of states to

restrict the numbers of asylum seekers coming to Europe. In this respect, Harvey (1998: 579) argues that 'there has been a paradigm shift in international refugee law away from the "exilic bias" and towards root causes'.

6 It is noteworthy here that European football clubs cannot restrict the number of foreign players in their teams: nationality clauses contravene the rights to free movement and establishment (Case C-415/93 *ASBL v Bosman* [1996] 1 CMLR 645).

7 For a critique of Kymlicka's thesis, see Leniham (1991); Waldron (1992).

8 Compare, however, Carens' (1992: 36–40) argument. Bauböck (1994a: 318) defends the right to migrate for refugees and close family members.

9 See Carens' contribution in Hailbronner et al. (1997).

10 Possible replication of the Californian Proposition 187 in the Union – that is, withdrawing schooling and non-emergency health care (including prenatal and postnatal services) to those who cannot prove their legal status – would be an affront to critical moral principles and human rights' norms. It is important not to deprive undocumented migrants and their children who would most probably 'become legal residents and citizens of such social rights as access to basic health services and education which favour future integration': Zincone (1997: 133).

11 For a critique of the unfair imposition of mandatory entry-clearance requirements on nationals of developing countries, see Guild (1994: 242).

12 Amnesty International, *Europe: The Need for Minimum Standards in Asylum Procedures*, June 1994, EU ASS/01/94.

7

European identity in praxis: from the land ethic to an ethic of dwelling

The story I have told so far has focused on the institutional construction of a civic and inclusive European identity. My proposals for institutional change in the fields of citizenship and immigration drew on the untapped potential of these institutions in order to sketch a normative path for the European Union in the new millennium. In particular, attention was paid to the ideas and policies that are required for the construction of a democratic polity in the Union.

Concerned with turning these ideas and proposals for institutional change into practical reality, I shall shift the focus of the discussion here to the individual and the process of her constitution as a political and ethical subject in an environment marked by institutional change. In other words, this chapter examines the mutually constitutive relationship between institutional reform and the construction of political selves.

Generally speaking, institutional reforms shape human behaviour not only by establishing inflexible legal duties, but also through their meaning-generating power – that is, by changing the way we think about things and by providing new resources for the formation of political subjectivities. But in order for new institutional designs to precipitate changes in human consciousness and stir processes of value change and cultural shifts, individuals must be willing to revise and reconstruct their understanding of, and relationship with, the social world, and to capitalise on new opportunities for civic engagement.

Instead of treating individuals as passive recipients of change and subsuming them into abstract categories, such as 'the Europeans' or 'the public', the discussion which follows places the responsibility for the realisation of the constructivist mode of European identity in the lap of individuals, too. Responsibility implies willingness to reflect critically on the status quo (Chapters 1 and 5), readiness to question dominant narratives (Chapters 5 and 6), and a desire to use whatever opportunities are available in political life in order to give an ethical response to the question of how to live humanely and democratically with others. European identity is thus no longer thought of exclusively in terms of policy orientations, institutional designs and routinised practices, but it becomes an imperative to live up to deeper socio-political and moral values.

The rationale behind this shift of attention from institutions to individual participants has a twofold justification. First, my argument would be incomplete if I did not consider the conditions for the success of the institutional reforms suggested in this book. What does the empirical implementation of constructive citizenship require in order to succeed? How can these changes take root in everyday practice and survive over a period of time in the face of deep-seated feelings about national history and of persisting national identities? After all, structural changes can take root only if they resonate among the population: they must relate to the internal culture of the polity or create a system of signification that belongs to the collective experience of the resident population. Such a system of signification will not merely constrain individuals to act in a manner which, albeit inconsistent with their attitudes, is consistent with critical moral principles, but it will also make theses attitudes gradually change to come into line with their behaviour. Hence, it will transform subjectivities. But in order to succeed, the new narrative must induce the readjustment of the individuals' cognitive structures and to provide answers to their living needs. In earlier discussions, we saw that a standard criticism of both constitutional patriotism and of the constructivist mode of identity is that they are too 'thin' to generate a community of shared identity at the European level. In contrast, national identities remain strong because they are rooted in existing historical cultures, conjure memories and respond to the psychological needs of individuals by promising immortality and salvation. Although I have criticised this argument for assuming that a political order that cannot command personal sacrifice is either short-lived or illegitimate, I have also conceded that the formation of a European identity in praxis may need narratives and operative myths that respond to the individuals' existential needs (pp. 36–7 above).

In this respect, my second aim is to articulate a democratic discourse of belonging which is capable of inducing ethical conduct and responding to individuals' living needs by creating the right conditions for a philosophical and critical relation to reality. Such a democratic narrative of belonging is vital to the realisation of constructive citizenship and the development of a responsive community of action in the Union. Before articulating this alternative vision, however, it is important to look closely at the narratives through which political subjectivities are actually produced and to describe honestly the difficulties that a constructivist European identity may encounter in praxis.

The land ethic

Territorial sovereignty and exclusive land ownership
Although we are anchored in space and our sense of place is essential to our self-development, we tend to forget that space and place are saturated with

content and meaning. We often view space as a container, an empty framework within which we move, act and interact and experience events. But as soon as events disrupt the everyday routine, the complex logic involved in the use of territory begins to unfold. Fences, walls and 'no-trespass' signs show the extent to which territory can be used to restrain, to separate and to exclude. As Sack (1986, p. 2) shows, territoriality is intimately related to how people use the land, how they organise themselves in space, and how they give meaning to place.

Whereas all forms of human organisation, be they in the form of tribe, *polis*, empire, medieval city or state, have had spatial dimensions, the privileging of the idea of fixed and exclusive territoriality is associated with the rise of the modern nation-state. Unlike the 'parcelised' and personalised authority of the feudal world, the modern system of political rule 'differentiated its subject collectivity into territorially defined, fixed and mutually exclusive enclaves of legitimate dominion' (Tilly, 1990; Ruggie, 1993: 149–51; Spruyt, 1994). Geographical space became demarcated and divided. More importantly, control over a bounded territory over which the state's jurisdiction extended became an inherent quality of statehood. Territoriality has thus been invested with political meaning owing to its association with statehood and sovereignty (territorial sovereignty).[1] This shows that far from being a neutral or an innocent concept, territoriality is a concept filled with power. It is both a means of exercising state power and a means of defining the object of that power, that is to say, 'the people', the members of a bounded community.

The legitimation and consolidation of modern states relied on the uniting of the people within a spatially delimited political framework. This was achieved through: (i) the 'territorialisation' of the ties identifying a collectivity to which certain metaphysical claims to 'immortality' are assigned, and (ii) the use of firm boundary lines in order to mould human behaviour by controlling access to a given territory. Statism has been underpinned by a boundary-obsessed territorialism which projects boundaries as barriers (see Chapters 1 and 6). In addition, it has transformed communities into 'bodies' firmly rooted in space and allegedly immutable in time. By making the motherland or fatherland an object of political devotion (Pizzorno, 1987: 52), states have given an ultimate identity to their members and made territory a source of authority.

Territoriality usually takes two forms: political territories and private ownership of land. Although these forms seem distinct, territorial sovereignty is in reality conceptually linked with private property ownership (Beitz, 1979; Schuck, 1984; Whelan, 1988). The connection between sovereignty (*imperium*) and property ownership (*dominium*) has feudal origins. Although Roman law distinguished between sovereignty (i.e. political rule over individuals) and property ownership (i.e. individual rule over things), early Teutonic law (i.e. the law of the Anglo-Saxons, Franks, Visigoths, Lombards and

other tribes) did not recognise such a distinction. In feudal law ownership of
the land and political sovereignty were inseparable. This comes as no surprise
bearing in mind that all property was thought of belonging to the Prince. The
'state long continued to be the prince's estate, so that even in the 18th
century the Prince of Hesse could sell his subjects as soldiers to the King of
England' (Cohen, 1978: 156). The conceptual overlap between political
authority and property ownership (i.e. between *imperium* and *dominium*)
can be discerned in the medieval usage of the term '*dominium*': *dominium*
signals political rule as well as property ownership (Whelan, 1988: 73). In his
A Defence of the Catholic and Apostolic Faith, for instance, Suárez states that
the Pope has the power to 'remove a prince, deprive him of his dominion in
order to prevent him from harming his subjects, and absolve his subjects from
their oaths of allegiance' (I: 286–7, cit. in Skinner, 1978: 180). In addition,
unlike the Roman conception of private property, medieval legal and political theory did not entail an absolute and exclusive conception of ownership:
property belonged to the King, but he could grant limited and conditional
rights to his vassals. In this respect, the feudal theory of dominion recognised
a conditional right to use property (Schlatter, 1951: 64, 75).

As regards the connection between land tenure (land) and personal
homage (loyalty), the medieval rule was that birthplace determined the contract of subjecthood. Every person born on landlord's land was the landlord's
subject and owed allegiance to him, that is, fidelity and obedience. Landlords
held their land from the King, owed 'fealty' and paid homage to the King.
The King was the supreme feudal lord; all the rest were his '*fideles*', his faithful (Salmond, 1902: 48–50). By the end of the thirteenth century, the
primacy of birthplace in determining who was the King's subject had become
established (Dummett and Nicol, 1990: 24). Birth in the King's 'ligeance'
made someone a subject. 'Ligeance' had the meaning of allegiance and of
a geographical tract. Natural subjects owed permanent and personal
allegiance, while alien subjects coming from friend countries owed 'local'
allegiance to the king so long as they were within his jurisdiction (Salmond,
1902: 50). Although aliens had the same obligations as natural subjects, they
had the ability to terminate the bond of allegiance and free themselves from
the fealty owed to the sovereign lord. In sum, given the privileged position
that land law had in the feudal legal order, it is not surprising that subjecthood was defined in terms of ideas and principles associated with land law
(Dummett and Nicol, 1990: 30).

At the close of the Middle Ages, the Roman conception of absolute and
exclusive private property began to gain prominence over the feudal theory
of dominion. The eventual triumph of the 'Roman pagan conception of
absolute property' is being marked, according to Figgis (1921: 99), by the
inception of Roman Law in Germany in 1495. The development of modern
ideas about private property, which formed the intellectual linchpin of capitalism, brought about the conceptual separation of political authority from

ownership. In Bodin's theory of sovereignty, for example, the dictum 'all to be the Prince's' referred only to the sovereign's absolute authority (*imperium*) only. This is because 'even in the most absolute monarchy ... the property and possession of every man's things must still be reserved to himself' (Bodin, 1962: 110). Although the collapse of the feudal concept of dominion made it possible to think of property apart from political authority and, thus, to distinguish between power relationships derived from property ownership and those derived from the political authority of the state (Schlatter, 1951: 76), the connection between the two did not fade away. After all, private property implies some measure of sovereign power since private owners have the right to exclude others from the benefit or use of something. Dominion over things is also *imperium* over our fellow human beings (Cohen, 1978: 159).

Like private property, state ownership of land entails a corporate right to exclude others from the use or benefit of state-owned land. Accordingly, the doctrine of national sovereignty refers to both 'supreme jurisdiction' over all persons and things residing within a demarcated territory, and to a sense of 'public ownership' of the national territory (i.e. territorial sovereignty). Theorists of the modern state, such as Vattel, have argued that both sovereignty and ownership of the country are retained by the sovereign nation as a whole which is politically embodied by the state (Whelan, 1988: 74–5). According to Vattel, the nation has public or 'supreme ownership' of the national territory or country: it possesses the collective right to use, enjoy it and even to exclude aliens. Indeed, the sovereign state's right to deny entry to 'undesirable' aliens is derived from the nation's 'right of ownership' (Vattel, II. 100, cit. in Whelan, 1988: 75). The survival of the connection between political authority and the idea of collective ownership of land into the modern era explains why exclusiveness seems to be logically entailed by the concept of territorial sovereignty. In the subsequent section I examine how community and territory have become synonymous in popular consciousness and how the formation of political selves has been shaped by the belief that territory 'houses' and binds a cohesive social entity.

Territoriality and the nationality principle
Whereas exclusive ownership of a certain territory underpins the principle of territorial sovereignty, the boundary-obsessed territorialism characterising statehood could be sustained only by making territory part of the nationalistic ideal. Boundaries and the composition of the population had to be aligned, and fixed territorial lines placed limits to people's identifications. Although territory has always been part of the national iconography, the process of state-building reinscribed nationhood in territorial terms and inspired rituals of enmity for outsiders. Indeed, prior to the modern reality of fixed and bounded spaces, religion – not territory – was the main organising principle; religion shaped the ties and defined the boundaries of the

universal community of Christendom. Modern statehood replaced the community of believers with a territorial collectivity to which redemptive ends were assigned, and the territorial state succeeded the church in performing the following functions:

- to provide ontological security by reconciling universality (the social whole, a community which is allegedly immutable in time and fixed in space) and particularity (individuals facing oblivion and death);
- to assign ultimate ends and purposes to the territorial collectivity;
- to lend a sovereign identity to its subjects and to command allegiance;
- to define the enemy: the enemy was no longer the infidel or heretic but the invader or the subversive (Pizzorno, 1987: 38–9, 48).

As Pizzorno (1987: 32) has stated, 'modern politics is essentially a process not of secularisation of values – at least as a prime motor, but of territorialisation of the binding ties'. This was achieved through the erection of boundaries which partitioned nations. Only in settler nations and along the Atlantic coast there was no need to redraw political boundaries (Gellner, 1994). In Central and Eastern Europe, however, the crucial test was to make boundaries and the composition of population coincide. Territoriality was used in the process of the restructuring of socio-spatial relationships and partook of the process of redefinition of nationhood in ways that accommodated the reality of fragmented and wounded nations. In such cases, nationhood became reinscribed in narrower territorial terms, and territory and community were made to coincide by strategies of assimilation of a culturally heterogeneous population and/or by population transfers. The articulation of territoriality with nationhood functioned as a strategy of compensation: a strategy of administration of the 'loss'of territories and portions of the nation. In other cases, nationhood became entangled with expansionist dreams of assembling the various national *irridenta* into a national state. Since territory was given a much more prominent role in defining nationhood, territorial integrity became an important element of the nationalist ideology which portrayed the military as the defender of the nation's ownership of land.

The rise of imperialism in the final quarter of the nineteenth century contradicted the territorial state ideal, thereby prompting a rearticulation of the link between territoriality and the nationality principle. As Bassin has pointed out, 'the notion of the body politic as a sovereign people occupying its own national territory was violated by the formal colonial annexation and incorporation of totally foreign lands and peoples' (Bassin, 1987: 474–7). As a consequence, new discursive articulations emerged which were better suited to the realities of the imperialist age. The German geopolitical discourse of *Lebensraum* is a good case in point, because it shows that territory and space are invested with political meaning as they become associated with strategies of power and military expansionism.

The term '*Lebensraum*' originates in Friedrich Ratzel's political geography, but it gained currency through Karl Haushofer's *Westpolik von Heute* and *Zeitschrift für Geopolitik*. Ratzel's primary concern was to furnish a scientific framework of political geography modelled on the basis of the laws of the non-human organic world (Bassin, 1987: 477–85). Accordingly, he conceptualised the state as an aggregate organism, consisting of homogeneous and spatially coalesced populations of individuals which drew sustenance from a certain amount of territory. Territory was the organism's living space (*Lebensraum*). Aggregate organisms need greater space in order to meet the needs of their increasing population. Failure to expand through the acquisition of new lands results in exhaustion of their sustenance base and decline (Ratzel, 1899 [1923], I, 72, cit. in Bassin, 1987: 178). According to Ratzel, greater space (i.e. the principle of *Grossraum*) guaranteed prosperity and higher levels of cultural development. This reference to culture is significant, for 'people rooted into earth' were seen as having higher cultural standards. In contrast, nomadic people were seen as having a 'weak' organic bond with space and thus lower cultural standards. Although Ratzel's association of space with 'organic communities' did not have racial connotations, national socialism appropriated Ratzel's theory of biological expansionism and linked it to racialism. Ratzel's idea of struggle for space was translated into a struggle for racial survival and space – the dwelling place of the racial community – became the surface of inscription of the will of the racial *Volk*. The subjugation of space to the will of the racial *Volk* imbued space with a dynamic character: it was capable of growth and possessed a unique energy that was released only through the historically destined strivings of the racial *Volk*. Rootedness of the *Volk* into the soil was thus the metaphysical rock and the cultural landscape the medium from which the racial *Volk* derived its energies.

All this suggests that territory is filled with ideologies (Lefebvre, 1976: 31) which provide the crucial resources through which both 'selfhood' and 'otherness' are being constructed. This is not to deny that space furnishes the presuppositional dimensions within which political life evolves and human interaction takes place. Rather, it suggests that the spatial is both constitutive of and constituted by the socio-political. As such, it is both enabling and constraining. In earlier discussions we saw that behind claims concerning the innocent spatiality of national life and the state's sovereign prerogative of protecting the national territory were specific assumptions about the nature and formation of political communities and strategies of power and control. Because 'territoriality is a historically sensitive use of space, especially since it is socially constructed and depends on who is controlling whom and why (Sack, 1986: 3), a different way of thinking about territoriality, centred upon the idea that space is there to be inhabited (i.e. dwelling space), may help foster a new democratic sensibility and contribute to the realisation of the constructivist mode of European identity in praxis. This issue is addressed below.

Dwelling, boundaries and belonging: Heideggerian insights

Space is neither objective (i.e. physical space) nor subjective (i.e. a category projected by a transcendental subject): it is, instead, relational. To put it differently, spaces open up by virtue of our engagement with things and/or of our interaction with persons. Space is thus a composite of various acts and states of connection; it is occasioned by and materialises in the process of establishing connections and interactions. This applies to both physical space and non-spatial spaces (i.e. cyberspace). This dual reference to territorial and non-territorial spaces is important for European governance in that it draws attention to the 'network quality of the EU': the complex system of inter-meshing, overlapping and functionally differentiated networks of relation-ships and exchanges (Ladeur, 1997). As such, it goes beyond the territorial logic underpinning the 'multi-level polity' concept (Diez, 1999). Space in the EU context is thus marked by multiplicity, and not singularity; it is also a-centric (i.e. non-hierarchical) and differential.

As far as physical space is concerned, we invariably think of space as an object and a noun (i.e. as a thing or as an emptiable framework). But according to Heidegger, space is a relation between *Dasein* and the things of *Dasein*'s concern (things ready-to-hand). *Dasein* is in a position to encounter concernfully those things ready to hand (the 'round about us': Heidegger, 1967: 136) because it is thrown into the world.[2] This *a priori* location enables *Dasein*'s involvement with things ready to hand (the equipment). In this sense, space also forms the presuppositional framework within which *Dasein*'s spatiality evolves (Sefler, 1973: 246–8).

What occasions the opening up of space as the public field of presence, in which things can be encountered as present and be experienced in different degrees of accessibility (i.e. as near or remote), is *Dasein*'s concern or care. Heidegger argues that care is manifested in two ways. As an ontic experience, care is manifested in *Dasein*'s pragmatic concern with the things ready to hand (equipment). As an ontological experience, care refers to concernful being in the world (i.e. when *Dasein* takes its very being as an issue) and of solicitude for others (i.e. being together, 'being-in-community'). Because the world is shared with others, Being-in-the world is essentially Being with (*Mit-sein*). This is not just a sociological statement: Heidegger argues that 'being-with is an existential characteristic of Being in the world' (Heidegger, 1967: 163). Hence, *Dasein* cannot disregard the existence of others, for co-being (being with) is something of the character of *Dasein* (Heidegger, 1967: 154).

Since co-being is logically and existentially entailed by the concept of *Dasein*, it follows that *Dasein* cannot achieve personal authenticity unless s/he exists as being-toward-others in a concernful relationship. An authentic mode of solicitude, however, is not to 'leap in', that is to say, to take away care from the Other, for this would be a relation of dependence. Rather, one should 'leap ahead' of the Other, in the sense of 'giving his burdens or care back to him and not of relieving him of his care' (Heidegger, 1967: 158–9). *Dasein* can respond to the call of care by only assuming responsibility, that is, by problematising one's own existence and discovering what it means to be a person in a world of other persons.

Hcidegger conceives of responsibility as the imperative 'ought to think'. This norm neither establishes any general moral duties nor does it take the form of a definite moral command, such as 'be nice to fellow human beings'. In fact, it precedes determinate rules of conduct – being, instead, their condition of possibility (Caputo, 1971: 132–4). Given that ethics refers to the abode of humans, meditating upon the 'essence of dwelling as the issue of Being' and discovering what it means to dwell in a world of co-dwellers is an origin-al ethic. For it is only by questioning the origin of humans' world (*Ursprung*) and the way in which humans dwell in the world (*ethos*) that individuals will discover what it means to dwell – and, then, hopefully, search anew for ways of dwelling.

Such a way of thinking renders suspect the automatic privileging of tradition and of conventional narratives about community, for beyond the bounds of any particular past lies responsibility. The latter projects a vision of the future the shape of which is not given, but emerges as an ethical aspiration. Care and responsibility as 'ought to think' are thus the keys towards uncovering what it means to dwell and how we should dwell with others. As such, they could form the basis of a democratic mode of belonging which, unlike existing nationalist discourses of belonging, does not offer escapism from the unbearable futility of our existence by promising immortality.[3] Instead, it induces individuals to take their being as an issue and to confront the mortality, fragility and contingency of their existence.

According to Heidegger the 'thereness' into which we are thrown entails a particular kind of responsibility: the responsibility to exist, that is, to 'stand forth', turn toward the truth of Being and assume it into her own existence. It is only when *Dasein* opens herself to the enveloping presentness, to the disclosure of Being itself, that she will reach her truest homeland and will be able to choose how she will exist. But Heidegger observed (1975) that individuals lead their everyday lives without taking their being as an issue and thinking of dwelling as the basic character of being. Dwelling has hardly become worthy of questioning and worthy of thinking. As a result, the meaning of dwelling as the 'manner in which mortals are on earth' has fallen into oblivion.

Language discloses this concealment: in his essay which is entitled *Building, Dwelling and Thinking*, Heidegger notes that the verb to be (*ich bin, du bist* and so on) derives from the old German word *buan, bauen* which means to dwell. If 'to be a human being means to be on earth as a mortal, to dwell' (1975: 147), then individuals ought to think what it means to dwell in a world of co-dwellers. In the same essay, Heidegger argues that the meaning of dwelling is sparing (i.e. refraining from hurting or damaging) and preserving: 'to dwell is to be set at peace, means to remain at peace within the free, the preserve, the free sphere that safeguards each thing in its nature' (1975: 149). Mortals dwell 'on the earth', 'under the sky', 'before the divinities' and 'belonging to men's being with one another' (Heidegger, 1975: 149–51), and their dwelling preserves the fourfold by bringing its presencing into things which, in their own way, make space for a site of its presencing. In this respect, spaces, and space itself, are always provided for within the stay of mortals. Heidegger reminds us here that our relation to space inheres in our dwelling: 'the relationship between man and space is none other than dwelling, strictly thought and spoken' (Heidegger, 1975: 157).

The idea that spaces open up by virtue of the fact that 'they are let into the dwelling of man' (Heidegger, 1975: 157) contrasts sharply with the land ethic (i.e. exclusive ownership of land). On that view, space is not to be owned. Rather, it is 'a place cleared or freed for settlement and lodging'. 'Space is something that has been made room for, something that is cleared and free, namely within a boundary, Greek *peras*' (Heidegger, 1975: 154). Interestingly, boundaries are not conceived of as barriers and stopping points, but as those 'from which something begins its presencing' (Heidegger, 1975: 154). By drawing upon the meaning of the ancient Greek noun *orion*, Heidegger puts forward a distinctive conception of boundary as *horismos* (Heidegger, 1975: 154), that is, as a horizon within which the fourfold unfolds. By so doing, Heidegger dismantles the boundary imagery that has surrounded the notion of territorial space. More importantly, however, he does so without dispensing altogether with the sense of boundedness that characterises dwelling.

This shift of emphasis from boundaries as limits to boundaries as the horizon within which the fourfold unfolds 'decentres' the meaning and significance attached to boundaries by the earlier-mentioned hegemonic discourses (see pp. 155–9 above) which seek to make political power real by making it visible. Bearing in mind that boundaries affect behaviour by controlling access to the territory (Sack, 1986: 19) and structure relationships (see pp. 133–42 above), a different thinking about boundaries and spatiality may help advance a new way of being together in the European polity and prompt a reorientation of European immigration policy. The weakening of territoriality's hold on our thinking about community and territorial sovereignty helps us realise that boundaries are not only symbolic markers of possession and exclusion, but they have also been used in order to displace attention from the internal, hierarchical relations and power dynamics ('the relationship between the controller and the controlled') to the territory (Sack, 1986: 26). Utterances, such as 'this is our way of doing things here'; 'this is our land, and if you want to live here you must conform'; strategies, such as assimilation, integration or differential exclusion of resident migrants (Chapters 1 and 5), official discourses and the negative perceptions about immigration (Chapter 6) have been based upon such strategic uses of boundaries and territoriality. By displacing the reinforced geometricism implied by traditional 'us/them' or 'inside/outside' divisions, and by prioritising dwelling over exclusive public ownership of land, the conception of boundary as *horismos* allows for permeable, porous boundaries and for inclusive communities with flexible membership (Chapters 1, 5 and 6). These are, indeed, the building blocks of the constructivist mode of European identity.

A political discourse built around these basic themes could inspire individuals to envision and give their support to forms of political organisation which are not defined by totalising boundaries and territorially informed patterns of exclusion, but are defined focally. Focal territoriality draws attention to the nature of dwelling and the ways in which respectful relationships among dwellers or groups of dwellers can be fostered. As such, it does not call for the dissolution of the state's boundaries; rather, it calls into question certain strategic uses of territoriality, boundaries and spatial relationships and their representation in hegemonic national narratives. Unlike the boundary imagery which draws our minds away from social interaction, a focal conception of territoriality prompts thinking and acting for the sake of dwelling. As such, it leads to the construction of more relaxed and dynamo-centric communities. Socio–political matters can most usefully be referred to such a focus, for the plight of dwelling, the values of the lived space transcend the reinforced geometricism and patterns of exclusion that boundaries imply. Indeed, in the concluding reflections in *Building, Dwelling, Thinking,* Heidegger talks about 'the real plight of dwelling'. It is important, he says, to think of 'dwelling as the plight and to plight the fulfilment of dwelling' (1975: 161):

> The real plight of dwelling lies in this, that mortals ever search anew for the nature of dwelling, that they must ever learn to dwell. What if man's homelessness consisted in this, that man still does not even think of the real plight of dwelling as the plight? Yet as soon as man gives thought to his homelessness, it is a misery no longer. Rightly considered and kept well in mind, it is the sole summons that calls mortals into their dwelling. But how else can mortals answer this summons than by trying on their part, on their own, to bring dwelling to the fullness of its nature? This they accomplish when they build out of dwelling, and think for the sake of dwelling.

This could be the basis for a democratic discourse of belonging, boundaries and community in the Union. As argued above, belonging in the Union is not only multiple and flexible, but is also critical and transformative. But the residents of Europe must 'respond to the plight of dwelling'. They have the responsibility to think about dwelling and to act for the sake of dwelling; to question narrow articulations of national interest and official discourses which undermine community by scapegoating migrants and admission seekers; to think what political belonging can be in the European polity; to think about exile and human suffering and to give an enlightened moral response to the plight of migrants and refugees. This responsibility grounds the 'ethic of the Other' discussed in the context of constructive citizenship (Proposition 6, Chapter 5) and underpins the empirical realisation of the institutional designs in the fields of citizenship and immigration in the Union I have suggested in this book.

Conclusion

Institutions and political identities stand in a mutually constitutive relation: good institutions and principled policies make good citizens, and, at the same time, the citizens' virtue contributes to the quality and success of institutions. The empirical implementation of the institutional reforms suggested in this book relies on and requires a change in human consciousness for its success and long-term viability. This will not be merely the outcome of a change in our thinking about ourselves, the formation of our identities and the role that difference plays in this process. Indeed, a recurrent theme of the discussion has been the need to abandon ideas about a unified and essential self and to resist aspirations to achieve a totalised identity. Coming to terms with the contingency of our being; acknowledging the incompleteness and the relational character of our identities; and embracing difference within ourselves and around us – all are crucial to avoiding the fundamentalisation of identities and to engaging respectfully with others. Nor will such a cognitive shift be simply the result of the cultivation of those citizenship virtues which are vital to the creation, and the maintenance, of a democratic and inclusive European polity. What is also needed is the fashioning of a new public ethic of political belonging which, unlike existing discourses of national belonging, will induce people to be critical and responsible. In this respect, the Heideggerian imperative to think for the sake of dwelling and to discover what it means to dwell concernfully in a world of co-dwellers unlocks new possibilities for a creative renewal of our socio–political practices and the realisation of the constructivist mode of European identity.

An intrinsic element for a democratic discourse of belonging is a new relationship to the land. As shown above, the articulation of sovereignty with a specific conception of territoriality modelled upon private ownership law has shaped the formation of political subjectivities, and has influenced significantly the way we think about political community and its rules of membership. Conversely, Heidegger's relational view of space challenges the possessiveness and exclusiveness which characterises territorial sovereignty, by suggesting that spaces open up by the fact that they are let into the dwelling of human beings. Such a relational view of space (i.e. spatiality as involvement, inclusion and concernful engagement) can foreground an alternative perspective. In addition, Heidegger's conception of boundary as *horismos* can be used to subvert the authoritative disciplining of boundaries by replacing the boundary-obsessed territorialism accompanying statism with a focal sense of territoriality. By prompting attention to dwelling and its ethics, the latter invites us to envisage a way of dwelling which: instead of portraying boundaries as walls views them as permeable membranes; in place of the logic of the securitisation of migration emphasises the relaxation of control and connection; in place of the requirement of cultural conformity (i.e. assimilation or absorption) for migrants and their families emphasises their equal participation in the fullness of communal life; and in place of the territorial state's monopoly over the definition of the terms of collective identities stresses the de-territorialization and pluralisation of identities.

What is additionally required for a democratic mode of political belonging is a new way of conceiving of community and the common European 'home'. The term 'home' here does not simply imply a place of belonging. Nor does it denote feelings of belonging. True, we regard as 'home' the place where we have our roots; where we are nurtured and sheltered; the place where our religions, festivals and traditions unfold. But, in reality, these spaces, places and practices have not been chosen by us: we simply find ourselves immersed in them. And although we cannot deny the fact that our identities have been 'informed' by our personal, cultural, political 'homes' in so far as they provide the resources on the basis of which we act, interact, judge, think and interpret, these homes neither determine us nor can they satisfy our yearning for answers to some deeper questions about the meaning, purpose and usefulness of our existence. Indeed, because these 'homes' are more likely to need faithful than critical persons, it is not uncommon to find that any person who 'is interested to know how (s)he should live instead of merely taking life as it comes, is automatically an Outsider' (Wilson, 1956: 66). In such circumstances, 'confronting life' can make our life take on the quality of a nightmare as we find ourselves questioning, rejecting, subverting and rethinking assumptions we have inherited in a desperate attempt to change the terms by which we live. But at such critical junctures our 'homes' also reveal themselves as they really are: namely, ongoing processes and sites of interaction and contestation. As such, they inform and distort; enable and constrain; present and conceal; include and exclude; determine and silence; liberate and dominate. It is not the place here to show that these 'homes' as ideals have been falsely worshipped, and that they can hurt and oppress. Chapters 1, 4, 5 and 6 have already addressed this with reference to essentialist national and cultural perspectives, and in Chapter 4 we saw that structures of domination, oppression and exclusion overflow the boundaries of the private home. Suffice it here to say that, unlike the romanticism of rootedness and the mythology of 'home' which underpins nationalist and other essentialist narratives, Heidegger draws our attention to the existential odyssey for finding a 'home'. We have seen that to dwell is not to rely on a mythology of a 'natural home' but to engage in the ongoing task of its discovery. This is essentially a process of *oikeiosis* (from *oikos* which means house), which may be translated as familiarisation with oneself and familiarisation with others. This process of *oikeiosis* opens up the possibility of 'home' and, by analogy, the possibility of community.

Communities are not granted by God or history. Nor are they founded on something prior and exterior to them. Rather, they are instituted and reinstituted by the people (in both their personal and corporate identities) in the course of their engagement with and participation in practices of social co-operation. This is the idea of communities of concern and engagement (see Proposition 2 in Chapter 5). On this reading, the European Community does not need to be grounded on foundational myths, traditions and 'thick' attachments, which ultimately reify culture and society. Rather, the European Community is a community beyond myths, attachments and tradition: a community which is constructed while the conversation concerning the process of inventing a tradition goes on. What creates a sense of community in the Union is its members' concern about the community's future possibilities and their share of responsibility for the solidity of its achievements. But such a community can flourish only if individuals belonging to numerous constituencies think about the nature of dwelling, see Others as co-dwellers and co-venturers and participate in the co-creation of a polity which is built for the sake of dwelling, is imagined for the sake of dwelling and is guided by the plight of dwelling.

No doubt, thinking of 'belonging' in terms of 'dwelling' and 'co-dwelling' (the ethic of dwelling), as opposed to defining dwelling in terms of territory and belonging to a cohesive and unified cultural entity which is rooted in the land (the land ethic), is bound to generate some inescapable tensions among individual Europeans, such as tensions between the demand for loyalty on the one hand and the ethic of responsibility on the other; between the pasts that we all embody and the future towards which we are heading; between the need to live life forward and our capacity to understand it backwards. Such tensions, however, are not disabling; they are also markers of our responsibility. Throughout this book I have argued that the future towards which we are heading, the formation of an inclusive and democratic European polity based on constructive citizenship and a principled approach to migration, the constructivist mode of European identity are tasks to be achieved. In this respect, it is our responsibility not to make the past (i.e. what has been) a barrier or limit that imperils what is to come. Following Heidegger, we should view it as *peras* (which means 'beyond') – that is, as a marker of what is to come and of all the things we should make happen. By so doing, the memory of what has been with all its narratives, understandings and troubling loyalties will not frustrate our anticipation of the possibilities to become other than what we are and to conceive of a new way of being together in the European polity.

Notes

1 As Walker (1990, p. 448) argues, 'despite all appearances, sovereignty is not a permanent principle of international order; the appearance of permanence is

simply an effect of a complex practice working to affirm continuities and to shift disruptions and dangers to the margins'.

2 Heidegger's novel argument is that the relationship between objective and human space lies in *Dasein*'s dwelling. This signals Heidegger's intellectual departure from both Husserl's idea that space as a category is projected by a transcendental ego and Descartes' ontology of *res extensa* (extent). An objection to this discussion on the Heideggerian philosophy of space might be that Heidegger in *Being and Time* asserts the absolute primordiality of time over space. Time in *Being and Time* is envisioned as the foundation of Being. Despite this subjugation of space to time, however, Sefler (1973: 250–3) has detected a logical tension in the Heideggerian philosophy of space. That is, when space is discussed in relation to time, then the former is thematically subordinated to the latter. In contrast, in Heidegger's later writings (i.e. *Discourse on Thinking* (1945), *On the Essence of Truth* (1951), *Building, Dwelling and Thinking* (1951)) space is seen as an 'authentic revelatory framework of Being' (all these essays can be found in Heidegger (1978b)). On this basis, Sefler's cursory reading of Being and Time leads him to conclude that Heidegger could just as easily have grounded temporality on spatiality (1973: 251).

3 The contribution of Heideggerian philosophy towards a postmodern politics has been the subject of much debate: see Schurmann (1990); Dallmayr (1981); Wolin (1990).

Conclusion

Citizenship and immigration affect everyone. More than any other institution, they touch us all, partly because of their scale and public nature, and partly because they hold up a revealing mirror to who we are and to the kind of society we want to live in. Forward-looking or backward-looking, European citizenship and migration policy are the visible expression of the European societies' priorities, aspirations and preoccupations. By defining membership in the European political community and shaping the institutions with which we live they, in turn, condition the way we behave.

This book has sought to develop a critical perspective on these constitutive dimensions of European polity formation and identity-building and to provide analytical frameworks which help us develop a greater understanding of the political evolution of the EC/EU. It suggested a theoretical framework for European citizenship which sheds light upon its present limitations and its unfinished agenda, and a set of policy proposals for institutional reform (Chapter 5). Constructive citizenship is propounded as a building block for the creation of a democratic, inclusive and heterogeneous European polity. Hand in hand with the challenge of articulating a theoretical framework for European citizenship went the task of rethinking the issue of immigration and suggesting an alternative institutional design in this area (Chapter 6). I challenged the assumption that internal deregulation of the mobility of labour is tied to a rigorous and stringent regulation of human mobility at the external frontiers. From this standpoint, I have sought to develop a paradigm for a principled and non-restrictive European migration policy, which is theoretically consistent, practical in meeting policy concerns and consonant with the norms underpinning the European Union's and the Member States' constitutional orders.

The strong link between philosophical discourse and practical problems, conceptual change and structural transformation enabled me to explore possibilities for a radical rethinking of European citizenship and immigration which are rarely acknowledged by lawyers and ways of institutionalising these which are rarely discussed by political scientists. More importantly, I have done so without sketching an ultimate end of integration or a utopian future of conflict-free relations. Although the 'departure from the nation-state' (neo-functionalism, federalism)/'return to the nation-state' (intergovernmentalism) dualism still characterises EU studies, the Union will remain a multilevel system of governance (Jachtenfuchs and Kohler-Koch, 1996) consisting of 'complex multitiered, geographically overlapping structures of governmental and non-governmental elites' (Wessels, 1997: 291).

It must be mentioned here that the aim of this book has not been to provide a blueprint for the European polity. Rather, what I have tried to articulate is a menu of concepts and propositions, typologies and policy options for institutional reform. The case for reform was made on the basis of the identification of the limitations of existing conceptual frameworks for European citizenship, identity and immigration as well as of weaknesses and contradictions in policy design and implementation. To some extent, such limitations are understandable given the novelty and complexity of the European enterprise. Our vocabulary and thinking about it is still in its infancy. Many of the concepts, ideas and frameworks used have sprung from the historical experience of the statist setting and the theoretical preoccupations of the twentirth century. As such, they carry an intellectual legacy which in parts represents a flawed and inadequate way of looking at the unfolding developments of the Union. The lens of normative political theory was particularly valuable in this respect. It enabled me to reflect on the course travelled so far, appreciate the insights derived from classic literature, develop new ideas, expand the theory in new directions and, by critically evaluating existing institutions, make policy relevant proposals. However, one must also be prepared to acknowledge the limitations of this methodology. By the latter I am not simply referring to the well justified critiques of topical bias to which this study is exposed, but also to the impact of intellectual interventions in general 'in the real world'(see below).

It would be naive to expect that governmental elites will embrace wholeheartedly my institutional recommendations, particularly since these question dominant patterns of discourse and interrupt the socially created webs of meaning which have framed and continue to frame debates on European citizenship, identity and immigration. However, I also believe that a valuable purpose will have been served if this book provokes debate, encourages a more reflective attitude towards our concepts and paradigms, highlights the importance of the ethics of the 'structuration' of the European polity and forms a backdrop against which the agenda and reform package of the 2000 Intergovernmental Conference (IGC) may be evaluated.

At its meeting in Cologne on 3 and 4 June 1999 the European Council announced its intention of convening an IGC on institutional reform in 2000 ahead of the anticipated enlargement of the Union. This was in accordance with the Protocol *On the institutions with the prospect of enlargement of the European Union* annexed to the Treaty of Amsterdam. Although the

Protocol had envisaged a limited reform before the first enlargement and a more comprehensive report before the number of Member States exceeded twenty, the broadening and acceleration of the accession process after Amsterdam blurred this distinction. The Helsinki European Council (December 1999) reaffirmed the inclusive nature of the accession process which now comprises thirteen candidate states within a single framework[1] (Helsinki European Council, *Presidency Conclusions*, 11/12/1999). This has given rise to calls for a more extensive reform of the Treaties at the 2000 IGC.

The IGC was formally opened on 14 February 2000 and the negotiations should be completed by December 2000. Although at the time of writing its agenda has not been finalised, the Cologne and Helsinki Council meetings reaffirmed that the IGC would settle the issues which the Amsterdam negotiations left unresolved – namely, the size and composition of the Commission, the weighting of the votes and the possible extension of qualified majority voting (QMV) in the Council and any other necessary amendment to the Treaties as regards European institutions in connection with the above issues and in implementing the Treaty of Amsterdam. Such reforms in the Council's working methods and the Commission's composition are necessary in order maintain the efficiency of European institutions in view of the accession of Central and Eastern European (CEE) states. For example, if the weighting of the votes in the Council remained the same, in an enlarged Union of twenty-seven members a decision could be blocked by a group of states representing 10 per cent of its population. In addition, unanimity in a Union of twenty-five or thirty members would lead to paralysis. Among the alternatives on offer are further extension of QMV to new areas (i.e. the right of Union citizens to free movement and residence (Article 18(2) EC), coordinating social security for workers (Article 42 EC), culture (Article 151 EC), some of the provisions of the Immigration Title, extending the mechanisms of the common commercial policy (CCP) to international negotiations and agreements on services and intellectual property (Article 133 EC) and certain decisions on taxation) and the adoption of a simplified Treaty amendment procedure involving a reinforced qualified majority for certain non-fundamental provisions of the Treaties (*Report by von Weizsäcker, Dehaene and Simon to the European Commission*, 18 October 1999). Because improving the efficiency of the European institutions is as important as maintaining the momentum of European integration after enlargement, flexibility or closer co-operation is likely to emerge as a key issue at the Conference. One should expect strengthened co-operation arrangements which will enable some Member States to move forward without their proposal being vetoed by other Member States, while respecting the Parliament's prerogatives. Of course, flexibility must remain 'a way of building on and strengthening the Union's achievements, not of loosening the ties that bind the Member States' (*Report by Weizsäcker, Dehaene and Simon*, 18 October 1999).

Eastward enlargement is a truly major challenge facing the Union at the new millennium, for it will impact on the operation of its institutions, its resources, the way its policies are conducted and its position in the international sphere. However, bearing in mind the impact of sheer numbers, the increasing diversity and the corresponding risk of fragmentation, it is plausible to argue that the challenge facing the Union is not simply one of adaptation; rather, it is one of transformation.

Full membership of the Union will most certainly result in the transformation of CEE states as well. The conditions for membership set by the 1993 Copenhagen European Council, such as stable democratic institutions, a functioning market economy, capacity to cope with competitive pressures inside the Union, acceptance of the *acquis*, and the 'pre-accession' strategy mapped out by the 1994 Essen European Council have already resulted in important changes in domestic structures and policies. In the field of migration policy, for example, CEE states have aligned their policies despite generalised concerns about EU interference in domestic internal and foreign affairs since these countries have to conform to principles, standards and requirements that have been adopted by the EU ministers without their participation (Lavenex, 1998). The new members must also accept the goal of EMU and the associated convergence criteria. Certainly, one cannot underestimate the risks involved in this process of 'forced' rapid transformation. For instance, although post-communist states have embraced economic reform, stability, liberalisation, the creation of a market economy and privatisation, and are attracted to Western models of prosperity, the process of structural adjustment may spark a process of de-idealisation and frustration. At the same time, however, strong collectivist traditions and a rooted sense of social justice in these states may prompt the strengthening of the European social model.[2]

The process of the penetration of European integration norms in domestic arenas is bound to give rise to tensions in view of specific particularities, understandings and/or structural systemic features (i.e. overgrowth of executive functions, embryonic civil society and so on). One can only hope that the new CEE members will respond to the challenges of constitutional pluralism and forgo the tendency to think in terms of national sovereignty, and even of the homogeneity of a national state. True, the new Europeans' experiences of self, community, citizenship and nationhood are different, but one hopes that EU membership will aid the process of 'righting wrongs' (Pogany, 1998) done to national and ethnic minorities and of consolidating a democratic culture.[3] Indeed, given the present activism of ethnic identities in Eastern Europe, minority constituencies are likely to view membership in the Union as an opportunity and a surface of inscription of demands for recognition, stronger identities and power-sharing. But when this happens, it is important that majority constituencies draw on the ideal of critical citizenship, suggested in this book, so as to form a new basis for social cohesion and for a rich, plural life free from state control, instead of viewing it as a threat to national identity-building and condemning the Union for unacceptable intrusions on national identities and sovereignty. In this respect, the constructivist modes of European identity and citizenship suggested in this book not only carry the promise of binding the enlarged Union together by taking the challenge of diversity and membership seriously without dispensing for the need for solidarity, but they can also travel beyond the Union, in the sense of addressing issues of identity formation and political community-building and inclusive, multicultural citizenship in East European settings.

The IGC is likely to contribute to the political construction of 'Europe' by promoting the area of freedom, security and justice and strengthening the Common Foreign and Security Policy (CFSP). As regards the latter, at the meetings of the European Council in Vienna and Cologne, the Heads of State and Government showed their willingness to develop a genuinely common policy in this field as well as to amplify and reinforce in this way the *acquis* in the Treaty of Amsterdam regarding foreign and security policy. This would mean the development of the Union's military and non-military crisis management capability – that is, its ability to develop a capacity to take decisions autonomously, launch and conduct EU-led military operations in response to international crises, the integration of the Western European Union (WEU) into the Union and the latter's endowment with legal personality.

A crucial impact on the process of the political construction of Europe will be the adoption of a European Union Charter of Fundamental Rights pursuant to the Conclusions of the Cologne and Tampere European Councils in June and October 1999, respectively. Although the rationale behind this initiative is to strengthen the Union's social legitimacy by consolidating existing rights and 'making their overriding importance and relevance more visible to the Union's citizens' (*Presidency Conclusions, Cologne European Council*, 3–4 June 1999; Draft Charter of fundamental rights of the EU, and crucial issues, such as the status of the Charter (i.e. whether it will be a legally binding instrument or declaratory), its enforceability and the jurisdiction of the Court are yet to be resolved, the Charter is bound to raise citizens' expectations and bring issues such as the relationship of the Union and its institutions to the ECHR (see the opinion of the Court 2/94 [1996] ECR I-1759) and the legal personality of the Union back on the political agenda. Differing visions about the nature and future of the European polity will inevitably surround the negotiations of the Nice European Council (December 2000) which will determine its legal enforceability and content. One hopes that the Charter is incorporated into the Treaties.

Though I share existing concerns about the necessity and desirability of producing a mere 'showcase of existing rights' which will not fill the current gaps and shortcomings in human rights protection in the Union, such as the restrictive rules on *locus standi*, the absence of a human rights' perspective in the Third Pillar and the limited extent of judicial supervision of Third Pillar activities, and the failure of the Community to accede to the ECHR, I never-theless believe that even a purely declaratory Charter which provides a mere index of existing rights would influence the ECJ and have a wide symbolic and educative function by strengthening the culture of rights in the Union. As Advocate General Francis Jacobs submitted to the House of Lords Select Committee on European Union 'even if not incorporated in the Treaties and made formally justiciable the Charter would have a "significant effect"' (OO 241, 257, House of Lords, Select Committee on the EU, 16 May 2000).

The Charter is envisaged to contain the fundamental rights and freedoms as well as basic procedural rights guaranteed by the ECHR; rights derived from the constitutional traditions of the Member States; rights which are protected as general principles of Community law; rights that pertain only to the Union citizens under the Treaties; and economic and social rights con-tained in the European Social Charter and the Community Charter of the Fundamental Social Rights of Workers. The inclusion of socio-economic rights may prove contentious, even though it is deemed that their inclusion will not enlarge the Community competence by the back door (Article 46 of the Charter). Another crucial issue is the extent to which the rights enunci-ated in the charter will apply to non-EU citizens.

Arguably, the Charter represents a unique opportunity for remedying the 'civic inclusiveness deficit' by tackling the inequitable position of long-term resident third-country nationals and providing better protection for asylum seekers and refugees for whom a right to asylum and due process rights are very important. The draft list of rights includes the right to asylum for nationals of third countries (Article 21), the right to vote and stand as a can-didate in EP elections for all residents (Article 25) and the right of migrant workers to equal treatment in the Member States (Article 40), but also reaf-firms the existing confinement of a core of civic and political rights to Union nationals (*The Times*, 1 June 2000: 4). If this position is endorsed by the Nice European Council, then the Charter will be a missed opportunity for the fashioning of a democratic and inclusive European public sphere and for pro-moting equal opportunities and an anti-discrimination culture in the Union.

Arguably, the realisation of the latter requires a more far-reaching and greater commitment than enhancing the structural visibility of fundamental rights. What is needed is a more holistic approach under which considera-tions of issues concerning rights' protection and the treatment of citizens, residents and others are subsumed under an overall understanding and broader debate over the constitutional identity of the Union: a debate which does not only recognise the linkage between European identity, citizenship and immigration, but also provides a plausible alternative vision to territor-ial populism, civic exclusiveness and bounded allegiances. After all, as it is often said, the value of the Community does not lie in its past but in the real-isation of new beginnings.

Do heterotopias matter?

It would be unrealistic to expect that this study – as, indeed, any study which represents a personal vision – will be immune from criticism. Two general lines of criticism in particular come to mind. First, it may be argued that my institutional recommendations in the domain of European citizenship and immigration represent mere wishful thinking given the present configuration of the power forces. Second, it may be said that my framework of analysis (and, in particular, my critique of illegitimate exclusion in the Union) involves commitment to some form of universalism which has been repudiated by the advent of postmodernism. I must briefly respond to both.

First, intergovernmentalists have undoubtedly refined our understanding of the integration process by identifying *loci* of power and influence. But their analyses are one-dimensional in that they sidestep the impact of supranational and subnational actors on European integration, and have failed to situate questions of feasibility within the matrix of fluid, dynamic, constantly changing institutional or other environments. Such bracketing may be problematic since there is no certainty that what has been decided will be achieved or that what actually happens is what was intended. Ignorance, misconceptions, lack of information, among other things, place severe restrictions on what can be achieved. The European level is a prime example of a fluid, unstable and unpredictable institutional setting. One never knows 'exactly which issue is going to emerge, or who will bring it up and how ... So political actors must be 'permanently on guard in order not to be caught napping by the sudden appearance of a new project that they "did not see coming"' (Mény, Muller and Quermonne, 1996: 11).

Given that change is intrinsically random and contingencies are seldom known in advance, to believe that there is a privileged vantage point from which one may pass judgement on what can or cannot be achieved seems like a modernist rationalist fallacy. Apparently, the future is neither futureless – as advocates of the 'ought implies can' thesis believe – nor the outcome of some determinist (functional or otherwise) logic. In this respect, it may be proper to approach questions of feasibility not through rationalist models designed to explain interactions among self-interested, unitary and rational nation-state actors, but through processes of 'scenario-writing'. The latter have the advantage of unravelling possible alternatives without eliminating the element of indeterminacy that accompanies policy options and solutions. They, in fact, provide a fuller picture of the realm of the possible by highlighting its limits as well as the possibilities for pushing them forward.

As regards the second criticism, I do not believe that renunciation of foundational thought and the 'grand narratives of modernity' (Aronowitz, 1988: 46) necessarily leads to some form of subjectivism. It is perhaps a major weakness of certain versions of postmodernism that discussions on the dissolution of the markers of certainty (Lefort, 1990: 19) and the critique of onto-theo-logical metaphysics have left questions, such as what to do with the world or how to lead our lives, off the agenda. But as the previous chapters have shown, the version of postmodernism I am espousing does not preclude normative vision. Instead, it provides reasons for action and inspires action.

Both realism and post-modernism quite rightly acknowledge the importance of 'particular' contexts in shaping European policy outcomes. They question the appropriateness as well as the effectiveness of utopian thinking. Utopias are idealised accounts of society. They are not 'real' places, for they cannot be effectively enacted or found. They are spaces of illusion since they present society itself in a perfected form. They have no location because they are always a horizon. This is not to say that utopias perform a worthless function. On the contrary, utopias are valuable for what they do: namely, not to let dreams dry up. But utopias do not make dreams a reality. This function is performed by heterotopias.[4]

Heterotopias may be defined as juxtapositions of what is; as contestations of the space in which we live. As such they are 'other' spaces, but 'real' and not mythic spaces. In their role as critical counteractive points to what exists, heterotopias are sites in which the present is exposed, contested, subverted and re-enacted. As such, they mark a difference from the realm of 'is'. At the same time, however, they can be actualised realities, not merely adhered to as an inspiration. The Union itself is the prime example of a heterotopia which has become a reality.

To criticise utopias is not to espouse a politics of low expectations. Similarly, to reflect critically on existing institutions, to defy power structures and engage in oppositional discourse is not to engage in utopian thinking. It is, instead, to choose a politics of in-volvement, rather than a politics of redemption.

Perhaps the most distinctive feature of heterotopias is that they entail a cautious but determined faith. Faith that institutional advances can be made since policies, even when they are made under the rubric of necessity or emergency, are choices and, as such, potentially challengeable. However, faith co-exists with caution, since institutions and laws, particularly those associated with Union citizenship and immigration arrangements, appear to reflect the wishes and misconceptions of national executives, rather than the latter being shaped by law and constitutional constraints.

Both pragmatic self-interested politics and ideological politics, however, have their own in-built limits. Pragmatic interests are prone to change and reversal, as they are not reinforced with deep ideological or philosophical commitments. A political process that is built and projected from pragmatic interests is bound to be a frail process susceptible to reversal. Ideological politics, on the other hand, may be more durable since they are reinforced by doctrinal commitments, but they, too, are prone to 'de-mythologisation' as a result of counter-ideologies and/or structural changes. So even if my 'heterotopic' proposals do not succeed, in the sense of being transformed into policies at the next IGC, they nevertheless deserve attention for the thinking they spark, the questions they raise and the openings they create. Indeed, I shall be pleased if the book promotes discussion of possible scenarios for institutional reform and inspires further investigations.

History is branded with its own mark of uncertainty. Acknowledgement of the forces of change and contingency does not weaken possibilities for action. Rather, it stimulates our creativity and opens up opportunities for more participation in the construction of the future. What is important in such a process is to 'to sustain the burden of action without certitude, and to keep always open the possibility of recognising past errors and changing course' (Arrow, 1974: 29). From this standpoint, the future may be seen as *poiisis*, that is, a creation and communities/polities as projects.

The European Union is the prime example of such a project for which there are neither tried solutions nor objective laws. Precisely because it is a construction (a creation of law), it carries an ethical responsibility, a responsibility to design institutions which respond to our needs as residents of Europe and reflect our capabilities as architects. Today is, after all, the tomorrow we were promised yesterday. And tomorrow, it is the next generation which will have to live with our present choices.

This is not to say that the European venture is not risk-ridden. It involves many risks, the most important of which is the risk of failure. But the European Union is not unique in this; all constructions are exposed to this risk. The Talmudic texts inform us that even God himself in creating the world contemplated the risk of failure and the return of nothing. Qualified hope may be an unbearable feeling, but it is impossible to evade it. It characterises all projects, ranging from the institutional implementation of a local tax policy to the implementation of the most elaborate, grand projects of political and economic restructuring; from experimentation under the most controlled setting in a biochemistry lab to the articulation of the arguments in this book ... One can only hope it works.

Notes

1   The applicant countries are: Poland, Hungary, the Czech Republic, Estonia, Slovenia, Cyprus, Malta, Romania, Slovakia, Latvia, Lithuania, Bulgaria and Turkey. The Commission has asked the Council to commit itself to being able to decide from 2002 on the accession of candidates that fulfil all the necessary criteria: COM (1999) 500 Final of 13 October 1999.

2   The European Council held a special meeting on 23-24 March 2000 in Lisbon to agree a new strategic goal for the Union in order to strengthen employment, economic reform and social cohesion as part of a knowledge-based economy. See the *Presidency Conclusions, Lisbon European Council*, SN 100/00.

3   Miller et al. (1998), in their study of values and political change in Hungary, Slovakia, the Czech Republic and Russia, found that there is no evidence that

people are not ready for democracy and the differences between these political cultures and an old-established democracy like Britain are not great (1998: 28).

4   The term is borrowed from M. Foucault (1986).

Bibliography

Ackerman, B. (1980), *Social Justice in the Liberal State*, New Haven, Yale University Press.

Ackerman, B. (1984), 'The Storrs Lectures: Discovering the Constitution', *Yale Law Journal*, 93, 1013–72.

Adelman, H. et al. (eds) (1994), *Immigration and Refugee Policy: Australia and Canada Compared*, Carleton, Victoria, Melbourne University Press.

Alexander, W. (1992), 'Free Movement of Non-EC Nationals: A Review of the Case Law of the Court of Justice', *European Journal of International Law*, 3, 53–64.

Anderson, B. (1983), *Imagined Communities*, London, Verso.

Andrews, G. (ed.) (1991), *Citizenship*, London, Lawrence & Wishart.

Anthias, F. and Yuval-Davis, N. (1992), *Racialized Boundaries; Race, Nation, Gender, Colour and Class and the Anti-racist Struggle*, London, Routledge.

Armstrong, K. and Bulmer, S. (1998), *The Governance of the European Single Market*, Manchester, Manchester University Press.

Aronowitz, S. (1988), 'Postmodernism and Politics', in A. Ross (ed.), *Universal Abandon* , Minneapolis, University of Minnesota Press.

Arrow, K. J. (1974), *The Limits of Organization*, New York, Norton.

Aspinwall, M. D. and Schneider, G. (1998) 'Same Menu, Separate Tables: The Institutionalist Turn in Political Science and the Study of European Integration', *Joint Sessions of the European Consortium for Political Research*, Warwick, March.

Avineri, S. and de Shalit, A. (eds) (1992), *Communitarianism and Individualism*, Oxford, Oxford University Press.

Bader, V. (1995), 'Citizenship and Exclusion', *Political Theory*, 23: 2, 211–46.

Balibar, E. and Wallerstein, I. (1991), *Race, Class, Nation: Ambiguous Identities*, London, Verso.

Bankowski, Z. (1994), 'Comment on Weiler', in S. Bulmer and A. Scott (eds), *Economic and Political Integration in Europe*, Oxford, Blackwell.

Barry, B. (1995), *Justice as Impartiality*, Oxford, Clarendon Press.

Bassin, M. (1987), 'Imperialism and the Nation-state in Friedrich Ratzel's Political Geography', *Progress in Human Geography*, 11, 473–95.

Bauböck, R. (1992), *Immigration and the Boundaries of Citizenship*, Warwick, Centre for Research in Ethnic Relations.

Bauböck, R. (1994a), *Transnational Citizenship: Membership and Rights in International Migration*, Aldershot, Edward Elgar.

Bauböck, R. (ed.) (1994b), *From Aliens to Citizens*, Aldershot, Avebury.

Bauböck, R. (1995), 'Legitimate Immigration Control', in H. Adelman (ed.), *Legitimate and Illegitimate Discrimination: New Issues in Migration*, Toronto, York Lanes Press.

Bauböck, R. (1997), 'Citizenship and National Identities in the European Union', *Harvard Jean Monnet Working Paper*, 4/97.

Bean, F. D. and Fix, M. (1992), 'The Significance of Recent Immigration Policy Reforms in the United States', in G. P. Freeman and J. Jupp (eds), *Nations of Immigrants: Australia, the United States, and International Migration*, Melbourne, Oxford University Press.

Beiner, R. (1992), *What's the Matter with Liberalism?*, Berkeley,University of California Press.

Beitz, C. (1979), 'Bounded Morality: Justice and the State in World Politics', *International Organization*, 33: 3, 405–24.

Bellamy, R., Bufacchi, V. and Castiglione, D. (eds) (1995), *Democracy and Constitutional Culture in the Union of Europe*, London, Lothian Foundation Press.

Bellamy, R. and Castiglione, D. (1997), 'The Communitarian Ghost in the Cosmopolitan Machine: Constitutionalism, Democracy and the Reconfiguration of Politics in the New Europe', in R. Bellamy and D. Castiglione (eds), *Constitutionalism, Democracy and Sovereignty: American and European Perspectives*, Aldershot, Avebury.

Bellamy, R. and Castiglione, D. (1998), 'The Normative Challenge of a European Polity: Cosmopolitan and Communitarian Models Compared, Criticised and Combined', in A. Follesdal and P. Koslowski (eds), *Democracy and the European Union*, Berlin: Springer-Verlag.

Bellamy, R. and Warleigh, A. (1998), 'From an Ethics of Integration to an Ethics of Participation: Citizenship and the Future of the European Union', *Millennium*, 27: 3, 447–70.

Bendix, R. (1964), *Nation Building and Citizenship*, New York, John Wiley.

Benhabib, S. (1994), 'Democracy and Difference: Reflections on the Metapolitics of Lyotard and Derrida', *The Journal of Political Philosophy*, 2: 1, 1–23.

Bermann, G. A. (1994), 'Taking Subsidiarity Seriously: Federalism in the European Community and the United States', *Columbia Law Review*, 94: 2, 332–455.

Birch, A. (1989), *Nationalism and National Integration*, London, Unwin Hyman.

Birrell, R. (1992), 'Problems of Immigration Control in Liberal Democracies', in G. P. Freeman and J. Jupp (eds.), *Nations of Immigrants: Australia, the United States, and International Migration*, Melbourne, Oxford University Press.

Bodin, J. (1962), *The Six Books of a Commonwealth*, K. D. McRae (ed.), Cambridge, Mass., Harvard University Press.

Bohning, W. R. (1972), *The Migration of Workers in the United Kingdom and the European Community*, London, Oxford University Press.

Bohning, W. R. (1973), 'The Scope of the EEC System of Free Movement of Workers: A Rejoinder', *Common Market Law Review*, 10, 81–6.

Bonnie, A. (1998), 'The Constitutionality of Transfers of Sovereignty: The French Approach', *European Public Law*, 4: 4, 517–32.

Borjas, G. (1990), *Friends or Strangers? The Impact of Immigration on the US Economy*, New York, Basic Books.

Borjas, G. (1991) 'Immigrant Participation in the Welfare System', *Industrial and Labor Relations Review*, 44, 195–211.

Bradley, A. (1994), 'The Sovereignty of Parliament: In Perpetuity?', in J. Jowell and D. Oliver (eds), *The Changing Constitution*, 3rd edn, Oxford, Clarendon Press, 91–4.

Brown, C. (1994), *Political Restructuring in Europe: Ethical Perspectives*, London, Routledge.

Brubaker, W. R. (1992), *Citizenship and Nationhood in France and Germany*, Cambridge, Mass., Harvard University Press.

Brubaker, W. R. (1995), 'Comments on Modes of Immigration Politics in Liberal Democratic States', *International Migration Review*, 29, 903–8.

Bulmer, S. and Scott, A. (1994), *Economic and Political Integration in Europe: Internal Dynamics and Global Context*, Oxford, Blackwell.

Bunyan, T. (1991), 'Towards an Authoritarian European State', *Race and Class*, 32: 3, 19–24.

Butcher, K. and Card, D. (1991), 'Immigration and Wages: Evidence from the 1980s', *American Economic Review*, 81, 292–6.

Buzan, B., Kelstrup, M., Lemaître, P., Tromer, E. and Wæver, O. (1990), *The European Security Order Recast: Scenarios for the Post-Cold War Era*, London, Pinter.

Buzan, B., Wæver, O., De Wilde, J. (1998), *Security: A New Framework for Analysis*, Boulder, Col., Lynne Rienner.

Calhoun, C. (1995), *Critical Social Theory*, Cambridge, Mass., Basil Blackwell.

Camilleri, J. A. and Falk, J. (1992), *The End of Sovereignty? The Politics of a Shrinking and Fragmented World*, Aldershot, Edward Elgar.

Caporaso, J. (1996), 'The European Union and Forms of State: Westphalian, Regulatory or Post-Modern?', *Journal of Common Market Studies*, 34: 1, 29–52.

Caputo, J. D. (1971), 'Heidegger's Original Ethics', *New Scholasticism*, 45, 127–38.

Carens, J. H. (1987), 'Aliens and Citizens: The Case for Open Borders', *The Review of Politics,* 49, 251–73.

Carens, J. H. (1988), Nationalism and the Exclusion of Immigrants: Lessons from Australian Immigration Policy', in M. Gibney (ed.), *Open Borders? Closed Societies? The Ethical and Political Issues*, New York and London, Greenwood Press.

Carens, J. H. (1992), 'Migration and Morality: A Liberal Egalitarian Perspective', in R. E. Goodin and B. Barry (eds), *Free Movement*, Pennsylvania, Pennsylvania State University Press.

Castles, S. (1984), *Here for Good: Western Europe's New Ethnic Minorities*, London, Pluto Press.

Castles, S. and Kosack, G. (1972), 'The Function of Labour Immigration in Western European Capitalism', *New Left Review*, 73, 3–21.

Castles, S. and Kosack, G. (1973), *Immigrant Workers in the Class Structure in Western Europe*, Oxford, Oxford University Press.

Castles, S. and Miller, M. J. (1993), *The Age of Migration: International Population Movements in the Modern World*, London, Macmillan.

Cesarani, D. and Fulbrook, M. (1996) *Citizenship, Nationality and Migration in Europe*, London, Routledge.

Christiansen, T. et al. (1999), 'The Social Construction of Europe', Special Issue, *Journal of European Public Policy*, 6: 4, 528–44.

Chryssochoou, D. (1996), 'Europe's Could-Be Demos: Recasting the Debate', *West European Politics*, 19, 787–801.

Chryssochoou, D., Tsinisizelis, M.J., Stavridis, S. and Ifantis, K. (1999), *Theory and Reform in the European Union*, Manchester, Manchester University Press.

Clapham, A. (1996), 'Opinion: The Privatization of Human Rights', *European Human Rights Law Journal*, 1: 1, 20–32.

Closa, C. (1992), 'The Concept of Citizenship in the Treaty on European Union', *Common Market Law Review*, 29, 1137–70.

Closa, C. (1994), 'Citizenship of the Union and Nationality of the Member States', in D. O'Keeffe and P. Twomey (eds), *Legal Issues of the Maastricht Treaty*, Chichester, Wiley.

Closa, C. (1998), 'Supranational Citizenship and Democracy: Normative and Empirical Dimensions', in M. La Torre, *European Citizenship: An Instituional Challenge*, The Hague, Kluwer.

Cohen, J. and Rogers, J. (eds.) (1995), *Associations and Democracy*, London, Verso.

Cohen, M. (1978), 'Property and Sovereignty', in C. B. Macpherson (ed.), *Property: Mainstream and Critical Positions*, Oxford, Basil Blackwell.

Cohen, P. (1988), 'The Perversions of Inheritance', in P. Cohen and H. S. Bains (eds), *Multiracist Britain*, London, Macmillan.

Cohen, R. (1987), *The New Helots: Migrants in the International Division of Labour*, Farnborough, Avebury.

Cohen, J. and Sabel, C. (1997), 'Directly-Deliberative Polyarchy', *European Law Journal*, 3: 3, 313–42.

Collinson, S. (1993a), *Europe and International Migration*, London, Pinter.

Collinson, S. (1993b), *Beyond Borders: West European Migration Policy Towards the 21st Century*, London, RIIA, Wyndham Place Trust.

Committee des Sages (1998), 'Leading by Example: A Human Rights Agenda for the European Union for the Year 2000', Florence, EUI.

Connolly, W. E. (1991a), *Identity/Difference*, Ithaca, Cornell University Press.

Connolly, W. E. (1991b), 'Democracy and Territoriality', *Millennium*, 20: 3, 463–84.

Connolly, W. E. (1993), 'Democracy and Territoriality', in M. Ringrose and A. J. Lehrner (eds), *Reimagining the Nation*, Buckingham, Open University Press.

Connolly, W. E. (1996), 'Pluralism, Multiculturalism and the Nation-State: Rethinking the Connections', *Journal of Political Ideologies* 1: 1, 53–73.

Cornell, D. (1998), 'Post-structuralism, the Ethical Relation and the Law', *Cardozo Law Review*, 9, 1587–1628.

Craig, P. (1991), 'United Kingdom Sovereignty after *Factortame*', *Yearbook of European Law*, 11, 221.

Craig, P. (1997) 'Directives: Direct Effect, Indirect Effect and the Construction of National Legislation', *European Law Review*, 22, 519–69.

Curtin, D. (1993), 'The Constitutional Structure of the Union: A Europe of Bits and Pieces', *Common Market Law Review*, 30, 17.

Curtin, D. (1997), *Postnational Democracy: The European Union in Search of a Political Philosophy*, The Hague, Kluwer.

Dagger, R. (1997), *Civic Virtues: Rights, Citizenship and Republican Liberalism*, Oxford, Oxford University Press.

Dahl, R. (1989), *Democracy and its Critics*, New Haven, Yale University Press.

Dahl, R. (1994), 'A Democratic Dilemma: System Effectiveness versus Citizen Participation', *Political Science Quarterly*, 109 1, 23–34.

Dahrendorf, R. (1958), *Class and Class Conflict in Industrial Society*, Stanford, Cal., Stanford University Press.

Dahrendorf, R. (1990), *Reflections on the Revolution in Europe*, London, Chatto & Windus).

Dallmayr, F. (1981), *Twilight of Subjectivity: Contributions to a Post-Individualist Theory of Politics*, Amherst Mass., Amherst University Press.

Dashwood, A. (1998), 'States in the European Union', *European Law Review*, 23, 201–16.

Dawkins, P. J., Foster, W., Lowell, L. and Papademetriou, D. G. (1992), 'The Microeconomic Analysis of Immigration in Australia and the United States', in G. P. Freeman and J. Jupp (eds), *Nations of Immigrants: Australia, the United States, and International Migration*, Melbourne, Oxford University Press.

de Benoist, A. (1985), *Democratie: Le Problème*, Paris, Le Labyrinthe.

de Benoist, A. (1994), 'The Idea of Empire', *Telos*, 98–99, 81–98.

de Burca, G. (1996), 'The Quest For Legitimacy in the European Union', *Modern Law Review*, 59, 349–76.

de Groot, G.-R. (1998), 'The Relationship between the Nationality Legislation of the Member States of the European Union and European Citizenship', in M. La Torre (ed.), *European Citizenship: An Institutional Challenge*, The Hague: Kluwer.

deWind, J. (1982) 'Undocumented Workers and the Labour Market: The Impact of Employers', unpublished paper presented at the 44th Congress of Americanists, University of Manchester, September cit. in R. Cohen, *The New Helots: Migrants in the International Division of Labour*, Farnborough, Avebury (1987).

Dedman, M. (1996), *The Origins and Development of the European Union 1945–1995*, London, Routledge.

Delanty, G. (1995), 'The Limits and Possibility of a European Identity: A Critique of Cultural Essentialism', *Philosophy and Social Criticism*, 21: 4, 15–36.

Delanty, G. (1996), *Inventing Europe: Idea, Identity, Reality*, London, Macmillan.

Delanty, G. (1997), 'Models of Citizenship: Defining European Identity and Citizenship', *Citizenship Studies*, 1: 3, 285–303.

Derrida, J. (1992), *The Other Heading: Reflections on Today's Europe*, Bloomington and Indianapolis, Indiana University Press.

Deutsch, K. (1966), *Nationalism and Social Communication*, Cambridge Mass., MIT Press.

Dicey, A.V. (1959 [1885]), *Introduction to the Study of the Law and the Constitution*, 10th edn, London, Macmillan.

Diez, T. (1999), 'Speaking "Europe": The Politics of Integration Discourse', *Journal of European Public Policy*, 6:4, 598–613.

d'Oliveira, J. H. (1993), 'Fortress Europe and Extra-Communitarian Refugees: Co-Operation in Sealing Off the External Borders', in H. G. Schermers et al. (eds), *Free Movement of Persons in Europe, Legal Problems and Experiences*, Dordrecht, Martinus Nijhoff, 166–82.

d'Oliveira, J. (1995), 'Union Citizenship: Pie in the Sky?', in A. Rosas and E. Antola (eds), *A Citizens' Europe: In Search of a New Order*, London, Sage.

Donnelly, J. (1985), *The Concept of Human Rights*, Kent, Croom Held.

Dummett, A. (1992), 'The Transnational Migration of People Seen from within a Natural Law Perspective', in R. E. Goodin and B. Barry (eds), *Free Movement*, Pennsylvania, Pennsylvania State University Press.

Dummett, A. and Nicol, A. (1990), *Subjects, Citizens, Aliens and Others: Nationality and Immigration Law*, London, Weidenfeld & Nicolson.

Ellis. E. (1994) 'Recent Case Law of the Court of Justice on the Equal Treatment of Women and Men', *Common Market Law Review*, 31, 43–75.

Emiliou, N. (1992a), Subsidiarity: Panacea or Fig Leaf?', in D. O'Keeffe and P. Twomey (eds), *Legal Issues of the Maastricht Treaty*, Chichester, Wiley.

Emiliou, N. (1992b), 'Subsidiarity: An Effective Barrier Against the Enterprises of Ambition?', *European Law Review*, 17, 383–407.

Evans, A. (1984), 'European Citizenship: A Novel Concept in the EEC Law', *American Journal of Comparative Law*, 32: 4, 674–715.

Evans, A. (1991), 'Nationality Law and European Integration', *European Law Review*, 16: 3, 190–215.

Evans, A. (1994), 'Third Country Nationals and the Treaty on European Union', *European Journal of International Law*, 5, 199–219.

Everling, U. (1992), 'Reflections on the Structure of the European Union', *Common Market Law Review*, 29, 1053–77.

Everson, M. (1995), 'The Legacy of the Market Citizen', in J. Shaw and G. More (eds), *New Legal Dynamics of European Union*, Oxford, Oxford University Press.

Favell, A. (1997), 'Citizenship and Immigration: Pathologies of a Progressive Philosophy', *New Community*, 23: 2, 173–95.

Favell, A. (1998), 'A Politics that is Shared, Bounded, and Rooted? Rediscovering Civic Political Culture in Western Europe', *Theory and Society*, 27, 209–36.

Ferris, E. (1993), *Beyond Borders: Refugees, Migrants and Human Rights in the Post-Cold War Era*, Geneva, World Council of Churches.

Figgis, J. N. (1921), *The Political Aspect of Saint Augustine's City of God*, London, Longmans Green.

Findlay, A. (1994), 'An Economic Audit of Contemporary Immigration', in S. Spencer (ed.), *Strangers and Citizens*, London, IPPR/Rivers Oram Press, 159–201.

Flax, J. (1996), 'Race/Gender and the Ethics of Difference: A Reply to Okin's "Gender Inequality and Cultural Differences"', *Political Theory*, 23: 3, 500–10.

Ford, G. (1992), *Fascist Europe: the Rise of Racism and Xenophobia*, London, Pluto Press.

Foucault, M. (1986), 'Of Other Spaces', *Diacritics*, Spring, 22–7.

Fraser, N. (1992), 'The Uses and Abuses of French Discourse: Theories for Feminist Politics', *Theory, Culture and Society*, 9, 51–71.

Frazer, N. (1995), 'Recognition or Redistribution? A Critical Reading of Iris Young's *Justice and the Politics of Difference*', *Journal of Political Philosophy*, 3: 2, 166–80.

Frazer, N. (1997), 'A Rejoinder to Iris Young', *New Left Review*, 126-129.

Freeman, G. (1979), *Immigrant Labour and Racial Conflict in Industrial Societies, 1945–1975*, Princeton, Princeton University Press.

Freeman, G. (1995), 'Modes of Immigration Politics in Liberal Democratic States', *International Migration Review*, 29, 881–902.

Freeman, M. (1994), 'The Philosophical Foundations of Human Rights', *Human Rights Quarterly*, 16, 491–514.

Freeman, G. and Jupp, J. (eds) (1992), *Nations of Immigrants: Australia, The United States and International Migration*, Melbourne, Oxford University Press.

Friedman, Marilyn (1989), 'Feminism and Modern Friendship: Dislocating the Community', *Ethics*, 99, 275–90.

Friedman Milton (1962), *Capitalism and Freedom*, Chicago, Chicago University Press.

Friedman, Milton and Friedman, Rose (1980), *Free to Choose a Personal Statement*, Harmondsworth, Penguin.

Fries, S. and Shaw, J. (1998), 'Citizenship of the Union: First Steps in the Court of Justice, *European Public Law*, 4: 4, 533–59.

Fuller, L. (1964), *The Morality of Law*, New Haven: Yale University Press.

Galston, W. (1991), *Liberal Purposes: Goods, Virtues, and Duties in the Liberal State*, Cambridge, Cambridge University Press.

Gamberale, C. (1995), 'National Identities and Citizenship in the EU', *European Public Law*, 4: 4, 633–61.

Garcia, S. (ed.) (1993) *European Identity and the Search for Legitimacy*, London, Pinter.

Gellner, E. (1983), *Nations and Nationalism*, Oxford, Basil Blackwell.

Gellner, G. (1994), *Conditions of Liberty: Civil Society and its Rivals*, London, Hamish Hamilton.

Giddens, A. (1985), *The Nation-State and Violence*, Cambridge, Polity Press.

Gilligan, C. (1982), *In a Different Voice: Psychological Theory and Moral Development*, Cambridge, Mass.: Harvard University Press.

Gilroy, P. (1987), *There Ain't No Black in the Union Jack: The Cultural Politics of Race and the Nation*, London, Hutchinson.

Gonzalez, J. P. (1995), 'The Principle of Subsidiarity: A Guide for Lawyers with a Particular Community Orientation', *European Law Review*, 20: 4, 335–70.

Goodin, R. E. (1985), *Protecting the Vulnerable*, Chicago, Chicago University Press.

Goodin, R. E. (1992), 'If People were Money…', in R. E. Goodin and B. Barry (eds), *Free Movement*, Pennsylvania, Pennsylvania State University Press.

Goodin, R. E. (1993), 'The Contribution of Political Science', in R. Goodin and P. Pettit (eds), *A Companion to Contemporary Political Philosophy*, Oxford, Blackwell, 157–82.

Goodin, R. E. (1996), 'Inclusion and Exclusion', *Archives Européenes de Sociologie*, 37: 2, 343–71.

Grimm, D. (1995), 'Does Europe need a Constitution?', *European Law Journal*, 1:1, 282–302).

Guild, E. (1996), *A Guide to the Right of Establishment under the Europe Agreements*, London, Baileys Shaw & Gillett.

Guiraudon, V. (2000), 'European Integration and Migration Policy: Vertical Policy-Making as Venue Shopping', *Journal of Common Market Studies*, 38: 2, 251–71.

Gutmann, A. (1985) 'Communitarian Critics of Liberalism', *Philosophy and Public Affairs*, 14: 3.

Gutmann, A. (1993), 'The Challenge of Multiculturalism in Political Ethics', *Philosophy and Public Affairs*, 22: 3, 171–206.

Haas, E. (1958), *The Uniting of Europe*, Stanford, Stanford University Press.

Habermas, J. (1992), 'Citizenship and National Identity: Some Reflections on the Future of Europe', *Praxis International,* 12, 1–19.

Habermas, J. (1993), 'Struggles for Recognition in Constitutional States', *European Journal of Philosophy*, 1: 2, 128–54.

Habermas, J. (1995), 'Remarks on D. Grimm's 'Does Europe need a Constitution'?', *European Law Journal*, 1, 303–7.

Habermas, J. (1996a), *Between Facts and Norms: Contributions to a Discourse Theory of Law and Democracy*, Cambridge: Polity Press.

Habermas, J. (1996b), 'The European Nation State', *Ratio Juris*, 9: 2, 125–37.

Hailbronner, K., Martin, D. A. and Motomura, H. (eds) (1997), *Immigration*

Admissions: The Search for Workable Policies in Germany and the United States, Providence RI, Berghahn.

Hailbronner, K. and Thiery, C. (1997), 'Schengen II and Dublin: Responsibility for Asylum Applications in Europe', *Common Market Law Review*, 34, 957–89.

Hall, P. and Taylor, R. C. (1996), 'Political Science and the Three New Institutionalisms', *Political Studies*, 44: 5, 936–57.

Hall, S. (1995), *Nationality, Migration Rights and Citizenship of the Union*, Dordrecht, Martinus Nijhoff.

Hall, S. (1996), 'Loss of Union Citizenship in Breach of Fundamental Rights', *European Law Review*, 21, 129–43.

Hammar, T. (ed.) (1985), *European Immigration Policy: A Comparative Study*, Cambridge, Cambridge University Press.

Hammar, T. (1990), *Democracy and the Nation-State*, Aldershot, Avebury.

Hansen, R. (1998), 'Citizenship, Immigration and Nationality Law in the European Union: A European Citizenship or a Europe of Citizens?', paper presented at the Conference on 'Migrants, Minorities and New Forms of Citizenship in the European Union', European Forum, Florence, European University Institute.

Harden, I. (1995), 'The Constitution of the European Union', *Public Law*, 609–24.

Harris, N. (1996), *The New Untouchables: Immigration and the New World Worker*, Harmondsworth, Penguin.

Hartley, T. C. (1976), 'The International Scope of the Community Provisions Concerning the Free Movement of Workers', in F. G. Jacobs (ed.), *European Law and the Individual*, Amsterdam, North-Holland.

Harvey, C. (1998), 'The European Regulation of Asylum: Constructing a Model of Regional Solidarity?', *European Public Law*, 4: 4, 561–92.

Harvey, D. (1989) *The Condition of Postmodernity*, Oxford, Basil Blackwell.

Hathaway, J. C. (1995), 'New Directions to Avoid Hard Problems: The Distortion of the Palliative Role of Refugee Protection', *Journal of Refugee Studies*, 8, 288–94.

Hayek, F. (1973), *Law, Legislation and Liberty*, vols 1 and 2, London, Routledge.

Hayek, F. (1986), *The Road to Serfdom*, London: Ark/Routledge and Kegan Paul.

Heater, D. (1990), *Citizenship: The Civic Ideal in World History, Politics and Education*, London and New York, Longman.

Heater, D. (1998), *What is Citizenship?*, Oxford, Polity Press.

Hechter, M. (1975), *Internal Colonialism: The Celtic Fringe in British National Development*, London, Routledge & Kegan Paul.

Heidegger, M. (1967), *Being and Time*, Oxford, Blackwell.

Heidegger, M. (1972), '*Time and Being*' in *On Time and Being*, trans. Joan Stambaugh, New York, Harper & Row.

Heidegger, M. (1975) *Poetry, Language, Thought*, trans. A. Hofstadter, New York, Harper & Row.

Heidegger, M. (1978a), 'Letter on Humanism', in *Basic Writings*, D. F. Krell (ed.), London: Routledge & Kegan Paul.

Heidegger, M. (1978b), *Basic Writings*, D. F. Krell (ed.), London, Routledge & Kegan Paul.

Held, D. (1991), 'Between State and Civil Society: Citizenship', in G. Andrews (ed.), *Citizenship*, London: Lawrence & Wishart.

Held, D. (1993), 'Democracy: From City-States to a Cosmopolitan Order?', in D. Held (ed.) *Prospects for Democracy*, Cambridge, Polity Press.

Held, D. (1995), *Democracy and the Global Order*, Cambridge, Polity Press.

Heller, A. and Feher, F. (1988), *The Postmodern Political Condition*, Cambridge, Polity Press.

Heritier, A. (1999), 'Elements of Democratic Legitimation in Europe: An Alternative Perspective', *Journal of European Public Policy*, 6, 269–82.

Hervey, T. (1991), 'Justification for Indirect Sex Discrimination in Employment: European Community and United Kingdom Law Compared', *International Comparative Law Quarterly*, 40, 807–26.

Hinsley, F. H. (1986), *Sovereignty*, Cambridge, Cambridge University Press.

Hirst, P. (1990), *Representative Democracy and its Limits*, Cambridge, Polity Press.

Hirst, P. (1994), *Associative Democracy*, Cambridge, Polity Press.

Hix, S. (1994), 'The Study of the European Community: The Challenge to Comparative Politics', *West European Politics*, 17: 1, 1–30.

Hix, S. (1998), 'The Study of the European Union II: The "New Governance Agenda and its Rival",' *Journal of European Public Policy*, 5: 1, 38–65.

Hobsbawm, E. (1990), *Nations and Nationalism since 1780*, Cambridge, Cambridge University Press.

Hoffmann, S. (1981), *Duties Beyond Borders*, Syracuse, Syracuse University Press.

Hoffmann, S. (1993) 'Thoughts on the French Nation Today', *Daedalus*, 122: 3, 63–79.

Hollifield, J. (1992), *Immigrants, States and Markets*, Cambridge Mass., Harvard University Press.

Honneth, A. (1994), *The Struggle for Recognition*, Oxford, Polity Press.

Honneth, A. (1998), 'Democracy as Reflexive Cooperation: John Dewey and the Theory of Democracy Today, *Political Theory*, 26: 6, 763–83.

Howe, P. (1995), 'A Community of Europeans: The Requisite Underpinnings', *Journal of Common Market Studies*, 33: 1, 27–46.

Howe, P. (1997), 'Insiders and Outsiders in a Community of Europeans: A Reply to Kostakopoulou', *Journal of Common Market Studies*, 35: 2, 309–14.

Huysmans, J. (1995), 'Migrants as a Security Problem: Dangers of "Securitizing" Societal Issues', in R. Miles and D. Thranhardt (eds), *Migration and European Integration: The Politics of Inclusion and Exclusion in Europe*, London, Pinter, 53–72.

Jachtenfuchs, M. et al. (1998), 'Which Europe? Conflicting Models of a Legitimate European Order', *European Journal of International Relations*, 4: 4, 409–45.

Jachtenfuchs, M. and Kohler-Koch, B. (1996), *Europäische Integration*, Opladen, Leske & Budrich.

Jorgensen, K.-E. (ed.) (1997), *Reflective Approaches to European Governance*, London, Macmillan.

Karst, L. K. (1989), *Belonging to America*, New Haven, Columbia University Press.

Keane, J. (1989), *Democracy and Civil Society*, London, Verso.

Kedurie, E. (1993), *Nationalism*, 4th edn, Oxford, Blackwell.

Keohane, R. O. (1989), 'Neoliberal Institutionalism: A Perspective on World Politics', in R. O. Keohane, *International Institutions and State Power: Essays in International Relations*, Boulder, Col., Westview.

King, D. (1987), *The New Right: Politics, Markets and Citizenship*, London, Macmillan.

King, D. S. and Waldron, J. (1988), 'Citizenship, Social Citizenship and the Defence of Welfare Provision', *British Journal of Political Science*, 18, 415–43.

Kitschett, H.P. (1986), 'Ploitical Opportunity Structures and Political Protest: Anti-Nuclear Movements in Four Democracies', *British Journal of Political Science*, 16, 57–85.

Koopmans, T. (1992), 'Federalism: The Wrong Debate', Guest Editorial, *Common Market Law Review*, 29, 1047–52.

Korella, G. D. and Twomey, P. M. (eds) (1995), *Towards a European Immigration Policy*, Brussels, Interuniversity Press.

Kostakopoulou, T. (1996), 'Towards a Theory of Constructive Citizenship in Europe', *Journal of Political Philosophy*, 4: 4, 337–58.

Kostakopoulou, T. (1998), 'European Citizenship and Immigration after Amsterdam: Silences, Openings, Paradoxes', *Journal of Ethnic and Migration Studies*, 24: 4, 639–56.

Kostakopoulou, T. (2000) 'Nested "Old" and "New" Citizenships in the European Union. Bringing Out the Complexity', *Columbia Journal of European Law*, 5: 3, 389–13.

Kristeva, J. (1993), *Nations Without Nationalism*, New York, Columbia University Press.

Kroogsgaard, L. B. (1993), 'Fundamental Rights in the European Community After Maastricht', *Legal Issues of European Integration*, 1, 99–113.

Kukathas, C. (1993), 'Multiculturalism and the Idea of an Australian Identity', in C. Kukathas, *Multicultural Citizens: The Philosophy and Politics of Identity*, Australia, St. Leonard's, Centre for Independent Studies.

Kundera, M. (1984), 'A Kidnapped West or Culture Bows Out', *Grata*, 11, 92–122.

Kurthen, H. (1997), 'Immigration and the Welfare State in Comparison: Differences in the Incorporation of Immigrant Minorities in Germany and the United States, *International Migration Review*, 3, 721–31.

Kymlicka, W. (1989), *Liberalism, Community, and Culture*, Oxford, Oxford University Press.

Kymlicka, W. (1990), *Contemporary Political Philosophy: An Introduction*, Oxford, Oxford University Press.

Kymlicka, W. (1995), *Multicultural Citizenship*, Oxford, Clarendon, 1995.

Kymlicka, W. and Wayne, N. (1994), 'Return of the Citizen: A Survey of Recent Work on Citizenship Theory', *Ethics*, 104, 352–81.

La Torre, M. (ed.) (1998), *European Citizenship: An Institutional Challenge*, The Hague, Kluwer.

Lacey, M. (1992), 'Keeping the Door Open: Welcoming Refugees and Immigrants Amid Growing Xenophobia', *Migration World*, 22: 1, 20–1.

Laclau, E. (1990), *Reflections on the Revolution of Our Times*, London, Verso.

Laclau, E. and Mouffe, C. (1986), *Hegemony and Socialist Strategy*, London, Verso.

Ladeur, H.-K. (1997), 'Towards a Legal Theory of Supranationality – The Visibility of the Network Concept', *European Law Journal*, 3: 1, 33–55.

Laffan, B. (1996), 'The Politics of Identity and Political Order in Europe', *Journal of Common Market Studies*, 34: 1, 81–102.

Laski, H. (1917) *Studies in the Problem of Sovereignty*, London, George Allen & Unwin.

Lavenex, S. (1998), 'Asylum, Immigration and Central-Eastern Europe: Challenges to EU Enlargement', *European Foreign Affairs Review*, 3, 275–94.

Layton-Henry, Z. (1992), *The Politics of Immigration: Immigration, 'Race' and 'Race' Relations in Post-War Britain*, Oxford, Blackwell.

Leca, J. (1990), 'Nationalità e cittadinanza nell'Europa delle immigrazioni', in *WAA, Italia, Europa e nuove immigrazioni*, Turin, Edizione della Fondazione Giovanni agnelli, cit. in E. Meehan, *Citizenship and the European Community*, London, Sage.

Leca, J. (1992), 'Questions of Citizenship', in C. Mouffe (ed.), *Dimensions of Radical Democracy. Pluralism, Citizenship and Community*, London, Verso.

Lefebvre, H. (1976), *The Survival of Capitalism*, London, Allison & Busby.

Lefort, C. (1990), 'Renaissance of Democracy?', *Praxis International*, 10: 2.

Lehning, P. (1997) 'European Citizenship: A Mirage?', in P. B. Lehning and A. Weale (eds), *Citizenship, Democracy and Justice in the New Europe*, London and New York', Routledge, 175–99.

Leibfried, S. and Pierson, P. (1992) 'Prospects for Social Europe', *Politics and Society*, 20: 3, 333–66.

Leniham, D. (1991), 'Liberalism and the Problem of Cultural Membership: A Critical Study of Kymlicka, *Canadian Journal of Law and Jurisprudence*, 4: 2, 401–19.

Lijphart, A. (1977), *Democracy in Plural Societies*, New Haven and London, Yale University Press.

Lipgens, W. (1982), *A History of European Integration, 1, 1945–1947*, Oxford, Clarendon Press.

Lodge, J. (1994), 'Transparency and the Democratic Deficit', *Journal of Common Market Studies*, 61: 3, 299–327.

Lu, C.-Y. (1999), 'Harmonisation of Migration Policies in the European Union – A State-Centric or Institutionalist Explanation?', paper presented to the ECSA Sixth Biennial International Conference, Pittsburgh, 2–5 June.

Lyotard, J.-F. (1984), *The Postmodern Condition*, Minneapolis, University of Minnesota Press.

Lyotard, J.-F. and Thebaud, J.-L. (1985), *Just Gaming*, Minneapolis, University of Minnesota Press.

MacCormick, N. (1993), 'Beyond the Sovereign State', *Modern Law Review*, 56, 1–18.

MacCormick, N. (1995), 'Sovereignty, Democracy and Subsidiarity', in R. Bellamy, V. Bufacchi and D. Castiglione (eds), *Democracy and Constitutional Culture in the Union of Europe*, London, Lothian Foundation Press.

MacCormick, N. (1996), 'Liberalism, Nationalism and the Post-Sovereign State', *Political Studies*, 44, 553–67.

Macedo, S. (1990), *Liberal Virtues: Citizenship, Virtue, and Community*, Oxford, Clarendon Press.

MacIntyre, A. (1981), *After Virtue*, London, Duckworth.

Macpherson, C. B. (ed.) (1978), *Property: Mainstream and Critical Positions*, Oxford, Basil Blackwell.

Majone, G. (1991), 'Cross-National Sources of Regulatory Policy-Making in Europe and the United States', *Journal of Public Policy*, 11, 79–106.

Majone, G. (1996), *Regulating Europe*, London, Routledge.

Majone, G. (1997) 'From the Positive to the Regulatory State: Causes and Consequences of Changes in the mode of Governance', *Journal of Public Policy*, 17: 2, 139–67.

Majone, G. (1998), 'Europe's Democratic Deficit: The Question of Standards', *European Law Journal*, 4: 1, 5–28.

Mancini, F. (1998), 'Europe: The Case for Statehood', *European Law Journal*, 4: 1, 29–42.

Mancini, F. and Keeling, D. T. (1994), 'Democracy and the European Court of Justice', *Modern Law Review*, 57, 175–90.

Mann, M. (1993), 'Nation-States in Europe and Other Continents: Diversifying, Developing, Not Dying', *Daedalus*, 122: 3, 115–40.

Marks, G., Hooghe, L. and Blank, K. (1996), 'European Integration from the 1980s: State-Centric v. Multi-Level Governance', *Journal of Common Market Studies*, 34: 3, 341–78.

Marks, G., Scharpf, F., Schmitter, P. C., Streek, W. (1996), *Governance in the European Union*, London, Sage.

Marshall, T. H. (1950), *Citizenship and Social Class*, Cambridge, Cambridge University Press.

Marshall, T. H. (1975), *Social Policy in the Twentieth Century*, London, Hutchinson.

Marshall, T. H. (1981), *The Right to Welfare and Other Essays*, London, Heinemann.

Martinello, M. (1995), 'European Citizenship, European Identity and Migrants: Towards the Post-national State?', in R. Miles and D. Thranhardt (eds), *Migration and European Integration: The Politics of Inclusion and Exclusion in Europe*, London, Pinter, 37–52.

Mayall, J. (1999), 'Sovereignty, Nationalism and Self-determination', *Political Studies*, 47: 3, 474–502.

Mazey, S. P. (1988), 'European Community Action on Behalf of Women: The Limits of Legislation', *Journal of Common Market Studies,* 27: 1, 63–83.

Mazey, S. P. and Richardson, J. (1993), *Lobbying in the European Community*, Oxford, Oxford University Press.

McClure, M. C. (1990), 'Difference, Diversity and the Limits of Recognition', *Political Theory*, 18: 3, 361–91.

McCrudden, C. (1993), 'The Effectiveness of European Equality Law: National Mechanisms for Enforcing Gender Equality Law in the Light of European Requirements', *Oxford Journal of Legal Studies*, 13: 3, 320–67.

McEldowney, J. (1994), *Public Law*, London, Sweet & Maxwell.

Mead, L. (1986), *Beyond Entitlement: The Social Obligations of Citizenship*, New York, Free Press.

Meehan, E. (1993), *Citizenship and the European Community*, London, Sage.

Meehan, E. (1997), 'Political Pluralism and European Citizenship', in P. B. Lehning and A. Weale (eds), *Citizenship, Democracy and Justice in the New Europe*, London and New York, Routledge.

Mény, Y., Muller P. and Quermonne J.-L. (eds) (1996), *Adjusting to Europe*, London, Routledge.

Miles, R. and Thränhardt, D. (eds) (1995), *Migration and European Integration: The Politics of Inclusion and Exclusion in Europe*, London, Pinter.

Miller, D. (1993), 'In Defence of Nationality', *Journal of Applied Philosophy*, 10: 1, 3–16.

Miller, D. (1994), 'The Nation-State: A Modest Defence', in C. Brown (ed.), *Political Restructuring in Europe*, London, Routledge.

Miller, D. (1995), 'Citizenship and Pluralism', *Political Studies*, 43, 432–50.

Miller, D. (1996), *On Nationality*, Oxford, Oxford University Press.

Miller, D. (1998), 'The Left, the Nation-State, and European Citizenship', *Dissent*,

Summer, 47–51.

Miller, W. L., White, S. and Heywood, P. (1998), *Values and Political Change in Post-Community Europe*, London: Macmillan.

Milward. A. (1992), *The European Rescue of the Nation-State*, London, Routledge.

Milward, A., Lynch, F. M. B., Romero, F., Ranieri, R., Sorensen, V. (1993), *The Frontier of National Sovereignty: History and Theory 1945–1992*, London, Routledge.

Modood, T. (1998), 'Anti-Essentialism, Multiculturalism and the "Recognition" of Religious Groups', *Journal of Political Philosophy* 6: 4, 378–99.

Moghadam, V. (1989), 'Against Eurocentrism and Nativism: A Review Essay on Samir Amin's *Eurocentrism* and Other Texts', *Socialism and Democracy*, Fall–Winter, 81–104.

Monar, J. (1998a), 'Justice and Home-Affairs in the Treaty of Amsterdam: Reform at the Price of Fragmentation, *European Law Review*, 23, 320–35.

Monar, J. (1998b), 'A Dual Citizenship in the Making: The Citizenship of the European Union and its Reform', in M. La Torre (ed.), *European Citizenship: An Institutional Challenge*, The Hague, Kluwer.

Monar, J. and Morgan, R. (eds) (1994), *The Third Pillar of the European Union: Co-Operation in the Fields of Justice and Home Affairs*, Brussels, Interuniversity Press.

Moore, R. (1989), 'Ethnic Divisions and Class in Western Europe', in R. Scase (ed.), *Industrial Societies, Crisis and Division in Western Capitalism and State Socialism*, London, Unwin Hyman.

Moravcsik, A. (1991), 'Negotiating the Single European Act', in R. Keohane and S. Hoffmann (eds), *The New European Community*, Boulder, Col., Westview.

Moravcsik, A. (1993), 'Preferences and Power in the European Community: A Liberal Intergovernmentalist Approach', *Journal of Common Market Studies*, 31: 4, 473–24.

Moravcsik, A. (1998), *The Choice for Europe: Social Purpose and State Power from Messina to Maastricht*, London, UCL Press.

Mouffe, C. (1992) 'Feminism, Citizenship and Radical Democratic Politics', in J. Butler and J. W. Scott (eds), *Feminists Theorise the Political*, New York and London, Routledge.

Mouffe, C. (1993), *The Return of the Political*, London, Verso.

Mulhall, S. and Swift, A. (1992), *Liberals and Communitarians*, Oxford, Blackwell.

Muller, W. C. and Wright V. (1994), 'Reshaping the State in Western Europe: The Limits to Retreat', *West European Politics*, 17, 1–11.

Müller-Graf, P. (1994), 'The Legal Bases of the Third Pillar and its Position in the Framework of the Union Treaty', *Common Market Law Review*, 31, 493–510.

Nagel, T. (1991), *Equality and Partiality*, New York, Clarendon.

Nascibene, B. (1996), *Nationality Laws in the European Union*, London, Butterworth.

Newman, M. (1996), *Democracy, Sovereignty, and the European Union*, New York, St Martin's Press.

Nozick, R. (1974), *Anarchy, State and Utopia*, Oxford, Basil Blackwell.

O'Keeffe, D. (1994), 'Union Citizenship', in D. O'Keeffe and P. Twomey (eds), *Legal Issues of the Maastricht Treaty*, Chichester, Wiley.

O'Keeffe, D. (1995a), 'The Emergence of a European Immigration Policy', *European Law Review*, 20: 1, 20–36.

O'Keeffe, D. (1995b), 'Recasting the Third Pillar', *Common Market Law Review*, 32, 893–920.

Okin, S. M. (1989), *Justice, Gender, and the Family*, New York, Basic Books.

Okin, S. M. (1994), 'Political Liberalism, Justice and Gender', *Ethics*, 105, 23–43.

Oldfield, A. (1990), 'Citizenship; An Unnatural Practice?' *Political Quarterly*, 61, 177–87.

O'Leary, S. (1992), 'Nationality Law and Community Citizenship: A Tale of Two Uneasy Bedfellows', *Yearbook of European Law*, 12, 353–84.

O'Leary, S. (1996a), *The Evolving Concept of Community Citizenship*, The Hague, Kluwer.

O'Leary, S. (1996b), *European Union Citizenship: The Options for Reform*, London, IPPR.

Parekh, B. (1991), 'British Citizenship and Cultural Difference', in G. Andrews (ed.), *Citizenship*, London, Lawrence & Wishart.

Parekh, B. (1994) 'Three Theories of Immigration', in S. Spencer (ed.), *Strangers and Citizens*, London, IPPR/Rivers Oram Press, 91–110.

Parekh, B. (1995), 'Ethnocentricity of the Nationalist Discourse', *Nations and Nationalism*, 1: 1, 25–52.

Parekh, B. (1998), 'Integrating Minorities in a Multicultural Society', in U. Preuss and F. Requezo (eds), *European Citizenship, Multiculturalism and the State*, Baden-Baden, Nomos.

Partan, D. G. (1995), 'The Justiciability of Subsidiarity', in C. Rhodes and S. Mazey (eds.), *The State of the European Union*, Harlow, Longman.

Pateman, C. (1985), *The Problem of Political Obligation: A Critical Analysis of Liberal Theory*, Cambridge, Polity Press.

Pateman, C. (1988), *The Sexual Contract*, Oxford, Basil Blackwell/Polity Press.

Peers, S. (1996), 'Towards Equality: Actual and Potential Rights of Third Country Nationals in the European Union', *Common Market Law Review*, 33, 7–50.

Peers, S. (1998), 'Who is Watching the Watchmen? The Judicial System of the "Area of Freedom, Security and Justice"', *Yearbook of European Law*, 18, 337–415.

Pescatore, P. (1987), 'Some Critical Remarks on the Single European Act', *Common Market Law Review*, 24, 9–18.

Petersmann, E.-U. (1995), 'Proposals for a New Constitution for the European Union: Building Blocks for a Constitutional Theory and Constitutional Law of the EU', *Common Market Law Review*, 32, 1123–75.

Philips, A. (1993), *Democracy and Difference*, Cambridge, Polity Press.

Philips, A. (1995), *The Politics of Presence*, Oxford, Oxford University Press.

Philips, A. (1997), 'Why Worry about Multiculturalism?', *Dissent*, 57–63.

Pierson, P. (1996), 'The Path to European Integration: A Historical Institutionalist Analysis'. *Comparative Political Studies*, 29: 2, 123–63.

Pieterse, N. J. (1991), 'Fictions of Europe', *Race and Class*, 32: 3, 3–10.

Pinder, J. (1995 [1991]). *European Community: The Building of a Union*, Oxford, Oxford University Press.

Pizzorno, A. (1987), 'Politics Unbound', in C. Maier (ed.), *Changing Boundaries of the Political: Essays on the Evolving Balance between the State and Society, Public and Private in Europe*, Cambridge, Cambridge University Press.

Plant, R. and Barry, N. (1990), *Citizenship and Rights in Thatcher's Britain: Two Views*, London: IEA Health and Welfare Unit.

Plender, R. (1976), 'An Incipient Form of European Citizenship', in F. G. Jacobs (ed.), *European Law and the Individual*, Amsterdam, North-Holland.

Plender, R. and Arnull, A. (1997), *The Jurisdiction of the European Court of Justice in Respect of Asylum and Immigration Matters*, position paper, London, Justice Publications.

Pogany, I. (1998), *Righting Wrongs in Eastern Europe*, Manchester, Manchester University Press.

Pogge, T. W. (1992), 'Cosmopolitanism and Sovereignty', *Ethics*, 103, 48–75.

Poiares-Maduro, M. (1998), *We the Court: The European Court of Justice and the European Economic Constitution*, Oxford, Hart Publishing.

Preuss, U. K. (1995), 'Problems of a Concept of European Citizenship', *European Law Journal*, 1: 1, 267–81.

Preuss, U. K. (1996), 'Two Challenges to European Citizenship', *Political Studies*, 44, 534–52.

Przeworski, A., Bardhan, P., Bresser Pereira, C. B., Bruszt, L. et al. (1995), *Sustainable Democracy*, Cambridge, Cambridge University Press.

Ratzel, F. (1899 [1923]), *Politische Geographie, oder die Geographie der Staaten, Des Verkehrs, und des Krieges*, 3rd edn, Oldenbourg, Munich and Berlin.

Rawls, J. (1971), *A Theory of Justice*, London, Oxford University Press.

Rawls, J. (1985), 'Justice as Fairness: Political not Metaphysical', *Philosophy and Public Affairs*, 14: 3, 515–72.

Rawls, J. (1988), 'The Priority of Right and Ideas of the Good', *Philosophy and Public Affairs*, 17, 251–76.

Rawls, J. (1993), *Political Liberalism*, New York, Columbia University Press.

Richardson, J. (ed.) (1996), *European Union: Power and Policy-Making*, London, Routledge.

Ricœur, P. (1986), 'Introduction', *in Philosophical Foundations of Human Rights*, Paris, United Nations Educational, Scientific, and Cultural Organisation.

Risse-Kappen, T. (1996), 'Explaining the Nature of the Beast: International Relations and Comparative Policy Analysis Meet the EU', *Journal of Common Market Studies*, 34: 1, 53–80.

Roche, M. (1992), *Rethinking Citizenship*, Cambridge, Polity Press.

Room, G. et al. (1989), 'New Poverty in the European Community', *Policy and Politics*, 17: 2, 165–76.

Rosenblum, N. L. (1994), 'Democratic Character and Community: The Logic of Congruence?', *Journal of Political Philosophy*, 2: 2.

Rubio-Marin, R. (1998), 'Equal Citizenship and the Difference that Residence Makes', in M. La Torre (ed.), *European Citizenship: An Institutional Challenge*, The Hague, Kluwer.

Ruggie, J. G. (1993), 'Territoriality and Beyond: Problematizing modernity in International Relations', *International Organization*, 47: 1, 139–74.

Sack, R. D. (1986), *Human Territoriality: Its Theory and History*, Cambridge, Cambridge University Press.

Safran, W. (1991), 'State, National Identity and Citizenship: France as a Test Case', *International Political Science Review*, 12, 219–38.

Salmond, W. J. (1902), 'Citizenship and Allegiance', *Law Quarterly Review*, 18, 49–63.

Sandel, M. (1982), *Liberalism and the Limits of Justice*, Cambridge, Cambridge University Press.

Sandel, M. (1997), *Democracy's Discontent: America in Search of a Public Philosophy*, Cambridge Mass., Harvard University Press.

Scanlan, A. J. and Kent, T. O. (1988), 'The Force of Moral Arguments for a Just Immigration Policy in a Hobbesian Universe', in M. Gibney (ed.), *Open Borders? Closed Societies? The Ethical and Political Issues*, New York, Greenwood Press.

Scharpf, F. (1988), 'The Joint Decision-Trap: Lessons from German Federalism and European Integration', *Public Administration*, 66, 239–78.

Schlatter, R. (1951), *Private Property: The History of an Idea*, London, Allen & Unwin.

Schlensinger, P. (1992), 'Europeanness – A New Cultural Battlefield', *Innovations*, 5, 11.

Schmitter, P. (1995) 'If the Nation-state Were to Wither Away in Europe, What Might Replace it?', *ARENA Working Paper*, 11.

Schmitter, P. (1996), 'Imagining the Future of the Euro-Polity with the Help of New Concepts', in G. Marks, F. W. Scharpf, P. Schmitter and W. Streeck, *Governance in the European Union*, London, Sage.

Schnapper, D. (1997), 'The European Debate on Citizenship', *Daedalus*, 126: 3, 199–222.

Schuck, H. P. (1984), 'The Transformation of Immigration Law', *Columbia Law Review*, 84: 1, 1–90.

Schuck, H. P. and Smith, M. R. (1985), *Citizenship without Consent. Illegal Aliens in the American Polity*, New Haven, Yale University Press.

Schuppert Folke, G. (1995), 'On the Evolution of a European State: Reflections on the Conditions of and the Prospects for a European Constitution', in J. J. Hesse and N. Johnson (eds), *Constitutional Policy and Change in Europe*, Oxford, Oxford University Press.

Schurmann, R. (1990), *Heidegger. On Being and Acting: From Principles To Anarchy*, Bloomington, Indiana University Press.

Scott, A., Peterson, J. and Millar, D. (1994), 'Subsidiarity: A "Europe of the Regions" v. the British Constitution?', *Journal of Common Market Studies*, 32: 1, 47–67.

Sefler, G. F. (1973), 'Heidegger's Philosophy of Space', *Philosophy Today*, 17, 246–54.

Seurin, L. J. (1995), 'Towards a European Constitution? Problems of Political Integration', *Public Law*, 625–36.

Shapiro, I. (1994), 'Three Ways To Be A Democrat', *Political Theory*, 22: 1, 124–51.

Shaw, J. (1996), 'European Union Legal Studies in Crisis? Towards a New Dynamic', *Oxford Journal of Legal Studies*, 16, 231–53.

Shaw, J. (1997a), 'European Union Citizenship: The IGC and Beyond', *European Public Law*, 3, 413–39.

Shaw, J. (1997b), 'The Many Pasts and Futures of Citizenship in the EU', *European Law Review* 22, 1 554–72.

Shaw, J. (1998), 'The Interpretation of European Union Citizenship', *Modern Law Review*, 61, 293–317.

Shaw, J. (1999), 'Postnational Constitutionalism in the EU', *Journal of European Public Policy* 6: 4, 579–97.

Shaw, J. and More, G. (eds) (1995), *New Legal Dynamics of European Union*, Oxford, Oxford University Press.

Shklar, J. (1991), *American Citizenship: The Quest for Inclusion*, Cambridge, Mass., Harvard University Press.

Silverman, M. (1991), 'Citizenship and the Nation-State in France', *Ethnic and Racial Studies*, 14: 3, 333–49.

Silverman, M. (1992), *Deconstructing the Nation: Immigration, Racism and Citizenship in Modern France*, London, Routledge.

Simon, J. (1989), *The Economic Consequences of Immigration*, Oxford, Blackwell.

Skinner, Q. (1978), *The Foundations of Modern Political Thought, 2: The Age of Reformation*, Cambridge, Cambridge University Press.

Smith, A. D. (1979), *Nationalism in the Twentieth Century*, Oxford, Martin Robertson.

Smith, A. D. (1981), *The Ethnic Revival in the Modern World*, Cambridge, Cambridge University Press.

Smith, A. D. (1986), *The Ethnic Origins of Nations*, Oxford, Blackwell.

Smith, A. D. (1991), *National Identity*, Harmondsworth, Penguin.

Smith, A. D. (1992), 'National Identity and the Idea of European Unity', *International Affairs*, 68: 1, 55–76.

Smith, A. D. (1993), 'A Europe of Nations – Or the Nation of Europe?', *Journal of Peace Research*, 30: 2, 129–35.

Smith, A. D. (1995), 'Gastronomy or Geology? The Role of Nationalism in the Reconstruction of Nations', *Nations and Nationalism*, 1: 1, 3–23.

Smith, J. P. and Edmonston, B. (eds) (1998), *The New Americans: Economic, Demographic and Fiscal Effects of Immigration*, Oxford, National Academy Press.

Sohrab, J. A. (1994), 'Women and Social Security: The Limits of EEC Equality Law', *Journal of Social Welfare and Family Law*, 1, 5–18.

Sorensen, G. (1999), 'Sovereignty: Change and Continuity in a Fundamental Institution', *Political Studies*, 47: 3, 590–604.

Soysal, Y. N. (1994), *Limits of Citizenship: Migrants and Postnational Membership in Europe*, Chicago, Chicago University Press.

Soysal, Y. N. (1996), 'Changing Citizenship in Europe', in D. Cesarani and M. Fulbrook (eds), *Citizenship, Nationality and Migration in Europe*, London, Routledge.

Spencer, M. (1990), *1992 and All That: Civil Liberties in Balance*, London, Civil Liberties Trust.

Spencer, M, (1995), *States of Injustice*, London, Pluto Press.

Spencer, S. (1994), 'The Implications of Immigration Policy for Race Relations', in S. Spencer (ed.), *Strangers and Citizens*, London, IPPR/Rivers Oram Press, 306–21.

Spicker, P. (1997), 'Exclusion', *Journal of Common Market Studies*, 35:1, 133–43.

Spruyt, H. (1994), *The Sovereign State and its Competitors*, Princeton, Princeton University Press.

Squires, J. (1993), 'Discussing Deliberative Democracy: Democracy and Difference', *Radical Philosophy*, 65, 61–2.

Steiner, J. (1998), *EC Law*, 6th edn, London, Blackstone Press, 62–9.

Stone Sweet, A. and Sandholtz, W. (1997), 'European Integration and Supranational Governance', *Journal of European Public Policy*, 4: 3, 297–317.

Strayer, J. R. and Munro, D. C. (1959), *The Middle Ages*, New York, Appleton-Century-Crofts, 115.

Suárez, F. (1872) A Defence of the Catholic and Apostolic Faith against the Errors of the Anglican Sect, 2 vols, Naples.

Syngellakis, A. (1996), 'The Place on the Agenda of the IGC of Environmental Rights and Values as an Expression of Citizenship and Human Rights', in Papers of the Symposium of Jean Monnet Chairs on the 1996 IGC, Brussels, 6–7 May 1996,

Luxembourg.

Taguieff, P.-A. (1985), 'Le néo-racisme différentialiste', *Langage et Société*, 34, 69–98.

Taguieff, P.-A. (1994), 'From Race to Culture: The New Right's View of European Identity', *Telos*, 98–9, 99–125.

Tamir, Y. (1993), *Liberal Nationalism*, Princeton, Princeton University Press.

Tassin, E. (1992), 'Europe: A Political Community?', in C. Mouffe (ed.), *Dimensions of Radical Democracy: Pluralism, Citizenship, Community*, London, Verso.

Taylor, C. (1985), 'Atomism', *Philosophy and the Human Sciences, Philosophical Papers*, 2, Cambridge, Cambridge University Press.

Taylor, C. (1989), 'Cross-Purposes: The Liberal–Communitarian Debate', in N. Rosenblum (ed.) *Liberalism and the Moral Life*, Cambridge, Mass.,Harvard University Press, 159–82.

Taylor, C. (1992), 'The Politics of Recognition', in A. Gutmann (ed.), *Multicultural-ism and the 'Politics of Recognition'*, Princeton, Princeton University Press.

Taylor, P. (1991), 'British Sovereignty and the European Community: What is at Risk?', *Millennium*, 20: 1, 73–80.

Taylor, P. (1996), *The European Union in the 1990s*, Oxford, Oxford University Press.

Teasdale, L. A. (1993), 'Subsidiarity After Maastricht', *Political Quarterly*, 64: 2, 187–97.

Tilly, C. (1975), *The Formation of National States in Western Europe*, Princeton, Princeton University Press.

Tilly, C. (1990), *Coercion, Capital and European States, 990–1900*, Oxford, Blackwell.

Toth, A. (1994), 'A Legal Analysis of Subsidiarity', in D. O'Keeffe and P. Twomey (eds), *Legal Issues of the Maastricht Treaty*, Chichester, Wiley.

Tully, J. (1995) *Strange Multiplicity: Constitutionalism in an Age of Diversity*, Cambridge, Cambridge University Press.

Turner, B. (1986), *Citizenship and Capitalism: The Debate over Reformism*, London, Allen & Unwin.

Turner, B. (1990), 'Outline of a Theory of Citizenship', *Sociology*, 24: 2, 189–217.

Turner, B. (1991), 'Further Specification of the Citizenship Concept: A Reply to M. L. Harrison', *Sociology*, 25: 2, 215–18.

Turner, B. (1993a), 'Contemporary Problems in the Theory of Citizenship', in B. Turner (ed.), *Citizenship and Social Theory*, London, Sage.

Turner, B. (1993b), 'Outline of a Theory of Human Rights', in B. Turner (ed.), *Citizenship and Social Theory*, London, Sage.

Turner, B. (1997), 'Citizenship Studies: A General Theory', *Citizenship*, 1: 1, 5–18.

Urwin, D. W. (1995 [1991]), *The Community of Europe: A History of European Integration since 1945*, London, Longman.

Van den Berghe, G. (1982), *Political Rights for European Citizens*, Aldershot, Gower.

Vander, P. E. (1991), *Resisting Leviathan; The Case against a European State*, London, Claridge Press.

Van Gunsteren, H. (1988), 'Admission to Citizenship', *Ethics*, 98, 731–41.

Van Selm-Thorburn, J. (1998) 'Asylum in the Amsterdam Treaty: A Harmonious Future?', *Journal of Ethnic and Migration Studies*, 24: 4, 627–38.

Vincent, A. (1997), 'Liberal Nationalism: An Irresponsible Compound?', *Political Studies*, 45: 2, 275–95.

Vincent, A. and Plant, R. (1984), *Philosophy, Politics and Citizenship: The Life and Thought of the British Idealists* , Oxford, Blackwell.

Vincenzi, C. (1995), 'European Citizenship and Free Movement Rights in the United Kingdom', *Public Law*, 259–75.

Wæver, O. (1995), 'Identity, Integration and Security: Solving the Sovereignty Puzzle in EU Studies', *Journal of International Affairs*, 48, 389–431.

Wæver, O. (1996), 'European Security Identities', *Journal of Common Market Studies*, 34, 1.

Wæver, O. et al., (1993), *Identity, Migration and the New Security Agenda in Europe*, London, Pinter.

Wæver, O., Bunzan, B. De Wilde, J. (1998), *Security: A New Framework for Analysis*, Boulder, Col., Lynne Rienner.

Waldron, J. (1992), 'Minority Cultures and the Cosmopolitan Alternative', *University of Michigan Journal of Law Reform*, 25, 751–93.

Walker, N. (1996), 'European Constitutionalism and European Integration', *Public Law*, 266–88.

Walker, R. B. J. (1990), 'Sovereignty, Identity, Community: Reflections on the Horizons of Contemporary Political Practice,' in R. B. J. Walker and H. S. Mendlovitz (eds), *Contending Sovereignties: Redefining Political Community*, Boulder, Col., Lynne Rienner.

Walker, R. B. J. (1993), *Inside/Outside*, Cambridge, Cambridge University Press.

Walker, R. B. J. and Mendlovitz, H. S. (1990), *Contending Sovereignties: Redefining Political Community*, Boulder, Col., and London, Lynne Rienner.

Wallace, H. (1995), 'Britain Out on a Limb?', *Political Quarterly*, 66: 1, 47–58.

Wallace, R. (1996), *Refugees and Asylum: A Community Perspective*, London, Butterworth.

Wallace, W. (1990), *The Transformation of Western Europe*, London, Pinter.

Wallace, W. (1999), 'The Sharing of Sovereignty: The European Paradox', *Political Studies*, 47: 3, 503–21.

Wallmans, S. (1983), 'Identity Options', in C. Fried (ed.), *Minorities: Community and Identity*, Dahlem Konferenzen 1983, Berlin, Springer-Verlag.

Walzer, M. (1983), *Spheres of Justice*, New York, Basic Books.

Ward, I. (1996), *A Critical Introduction to European Law*, London, Butterworth.

Ward, I. (1997), 'Law and Other Europeans', *Journal of Common Market Studies*, 35: 1, 79–96.

Weale, A. (1995), 'Democratic Legitimacy and the Constitution of Europe', in R. Bellamy et al. (eds), *Democracy and Constitutional Culture in the Union of Europe*, London, Lothian Foundation Press.

Weatherill, S. (1989) 'Note on *Cowan* v. *Le Trésor Public*', *Common Market Law Review*, 26, 563–81.

Weatherill, S. (1996), *EC Consumer Law*, Harlow, Longman.

Webber, F. (1991), ' From Ethnocentrism to Euro-racism', *Race and Class*, 32: 3, 11–19.

Weber, C. (1995), *Simulating Sovereignty*, Cambridge, Cambridge University Press.

Weil, P. and Hansen, R. (1999), *Citizenship, Immigration and Nationality: Nationality Law in the European Union*, London, Macmillan.

Weiler, J. H. H. (1990), 'The Legal Dimension', in W. Wallace (ed.), *The Dynamics of Political Integration*, London, Pinter, 242–60.

Weiler, J. H. H. (1991), 'The Transformation of Europe', 100 *Yale Law Journal*, 2405–82.

Weiler, J. H. H. (1993), 'Journey to an Unknown Destination: A Retrospective and Prospective of the European Court of Justice in the Arena of Political Integration', *Journal of Common Market Studies*, 31, 417–46.

Weiler, J. H. H. (1994), 'Fin-de-siècle Europe', in R. Dehousse (ed.), *Europe after Maastricht: An Ever Closer Union?*, Munich, Beck, 203–16.

Weiler, J. H. H. (1995a), 'Does Europe Need a Constitution? Reflections on Demos, Telos and the German Maastricht Decision', *European Law Journal*, 1: 3, 219–58.

Weiler, J. H. H. (1996), 'European Neo-Constitutionalism: In Search of Foundations for the European Constitutional Order', *Political Studies*, 44, 517–33.

Weiler, J. H. H. (1997), 'To be a European Citizen – Eros and Civilization', *Journal of European Public Policy*, 4: 4, 495–519.

Weiler, J. H. H. (1998), 'European Citizenship – Identity and Differentity', in M. La Torre (ed.), *European Citizenship: An Institutional Challenge*, The Hague, Kluwer.

Weiler, J. H. H., Haltern, U. R. and Mayer, F. C. (1995), 'European Democracy and its Critique', *West European Politics*, 18: 3.

Wessels, F. (1997), 'An Ever Closer Union? A Dynamic Macropolitical View on European Integration Processes, *Journal of Common Market Studies*, 35: 2, 267–99.

Westlake, M. (1995), 'The European Parliament, the National Parliaments and the 1996 Intergovernmental Conference', *Political Quarterly*, 66: 1, 59–73.

Whelan, F. (1981), 'Citizenship and the Right to Leave', *American Political Science Review*, 75: 3, 636–53.

Whelan, F. (1988a), 'Vattel's Doctrine of the State', *History of Political Thought*, 9: 1.

Whelan, F. (1988b), 'Citizenship and Freedom of Movement: An Open Admissions Policy?', in M. Gibney (ed.), *Open Borders? Closed Societies?*, Westport, Conn. and New York, Greenwood Press.

Wiener, A. (1997), 'Assessing the Constructive Potential of Union-Citizenship – A Socio–Historical Perspective', *European Integration On-line Papers* 1: 17 <http://eiop.or.at/eiop/>.

Wiener, A. (1998), *Building Institutions: The Developing Practice of European Citizenship*, Oxford, Westview.

Wiener, A. and Sala, D. V. (1997), 'Constitution-Making and Citizenship Practice – Bridging the Democracy Gap in the EU?', *Journal of Common Market Studies* 35: 4, 595–614.

Wilke, M. and Wallace, H. (1990), 'Subsidiarity: Approaches to Power-Sharing in the European Community', *RIIA Discussion Papers*, 27, London, The Royal Institute of International Affairs.

Wilkinson, B. (1995), 'Towards European Citizenship? Nationality, Discrimination and Free Movement of Workers in the European Union', *European Public Law*, 1: 3, 417–37.

Williams, S. (1990), 'Sovereignty and Accountability in the European Community', *Political Quarterly*, 6: 3, 299–327.

Wilson, C. (1956), *The Outsider*, London, Indigo.

Wilterdink, N. (1993), 'The European Ideal: An Examination of European and National Identity', *Archives Européennes Dé Sociologie*, 34, 119–36.

Wincott, D. (1995), 'Institutional Interaction and European Integration: Towards an Everyday Critique of Liberal Intergovernmentalism', *Journal of Common Market Studies*, 33: 4, 597–609.

Withol de Wenden, C. (1991), 'Immigration Policy and the Issue of Nationality', *Ethnic and Racial Studies*, 14: 3, 319–32.

Wolin, R. (1990), *The Politics of Being: The Political Thought of Martin Heidegger*, New York, Columbia University Press.

Wolin, T. (1993), 'Democracy, Difference and Re-cognition', *Political Theory*, 21: 3, 464–83.

Wooldridge, F. and D'Sa, R. (1996), 'ECJ Decides *Factortame (No. 3)* and *Brasserie du Pecheur*', '*European Business LAw Review*, 7: 7, 161–7.

Yeatman, A. (1993), 'Voice and Representation in the Politics of Difference', in S. Gunew and A. Yeatman (eds), *Feminism and the Politics of Difference*, Melbourne, Allen and Unwin.

Yeatman, A. (1994), *Postmodern Revisioning of the Political*, London, Routledge.

Young, I. M (1986), 'The Ideal of Community and the Politics of Difference', *Social Theory and Practice*, 12: 1, 1–26.

Young, I. M. (1989), 'Polity and Group Difference: a Critique of the Ideal of Universal Citizenship', *Ethics*, 99: 2, 250–74.

Young, I. M. (1990), *Justice and the Politics of Difference*, Princeton, Princeton University Press.

Young, I. M. (1993), 'Together in Difference: Transforming the Logic of Group Political Conflict', in J. Squires (ed.), *Principled Positions*, London, Lawrence & Wishart.

Young, I. M. (1997), 'The Complexities of Coalition', *Dissent*, 64–9.

Zincone, G. (1993), 'The Political Rights of Immigrants in Italy', *New Community*, 20:1, 131–45.

Zincone, G. (1997), 'The Powerful Consequences of Being too Weak. The Impact of Immigration on Democratic Regimes', *Archives Européennes de Sociologie*, 38: 1, 104–38.

Table of EU documents

Commission Decision 85/381 OJ 1985 L217/25

Community Charter of the Fundamental Social Rights of Workers (1989) Bull. EC 12-1989, Presidency Conclusions

Denmark and the TEU (1994), Annex 3: Unilateral Declarations of Denmark OJ C348/4, 31/12/94

Dublin Convention (1991) 30 ILM 425

Eurobarometer, No. 48, Autumn 1997

European Commission (1975) Report on Granting of Special Rights, Bull. EC Supplement 7/26

European Commission (1979) Proposal for a Directive on the Right of Residence for Nationals of the Member States in the Territory of Another Member State COM(89) 275 Final, 17/8/79

European Commission (1985) Background Report on 'An Ambition for Europe' ISEC/B6/85

European Commission (1986) A People's Europe, Bull. EC Supplement 7/86

European Commission (1988) Communication on 'A People's Europe' COM(88) 331 Final, Bull. EC, Supplement 2/88

European Commission (1988) Proposal for a Directive on Voting Rights for Community Nationals in Local Elections in their Member State of Residence COM(88) 371, Doc. C2-104/8, Bull. EC Supplement 2/88

European Commission (1989) Amended Proposal for a Council Directive on Voting Rights for Community Nationals in local elections in their Member State of Residence, COM(89) 524 Final, 1989

European Commission (1990) Opinion on Union Citizenship, 21/10/1990

European Commission (1993) Report on the Citizenship of the Union COM(93) 702 Final, 21/12/93

European Commission (1993) Report to the Council on the Possibility of Applying Article K9 to Asylum Policy SEC(93) 1687 Final, 4/11/93

European Commission (1993) Communication to the Council and the European Parliament on Immigration and Asylum policies COM(93) 684 Final, 10/12/93

European Commission (1994) Communication to the Council and the European Parliament on Immigration and Asylum Policy COM(94) 23 Final, 23/02/94

European Commission (1994) White Paper on Growth, Competitiveness and Employment COM(94) 333 Final

European Commission (1994) Communication on Immigration and Asylum Policy COM(94) 23 Final, 23/2/94

European Commission (1995) Report for the Reflection Group, 10/5/95, Bull. EU 5

European Commission (1997) Report on Union Citizenship COM(97) 230, 27/5/97, 14

European Commission (1997) Proposal for a Decision on Establishing a Convention on Rules for Admission of Third Country Nationals to the Member States of the European Union COM(97) 387, 30/7/97, Bull. EU 7/8, 111–12

European Commission (1998) Proposal for a Regulation Amending Regulation 1612/68 COM(1998) 394 Final, OJ C344/12

European Commission (1998) Proposal for a Directive amending Directive 68/360 COM (1998) 394 Final, OJ C344/12

European Commission (1998) Proposal for a Council Regulation Amending Regulation 1408/71, OJ C6, 10/1/98

European Commission (1999) Report on the Progress Achieved by the Countries Applying for Accession COM(1999) 500 Final, 13/10/99

European Commission and European Council (1998) Action Plan on How Best to Implement the Provisions of the Treaty of Amsterdam Establishing an Area of Freedom, Security and Justice, 12/7/98 <http://ue.eu.int/jai/article.asp?=en&id= 39813844>.

European Council (1964) Directive 64/221 OJ Special Edition 850/64, 117

European Council (1968) Regulation 1612/68 on Free Movement of Workers OJ Special Edition 475, OJ L257/2

European Council (1968) Directive 68/360/EEC OJ Special Edition (II) 485

European Council (1970) Regulation 1251/70 in the Right to Remain after Employment OJ L142/24

European Council (1971) Regulation 1408/71 on the application of social security schemes OJ L149/2

European Council (1973) Declaration on European Identity, Annex 2 to chapter II, 7th General Report EC

European Council (1977) Decision Concerning Direct Elections to the European Parliament OJ L27, 8/10/77

European Council (1980) Directive 80/987/EEC on Employment Insolvency OJ L283/23

European Council (1984) Recommendation on the Promotion of Positive Action for Women, Rec. 84/635, OJ L331/34, 13/12/84

European Council (1990) Directive 90/364 on the right of residence, OJ L180/26

European Council (1990) Directive 90/365 on the Right of Residence for Employees and Self-Employed Persons who have Ceased their Occupational Activity, OJ L180/28

European Council (1990) Directive 90/366 on the Right of Residence for Students, OJ L180/30

European Council (1992) Edinburgh European Council, Declaration on Nationality of a Member State, OJ C 348, 2/12/92

European Council (1992) Birmingham European Council, Birmingham Declaration – A Community Close to its Citizens, Bull. EC 10-1992, 1.8.9

European Council (1992) Resolution on Manifestly Unfounded Applications for Asylum, 30 Nov/1 Dec, not published in the Official Journal

European Council (1992) Resolution on a Harmonised Approach to Questions Concerning Third Countries, 30 Nov/1 Dec, not published in the Official Journal

European Council (1993) Directive 93/96/EEC on the Right of Residence for Students OJ L317/59

European Council (1993) Directive 93/109/EC on Exercising the Right to Vote in European Parliament Elections OJ L329/34, 30/12/93

European Council (1994) Directive 94/80/EC on Right to Vote and Stand in Municipal Elections OJ L368, 31/12/94

European Council (1994) Directive 94/45/EC on the Introduction of European Works Councils OJ L254/64, 30/9/94

European Council (1995) Regulation 2317/95 on a Common Visa OJ L234/1 Replacing Regulation 1683/95 OJ L164/1

European Council (1995) Resolution on the Response of Educational Systems to the Problems of Racism and Xenophobia OJ C312, 23/11/95

European Council (1995) Resolution on the Fight Against Racism and Xenophobia in the Fields of Employment and Social Affairs OJ C296, 10/11/95

European Council (1996) Directive 96/34/EC on the Framework Agreement on Parental Leave OJ L145/4

European Council (1996) Decision on an Emergency Travel Document O J L168, 6/7/96

European Council (1996) Resolution on Minimum Guarantees for Asylum Procedures OJ C274/13, 19/9/96

European Council (1996) Recommendation on the Status of Long-Term Resident Third Country Nationals OJ C80/2

European Council (1996) Recommendation on combating the Illegal Employment of Third Country Nationals Bull. EU 6/1996, point 1/10/7

European Council (1995) Madrid European Council – Presidency Conclusions, SN 400/95 Part B 16/2/95

European Council (1996) The European Union Today and Tomorrow. Adapting the European Union for the Benefit of its Peoples and Preparing it for the Future: A General Outline for a Draft Revision of the Treaties, Dublin II, Conf. 2500/96, 5/12/96.

European Council (1996) Recommendation on Harmonising the Means of Combating Illegal Immigration and Illegal Employment and Improving the Relevant Means of Control [1996] OJ C5/1, 22/12/95

European Council (1998) Strategy Paper on Immigration and Asylum Policy, 9809/98, Brussels, 1/7/1998

European Council (1999) Cologne European Council, Presidency Conclusions, 3–4 June 1999

European Council (1999) Decisions on Integrating the Schengen Acquis into the EU's Legal Order OJ L176, 12/7/99

European Council (1999) Helsinki European Council, Presidency Conclusions, 11/12/1999 <http://presidency.finland.fi/net com>

European Council (2000) Lisbon European Council Presidency Conclusions, SN 100/00, 23–24 March 2000

European Consumers Organisation (1995) The 1996 IGC – Revision of the Treaty: Observations by BEUC, 27/6/95, Brussels <htttp://europa.eu.int>

European Parliament (1977) Declaration of Fundamental Rights and Freedoms OJ C103, 27/4/77

European Parliament (1977) Resolution on Special Rights for the Citizens of the Community, OJ C200/25

European Parliament (1977) Resolution on the Granting of Special Rights OJ C299, 12/12/77

European Parliament (1982) Resolution on a Draft Uniform Electoral Procedure for the Election of Member of the European Parliament, OJ C87/61

European Parliament (1983) Resolution on the Right of Citizens of a Member State Residing in a Member State other their own to Stand for and Vote in Local Elections OJ C184/28

European Parliament (1989) Resolution on the Joint Declaration Against Racism and Xenophobia and an Action Programme by the Council of Ministers A2-261/88, O J C69, 14/2/89

European Parliament (1989) Resolution on the Declaration of Fundamental Rights and Freedoms, A2-0003/89

European Parliament (1991) Resolution on Union Citizenship A3-0300/91 OJ C183, 15/7/91

European Parliament (1992) Resolution on the results of the Intergovernmental Conferences A3-01123/92, OJ C125/81, 7/4/92

European Parliament (1992) Resolution on the harmonisation within the European Community of Asylum Law and Policies A3-0284/92, OJ C337/211, 21/12/92

European Parliament (1993) Opinion of the Committee on Civil Liberties and Internal Affairs A3-0215/93

European Union's Migrants' Forum (1993) Proposal for a draft Council Directive concerning the Elimination of Racial Discrimination, Brussels <http://europa.eu.int>

Interinstitutional Agreement on the Ombudsman's Duties (1993) Bull. EC 10/1993

Schengen Convention 1985 (1991) 30 ILM 68

Schengen Convention 1990 (1991) 30 ILM 84

Spaak Report (1956), cited in Urwin, 1991 and Ward, 1996, p. 13

Spanish Proposal on Union citizenship (1990) Europe 1653, 6/10/90, Luxembourg

von Weizsacker, R., Dehaene, J. and Simon, D. (1999) The Institutional Implications of Enlargement, Report to the European Commission, Brussels, 18/10/99

Table of cases

R v Secretary of State for Transport, ex parte Factortame (Case C-213/89) [1990]
  ECR I-2433; [1990] 3 CMLR 1
R v Secretary of State for Transport, ex parte Factortame (Case C-221/89) [1991]
  ECR I-3095; [1991] 3 CMLR 589
Reyners v Belgium (Case 2/74) [1974] ECR 631; [1974] 2 CMLR 305
Rush Portuguesa Lda v Office National d'Immigration (Case C-113/89) [1990] ECR
  I-1417; [1991] 2 CMLR 818
Sager v Societe Dennmeyer and Co Ltd (Case C-76/90) [1991] I-4221
Saldanha (Case C-122/960 [1997] ECR I-5325
Schindler (Case C-275/92) [1994] ECR 1039;
Schmid v Belgian State (Case C-310/91) [1993] 1 ECR 3011; [1995] 2 CMLR 803
Scholz v Universitaria di Cagliari (case C-419/92) [1994] ECR I-505; [1994] 1 CMLR
  873
Schoning-Kougebetopoulou v Freie and Hansestadt Hamburg (Case C-15/96) [1998]
  1 CMLR 931
Skanavi and Chryssanthakopoulos (Case C-193/94) [1996] ECR I-929; [1996] 2
  CMLR 372
Spotti v Freistaat Bayern (Case C-272/92) [1993] ECR I-5185; [1994] 3 CMLR 629
Stober and Pereira v Bundesanstalt fur Arbeit (Cases 4 and 5/95) [1997] ECR I-511;
  [1997] 2 CMLR 213
Uecker and Jacquet v Land Nordrhein-Westfalen (Cases C-64 and 65/96) [1997] ECR
  I-317; [1997] 3 CMLR 963
Union Royale Belge des Societes de Football/Association ASBL v Bosman (Case C-
  415/93) [1995] ECR I-4921; [1996] 1 CMLR 645
Van Binsbergen v Bestuur van de Bedrijfsvereniging voor de Metaalnijverheid (Case
  33/74) [1974] ECR 1299
Van der Elst v Office des Migrations Internationales (Case C-43/93) [1994] ECR I-
  3803
Van Gend en Loos (Case 26/92) [1963] ECR 1
Walrave and Koch v Association Union Cycliste Internationale (Case 36/74) [1974]
  ECR 1405; [1975] 1 CMLR 320
Wijsenbeek (Case C-378/97) [1999] Judgement of 21 September 1999

Opinions

Opinion 2/94 on accession by the Community to the European Convention for the
  Protection of Human Rights and Fundamental Freedoms [1996] ECR I-1759

Cases from other jurisdictions

France
Amsterdam, Decision 97-394 DC, 31 December 1997
Maastricht I, Decision 92-308 DC, 9 April 1992
Maastricht II, Decision 92-312 DC, 3 September 1992
Maastricht III, Decision 92-313 DC, 23 September 1992

Germany
Brunner v European Union Treaty 2 BvR 2134 & 2159/92 [1994] 1 CMLR 57

Index